# AGENTS,
# CAUSES,
## AND
# EVENTS

D1602116

— ? introduction
— Chisholm (in Pereboom)
— Pereboom (in Pereboom)
— O'Connor (in O'Connor, ed.)

# AGENTS, CAUSES, AND EVENTS

## Essays on Indeterminism and Free Will

Edited by
*Timothy O'Connor*

*New York    Oxford*
OXFORD UNIVERSITY PRESS
1995

Oxford University Press

Oxford   New York
Athens   Aukland   Bangkok   Bombay
Calcutta   Cape Town   Dar es Salaam   Delhi
Florence   Hong Kong   Istanbul   Karachi
Kuala Lumpur   Madras   Madrid   Melbourne
Mexico City   Nairobi   Paris   Singapore
Taipei   Tokyo   Toronto

and associated companies in
Berlin   Ibadan

Published by Oxford University Press, Inc.
198 Madison Avenue, New York, New York 10016-4314

Oxford is a registered trademark of Oxford University Press

Library of Congress Cataloging-in-Publication Data
Agents, causes, and events : essays on indeterminism and free will /
edited by Timothy O'Connor.
p. cm.   Includes bibliographical references and index.
Contents: Libertarianism, action, and self-determination / Galen Strawson—
The problem of autonomy / Thomas Nagel—On giving libertarians what they
say they want / Daniel Dennett—Libertarianism and rationality / Richard
Double—Reasons explanation of action / Carl Ginet—Agents, causes, and
events / Roderick Chisholm—Choice and indeterminism / Robert Nozick—
Two kinds of incompatibilism / Robert Kane—Two concepts of freedom /
William Rowe—Agent causation / Timothy O'Connor—Toward a credible
agent-causal account of free will / Randolph Clarke—When is the will free? /
Peter van Inwagen—When the will is free /
John Martin Fischer and Mark Ravizza.
ISBN 0-19-509156-6.—ISBN 0-19-509157-4 (pbk. )
1. Free will and determinism.   I. O'Connor, Timothy (Timothy W.)
BJ1461.A34   1995
123'.5—dc20   94-13498

2 4 6 8 9 7 5 3

Printed in the United States of America
on acid-free paper

For
CARL GINET

# Acknowledgments

I wish to thank John Martin Fischer, Carl Ginet, Norman Kretzmann, and the editor at Oxford University Press, Angela Blackburn, for advice and assistance in selecting and preparing this collection of essays.

The following essays have been published previously:

"Libertarianism, Action and Self-Determination" by Galen Strawson is excerpted from Ch. 2 of his *Freedom and Belief* (Oxford: Clarendon Press, 1986). Reprinted by permission of Oxford University Press.

"The Problem of Autonomy" by Thomas Nagel is excerpted from Ch. 7 of his *The View from Nowhere* (New York: Oxford University Press, 1986). Reprinted by permission of Oxford University Press.

"On Giving Libertarians What They Say They Want" by Daniel Dennett appeared in his *Brainstorms* (Cambridge, MA: Bradford Books, 1978). Reprinted by permission of MIT Press.

"Libertarianism and Rationality" by Richard Double appeared in *The Southern Journal of Philosophy* 26 (1988), pp. 431–39. Reprinted by permission of the Dept. of Philosophy, Memphis State University.

"Reasons Explanation of Action: An Incompatibilist Account" by Carl Ginet appeared in *Philosophical Perspectives, 3, Philosophy of Mind and Action Theory, 1989,* edited by James E. Tomberlin (copyright by Ridgeview Publishing Co., Atascadero, CA). Reprinted by permission of Ridgeview Publishing Company.

"Choice and Indeterminism" by Robert Nozick is reprinted by permission of the publishers from *Philosophical Explanations* (Cambridge, MA: Harvard University Press, 1981); copyright 1981 by Robert Nozick.

"Two Kinds of Incompatibilism" by Robert Kane appeared in *Philosophy and Phenomenological Research* 50 (1989), pp. 219–54. Reprinted by permission of The International Phenomenological Society.

"Two Concepts of Freedom" by William Rowe appeared in *The Proceedings and Addresses of the American Philosophical Association* 61 (1987), pp. 43–64. Reprinted by permission of the American Philosophical Association.

"Toward a Credible Agent-Causal Account of Free Will" by Randolph Clarke appeared in *Noûs* 27 (1993), pp. 191–203. Reprinted by permission of Blackwell Publishers.

"When Is the Will Free?" by Peter van Inwagen appeared in *Philosophical Perspectives, 3, Philosophy of Mind and Action Theory, 1989,* edited by James E. Tomberlin (copyright by Ridgeview Publishing Co., Atascadero, CA). Reprinted by permission of Ridgeview Publishing Company.

"When the Will Is Free" by John M. Fischer and Mark Ravizza appeared in *Philosophical Perspectives, 6, Ethics, 1992,* edited by James E. Tomberlin (copyright by Ridgeview Publishing Co., Atascadero, CA). Reprinted by permission of Ridgeview Publishing Company.

# Contents

*[handwritten note:]* → Mill → "necessitarian"
vs.
Reid → agent causation

## III   *Indeterminism and the Extent of Free Will*

# Contributors

RODERICK M. CHISHOLM is Emeritus Professor of Philosophy and Andrew W. Mellon Professor of Humanities at Brown University.

RANDOLPH CLARKE is Assistant Professor of Philosophy at the University of Georgia.

DANIEL DENNETT is the Distinguished Professor of Arts and Sciences and the Director of the Center for Cognitive Studies at Tufts University.

RICHARD DOUBLE is Assistant Professor of Philosophy at Edinboro University of Pennsylvania.

JOHN MARTIN FISCHER is Professor of Philosophy at the University of California, Riverside.

CARL GINET is Professor of Philosophy at Cornell University.

ROBERT KANE is Professor of Philosophy at the University of Texas at Austin.

THOMAS NAGEL is Professor of Philosophy at New York University.

ROBERT NOZICK is Arthur Kingsley Porter Professor of Philosophy at Harvard University.

TIMOTHY O'CONNOR is Assistant Professor of Philosophy at Indiana University.

MARK RAVIZZA is a novice in the Jesuit Novitiate, Pacific Province, in Culver City, California.

WILLIAM L. ROWE is Professor of Philosophy at Purdue University.

GALEN STRAWSON is a Fellow at Jesus College, University of Oxford.

PETER VAN INWAGEN is Professor of Philosophy at Syracuse University.

# AGENTS,
# CAUSES,
## AND
# EVENTS

# Introduction

Understanding how free will is possible is perhaps the most vexing of the traditional problems of philosophy. Clearly, one important reason for this is that it is tangled up with questions about a number of other difficult matters, such as the nature of mind, causation, and explanation. And a second reason for its resistance to clear and decisive resolution stems from the fact that it involves a phenomenon that (apparently) is a fundamental part of our ordinary experience: all of us are constantly making choices to act in various ways, conscious all the while that it is *we* who have determined that we should act thus, and that we might have chosen quite differently—that it was fully within our power at the time to have done so. We care deeply about this ostensible *feature* of ourselves, whether we call it "autonomy," "self-determination," or "control," despite the somewhat inchoate nature of our pretheoretical grasp of it. So when a philosopher (typically with a broader philosophical agenda to push) comes along and proposes an analysis of some term we use to capture this feature—self-determination," say—and triumphantly announces that such an analysis is quite compatible with various theses about the nature of human action that we originally took to be inconsistent with our freedom of action, we are generally not inclined to respond thus: "Well, yes, I can see that you have certainly captured at least one important sense of our use of that term, and since you are certainly right that demanding anything stronger than that makes things rather difficult, perhaps we ought to adopt that as the best analysis and consider the troublesome matter decided." We are not so inclined because "free will," "self-determination," and so on (pick your favorite term) do not function in the first instance as *theoretical* terms connected in a certain way to other such terms (e.g., "moral responsibility"); rather, they are used to describe that of which we take ourselves to have immediate experience.

An issue which has dominated free will discussions since the seventeenth century is the compatibility of free will and causal determinism (as a cursory survey of modern anthologies on the subject bears out). And this has continued right up to the present time, in which a formal modal version of the traditional argument for the incompatibilist position has attracted a great deal of discussion.[1] Contemporary philosophers appear to be divided into roughly equal camps on this matter, with little prospect for significant advance by continuing to tackle the issue head-on. Part of the significance of the present collection of essays is its potential for influencing the compatibility debate in a somewhat indirect fashion. For a great many philosophers who are compatibilists concede that there is a significant degree of initial plausibility to the incompatibilist argument. And yet they ultimately reject the argument on something like the following grounds:

> We have free will. But if causal determinism really were a threat to free will, it's hard to see how *in*determinism could be of any help. (Indeed, it seems to just make matters worse). But since these are exhaustive possibilities, they can't *both* be incompatible with free will. Therefore, it seems best to conclude that we're getting taken in by the incompatibilist argument.

The only remaining job, for such philosophers, is to come up with the most plausible account of exactly what is wrong with the incompatibilist argument. Many of the essays collected here are, among other things, addressed to such half-hearted compatibilists: for they try to provide a coherent model of free action that involves indeterminism and to show why the indeterministic aspects of their accounts are necessary to securing the autonomy that we prereflectively attribute to ourselves.

These essays are addressed to a second group of philosophers as well: those who accept the argument for the incompatibility of free will and determinism, but who also claim that free will is incompatible with indeterminism. Given the exhaustive nature of the two possibilities, these philosophers are committed to the incoherence of the very notion of free will. While this is a position that was rarely held in the history of philosophy, it is beginning to find a voice in a small, but growing number of contemporary thinkers.

A few of these skeptical philosophers are included here and set the stage for the more constructive proposals that follow. In "Libertarianism,

Action, and Self-Determination," Galen Strawson argues that self-determination is impossible because it would require one's having completed an infinite number of choices. The core of the argument is as follows: (1) How one acts is determined by one's character and particular mental state at the time of acting. So (2) if one is to be self-determining with respect to a particular action at time *t*, one must have chosen to have the character that issued in this action. But (3) this would require some principle of choice leading one to prefer being that way, rather than some other way, at *t*. But then (4) for the choice described in (2) to have been a self-determining one, one must have chosen the principle of choice on which it was based. And clearly the same requirement will be placed on this further choice, requiring still further principles of choice, with no end in sight.

In "The Problem of Autonomy," Thomas Nagel defends the incoherence thesis by a somewhat different route. He describes two different standpoints from which we can view our own activity: from the 'internal' standpoint, it seems that we determine how we shall act through our choices, which are explained by our reasons for so acting, while not being causally determined by any set of prior conditions. But from the 'objective' standpoint, the only form of explanation we understand is causal explanation, and to the extent that any event is not strictly determined by antecedent factors, it is also not explained. Thus, if my reasons for acting do not (in conjunction with other factors) determine how I act, then they cannot explain why I acted as I did, *rather than in some other way that was also causally open to me.* And we simply cannot make intelligible from the objective standpoint any other way in which *I* may be said to have been the factor determining which of causally open possibilities was realized.

A very different type of skeptical challenge to indeterministic accounts of free agency is advanced in Daniel Dennett's "On Giving Libertarians What They Say They Want." At first sight, Dennett looks like a friend, rather than a foe, of indeterministic accounts of free will. For he addresses a question which is frequently and pointedly put to the indeterminist—"Precisely *where* in the process of deliberation do you propose to have the autonomy-securing indeterminism reside?"—and offers a constructive suggestion: we may suppose some mechanism that generates the considerations to be reflected on in deliberation whose operation is to some degree undetermined. (Whichever considerations are generated will then determine the ensuing choice.) And he persuasively argues that the presence of indeterminism at just this point can hardly be claimed to render the choice inexplicable: it will be fully explicable (determined, if you like) by the reasons that are in view at the time the choice is made. The challenge comes when he claims near the end of his discussion that the considerations favoring such an account over traditional deterministic accounts do not really require that the factor-generator be *indeterministic* after all. All that is desirable about such a picture would be secured by a physically determined but *patternless* generating process. Thus, the upshot of Dennett's discussion is that the indeterminists may have been right about the inadequacy of typical determinist accounts of action, but that once the desired missing feature is clearly articulated, it appears to be compatible with determinism, after all.

Finally, Richard Double's essay—like Dennett's—is not an expression of skepticism concerning the coherence of the concept of autonomous, responsible behavior, but is instead focused solely on indeterministic accounts. Double suggests that we divide such accounts into two categories, corresponding to two different views on where the autonomy-conferring indeterminacy should be located. On the traditional approach, the locus of indeterminism is in the very act of choice itself. An alternative, as we have already seen, is in the process of gathering reasons before and during a period of deliberation. Double argues that neither approach is satisfactory. Consider first the usual view that the action-triggering choice is itself undetermined. Double claims (and tries to motivate through an example) that any plausible account of reasons explanation must satisfy what he calls the 'Principle of Rational Explanation': Citing a person's reasoning process $R$ rationally explains a choice $C$ only if the probability of $C$ given $R$ is greater than the probability of not-$C$ given $R$. And he notes that at least in van Inwagen's version of the undetermined-choice approach, this principle is not satisfied, since van Inwagen appears to allow that when an agent acts with free will, it may have been equally likely for each of two alternatives that he would perform that alternative. While Double does not try to extend this criticism to the general sort of approach typified by van Inwagen, it is worth noting that many such accounts do contravene Double's principle. As for the alternative approach of locating indeterminism back at the stage of gathering reasons for acting (as suggested by Dennett and Robert Kane, whose work will be discussed below), Double claims it is unsatisfactory because it is hard to see how such chance occurrences of recognizing reasons for acting could ground my responsibility, and, in any case, most indeterminists have wanted more than this: they want to maintain that up to the moment of choice, I could have acted differently. (The reader will recall my earlier suggestion that this capacity to have chosen differently is part of the phenomenology of decision, and is thus included in our pretheoretic notion of 'free will'.)

These four representative challenges to indeterministic theories are then followed by seven different accounts of free will that are intended to address one or more of these criticisms. It is helpful to divide such theories into three basic types: (1) *simple indeterminism*, which maintains that free agency doesn't require there to be any sort of causal connection (even of an indeterministic variety) between the agent and his free actions; (2) *causal indeterminism,* according to which an agent causes his free actions via his reasons for so acting, but indeterministically; and (3) *the agency theory,* which posits a *sui generis* form of causation by an agent that is irreducible (ontologically as well as conceptually) to event-causal processes within the agent.

Carl Ginet is our sole representative of simple indeterminism. In his "Reasons Explanation of Actions: An Incompatibilist Account," he responds to the common complaint that such a view is incompatible with the agent's determining his own action by contending that it rests upon a conflation of the conditions necessary to determining one's own action with those necessary to determining some further state of affairs *via* one's action. He bolsters this line of defense by providing a non-causal account of several forms of reasons explanation of action. On Ginet's view, reasons explain actions wholly in virtue of the similarity of content between the prior desire/intention and action, along with the directly referential relation between the action and its concurrent intention.

Three of our authors take an alternative route by advancing very different versions of the currently popular causal indeterminist view. In "Agents, Causes and Events: The Problem of Free Will" (an essay commissioned for this volume), Roderick Chisholm begins with an analysis of the concept of causation and then tries to show how reasons might causally contribute to the occurrence of an action for which there is no sufficient causal condition. Some, however, will object to the adequacy of the causal indeterminist view by claiming that the agent is not responsible for the fact that the indeterministic process, on a particular occasion, was settled by choice A, given that choice B was equally possible. Perhaps there is a statistical tendency governing relative likelihoods over a number of similar situations, but the outcome in any particular case seems a matter of chance. Robert Nozick ("Choice and Indeterminism") and Robert Kane ("Two Kinds of Incompatibilism") both try to identify special features of the nature of the process of deliberation and choice that will make it plausible to say that the agent does control the particular *way* in which the causally indeterministic process unfolds. Nozick's strategy starts with the characterization of choice as a process of assigning relative weights to various reasons for acting; in doing so, he draws on an analogy to the "collapsing of the wave packet" within the orthodox interpretation of the quantum mechanical theory of measurement. He then suggests that the more important of an agent's choices tend to have a self-subsuming character; having chosen to order my values in a certain fashion, I come to see that choice as an instance of (because approved by) that very ordering. Nozick argues that this self-subsumptive character of indeterministic choice provides the means for rebutting the charge of randomness. Kane's approach tries to draw consequences from careful attention to the phenomenology of "deliberative struggle" accompanying decision making in many cases involving a conflict between moral or prudential considerations and short-term desire. In such cases, these opposing reasons explain why we're in a state of internal conflict, but they cannot (for precisely the reason that they don't move us decisively in either direction) explain the outcome. So what *does* explain the decision that is eventually reached? In some of his earlier work, Kane pointed to the agent's *identification* with the very process of struggle. Whichever way I choose, it is *my* choice, an expression of who I have chosen to be. In the more recent essay included here, Kane focuses instead on a peculiar duality that he sees in such choices: viewed in one way, a decision to perform action A rather than action B is a judgment or event of coming to believe that the reasons for A are weightier than those for B; viewed in another way, it is simply a choice to do A. Kane argues that these two aspects of choice (cognitive and volitional) are mutually explanatory. I come to believe that the reasons for A are weightier because I have chosen to do A, and I have chosen to do A because I have come to believe that my reasons favor doing so.[2]

The presentation of constructive proposals is concluded with three attempts to rehabilitate the traditional appeal to the concept of agent causation. William Rowe's "Two Concepts of Freedom" is a discussion of Thomas Reid's influential account of the agency theory. Rowe's main concern is to deal with an apparent problematic implication of Reid's account, viz., that the agent must engage in an infinite number of simultaneous "exertions of active power," or causings, in the production of each free act. In "Agent Causation," I try to show how agent causation can be understood as a distinct species (from 'event' causation) of the primitive idea of causal production underlying contemporary realist conceptions of event causation. I then respond to several contemporary objections to the agency theory and provide an account of reasons explanation that incorporates it. Randolph Clarke ("Toward a Credible Agent-Causal Account of Free Will") also uses contemporary realist accounts of event causation as a springboard to developing an agent-causal account of free action, but he makes the quite novel suggestion that an agent's causing his own action is consistent with that action's also being indeterministically caused by his reasons for so acting. He suggests that we may think of the agent as directly determining, from among a range of causally possible alternatives, which reason will issue in which action on any given occasion.

Finally, Peter van Inwagen, and John M. Fischer and Mark Ravizza round out the discussion with a intriguing and lively exchange over the implications of incompatibilism for the question of how *frequently* one may plausibly suppose free choice to occur.[3] Van Inwagen argues that if free will is incompatible with determinism (as he believes to be the case), then we have "precious little free will." His argument has two basic stages. He first claims that anyone who is an incompatibilist must accept the validity of a certain modal inference rule, "Beta" (or something very much like it) that he and others employ in contemporary discussions of the incompatibility argument. He then tries to show through successive discussion of three examples (representative of increasingly wider ranges of ordinary choice scenarios) that there are very plausible premises corresponding to each case which, by rule Beta, entail that the agent has no choice about either refraining from or performing a certain action. The third case is supposed to represent any case in which one regards an act "as the one obvious thing or only sensible thing to do"—and such cases are, van Inwagen says, our normal everyday situation. The only remaning sort of cases in which it is plausible to think we make free choices are (1) "Buridan's Ass" cases, (2) cases where duty or long-term prudence are pitted against short-term desire, and (3) cases involving incommensurable values—where my values do not make clear to me what I should do precisely because the decision I face is one of *ordering* my values. Since it is clear enough that these cases comprise only a small segment of the total number of my decisions, if I freely choose *only* under such circumstances, than I do indeed have far less freedom of choice than I prereflectively take myself to have.

In "When the Will is Free," John M. Fischer and Mark Ravizza challenge van Inwagen's argument at both stages. They first claim that there are plausible forms of argument for incompatibilism that do not imply the validity of Beta. They then go on to argue that even if Beta is valid, it cannot be used to show that the agent does not choose freely in van Inwagen's representative cases. Their strategy is to question, for each case, the truth of a modalized conditional van Inwagen uses to show that the agent is not free in that case. Each of these premises have the form, "If circumstances C obtain, then agent X will perform [or will refrain from] action A, and no one has or ever had any choice about whether this conditional is true." In each of these cases, C includes the agent's having reasons that either completely or heavily favor doing (or refraining from doing) action A. The basic issue between van Inwagen and Fischer and Ravizza, then, concerns how such one-sided motivation affects one's freedom of choice, with Fischer and Ravizza taking the position that while it may make a certain course of action highly likely, in all but the most extreme examples it will not preclude one's *ability* to do otherwise.

## Notes

1. For presentations of the argument, see Carl Ginet, "The Conditional Analysis of Freedom," in P. van Inwagen, ed., *Time and Cause* (Dordrecht: Reidel,

1980), and P. van Inwagen, *An Essay on Free Will* (Oxford: Oxford University Press, 1983). I have discussed critical reactions to their argument in "On the Transfer of Necessity," *Noûs* 27 (1993), pp. 204–18.

2. In "Indeterminism and Free Agency: Three Recent Views" (*Philosophy and Phenomenological Research* 53 [1993], pp. 499–526), I critically discuss the causal indeterministic views of Nozick and Kane as well as Ginet's simple indeterminism.

3. Van Inwagen has continued this debate with his "When the Will Is Not Free" (forthcoming in *Philosophical Studies*).

# I

## Problems
## for Indeterministic
## Accounts of Free Will

# 1

## Libertarianism, Action, and Self-Determination

GALEN STRAWSON

### 1. The Argument Summarized

'Objectivist' theories of freedom suppose, naturally enough, that the task of showing that we are free involves showing that we have certain properties, *not* including the property of believing we are free, that are necessary and sufficient for freedom. Such theories usually take the question of whether determinism is true or false to be important when one is trying to answer the question whether we are free. And they regularly come up against the sceptical objection that, whether determinism is true or false, we cannot possibly be free either way.

It is a compelling objection. Surely we cannot be free agents, in the ordinary, strong, true-responsibility-entailing sense, if determinism is true and we and our actions are ultimately wholly determined by "causes anterior to [our] personal existence"?[1] And surely we can no more be free if determinism is false and it is, ultimately, either wholly or partly a matter of chance or random outcome that we and our actions are as they are?

So far as Objectivist theories go (and nearly all theories are Objectivist theories), the sceptical objection seems fundamentally correct. Neither of the two options, *determined* and *random*, seems able to give us or allow us what we want. But together they exhaust the field of options. It is true that an action may be the result of a complex cause, some of whose components themselves have causes that can be traced back indefinitely far, while others are either themselves genuinely undetermined events, or can be traced back causally to undetermined events. But it seems clear that a mixture of determined and undetermined antecedents cannot help to make an action free, whatever the proportion of the mixture.

If neither determinedness nor randomness (nor any mixture of the two) can either permit or provide for what we want in the way of freedom, in the ordinary, strong sense (this qualification will be taken for granted henceforth), then there is no more to say—so far as Objectivist theories of freedom are concerned. But what exactly do we want?

One can partially describe the state of affairs that would give us what we want in terms of the notion of self-determination: for if one is to be truly *responsible* for one's actions, then, clearly, one must be truly *self-determining* or truly *self-determined* in one's actions. True responsibility presupposes true self-determination.[2]

Is this any help? It may be said that to talk of self-determination in this context is to do little more than reexpress our ordinary, strong notion of freedom or true responsibility in one more way. But it is nevertheless worth asking what such self-determination might be.

The first thing to note is that the notion of self-determination is ambiguous. If one is going to employ it at all, one has to eliminate the ambiguity. It can be understood in a compatibilistic sense, as follows: (1) one is self-determined, or self-determining, in any particular case of action, just so long as what one does is indeed a result of one's own choices, decisions, and deliberations. In this sense, one can be self-determining is one's (physical) *actions* even if one is not self-determining with respect to one's *choices* or *decisions*—one can be self-determining in one's actions even if one's choices, decisions, and deliberations are entirely determined phenomena, and are phenomena for whose occurrence and nature one is not truly responsible. Such self-determination is clearly compatible with determinism.

Here, however, 'self-determination' will be used in a different way: according to which (2) one is truly *self-determining*, in one's actions, only if one is truly *self-determined*, and one is truly self-determined if and only if one has somehow or other *determined how one is in such a way that one is truly responsible for how one is.*[3] Such self-determination may seem evidently impossible. But it can also seem to be clearly necessary if one is indeed to be truly responsible for one's actions and, hence, free in the present sense. The argument for this will be given shortly.

There is another natural picture of self-determination according to which (3) one can somehow or other be truly self-determining in one's decisions or choices, and hence in one's actions, even if one is not truly responsible for how one is (in respect of character, etc.). I shall not discuss this picture directly until sections 7 and 8, where it will be argued that the objections to it are at bottom exactly the same as the objections to self-determination understood in sense (2).

It is clear, I think, that the truth of determinism excludes self-determination understood in sense (2). One cannot have determined how one is, in such a way that one is truly and ultimately responsible for how one is, and hence for how one acts, if how one is is ultimately wholly determined by 'causes anterior to one's personal existence.' I shall assume that this is so. To make this assumption is not to ignore the claims of compatibilism, for nearly all compatibilists agree with it. They agree that true responsibility and true self-determination are impossible if determinism is true. That is why they standardly attempt to define freedom in such a way that it does not involve true responsibility (or true self-determination), for they want to reach the conclusion that we are indeed free.

It is true that some compatibilists claim that one can in some manner take over true responsibility for one's actions despite determinism.[4] Others are tempted by the idea that mere possession of the ability to engage in fully self-conscious deliberation is sufficient for true responsibility understood in the strongest possible sense, irrespective of whether or not determinism is true, and irrespective of whether or not we can be self-determining in way (2)[5].

Given that (true) self-determination is impossible if determinism is true, the only remaining question is whether it is possible if determinism is false. Many will think it obvious that indeterminism cannot help with self-determination. But it will merely for the sake of discussion be supposed that it is not obvious. Indeed, it will be supposed that what any serious libertarian has to try to do is to give some account of how self-determination is possible given the falsity of determinism. What follows will therefore be a discussion of libertarianism. Detailed reasons, stated in the terms of a particular theoretical frame, will be offered as to why self-determination is not possible. But the general argument for the impossibility of self-determination is very simple and does not depend essentially on the particular theoretical frame; it should be restatable to fit any preferred picture of the nature of mind and action. It goes as follows.

(1) Interested in free action, we are particularly interested in rational actions (i.e., actions performed for reasons as opposed to reflex actions or mindlessly habitual actions),[6] and wish to show that such actions can be free.

(2) How one acts when one acts rationally (i.e., for a reason)[6] is, necessarily, a function of, or determined by, how one is, mentally speak-

ing. (One does not at present need to be more precise than this; one could add "at the time of action" after "mentally speaking.")

(3)  If, therefore, one is to be truly responsible for how one acts, one must be truly responsible for how one is, mentally speaking—in certain respects, at least.

(4)  But to be truly responsible for how one is, mentally speaking, in certain respects, one must have chosen to be the way one is, mentally speaking, in certain respects. (It is not merely that one must have caused oneself to be the way one is, mentally speaking; that is not sufficient for true responsibility. One must have consciously and explicitly chosen to be the way one is, mentally speaking, in certain respects, at least, and one must have succeeded in bringing it about that one is that way.)[7]

(5)  But one cannot really be said to choose, in a conscious, reasoned fashion, to be the way one is, mentally speaking, in any respect at all, unless one already exists, mentally speaking, already equipped with some principles of choice, '$P_1$'—with preferences, values, pro-attitudes, ideals, whatever—in the light of which one chooses how to be.

(6)  But then to be truly responsible on account of having chosen to be the way one is, mentally speaking, in certain respects, one must be truly responsible for one's having *these* principles of choice $P_1$.

(7)  But for this to be so one must have chosen them, in a reasoned, conscious fashion.

(8)  But for this—i.e., (7)—to be so, one must already have had some principles of choice, $P_2$, in the light of which one chose $P_1$.

(9)  And so on. True self-determination is logically impossible because it requires the actual completion of an infinite regress of choices of principles of choice.

That's really all there is to the argument, although another model of self-determination, which one might call the Leibnizian model, will also be considered and rejected below.

It is (3), perhaps, that is most likely to be resisted. It may be objected that one does not have to be at least partly truly responsible for how one is, mentally speaking, but only for how one decides; and that one can make a fully deliberate decision and be truly responsible for it even if one's character, say, is entirely determined (or entirely not self-determined). But it will be argued that this is, in a crucial sense, simply not so.

Item (4) may also be objected to—in particular the idea that one must have *chosen* to be the way one is. Of course this seems, in a way, an absurdly artificial condition to place on true self-determination. But one should ask oneself what else being at least partly truly responsible for how one is, mentally speaking, could possibly consist in. Item (4) can be put in a slightly different way: "one must oneself have consciously and intentionally brought it about that one is the way one is, in certain respects, at least." But then the rest of the argument goes through as before, with only minor alterations.

In fact, essentially the same argument can be given in a much less artificial and extremely familiar form: (1) It is undeniable that one is the way one is as a result of one's heredity and experience. (2) One cannot somehow accede to true responsibility for oneself by trying to change the way one is as a result of heredity and experience. For (3), both the particular way in which one is moved to try to change oneself, and the degree of one's success in the attempt at change, will be determined by how one already is as a result of heredity and experience. (And any further changes that one can successfully bring about only after certain initial changes have been brought about will in turn be determined, via the initial changes, by heredity and experience.)

It may be objected that the kind of freedom this argument shows to be impossible is so obviously impossible that it is not even worth considering. But the freedom that is shown to be impossible by this sort of argument against self-determination is just the kind of freedom that most people ordinarily and unreflectively suppose themselves to possess, even though the idea that some sort of ultimate self-determination is presupposed by their notion of freedom has never occurred to them. It is therefore worth examining the argument in detail because the idea that we possess such freedom is central to our lives.

Curiously, it seems that we have this general conception of ourselves as free in the strong sense although our most ordinary notions of decision, choice, and action already contain within themselves everything that is necessary in order to demonstrate the impossibility of such freedom—as in the argument just set out.[8] Our apparently unrenounceable commitment to this general conception coexists with our everyday employment of notions that can quickly furnish a clear proof that such freedom is not possible. It appears that we tolerate some very deep inconsistencies in this area, and that our general conception of ourselves as free has many highly diverse and indeed incompatible aspects (cf. *Freedom and Belief* §§6.4 and 6.5).

## 2. Libertarianism: A Constraint

Incompatibilism is the view that the falsity of determinism is a necessary condition of freedom. In itself, it involves no view about whether determinism is true or false, or about whether or not we are free. 'Libertarianism', by contrast, is the name of a positive incompatibilistic theory of freedom, one that purports to show that we are free and so assumes (or argues) that determinism is false.

This is agreed on all sides. But I shall also take it that no theory can be properly counted as a libertarian theory unless it gives an account of action-production which shows in detail how and why some sort of actual indeterministic occurrence is a necessary feature of the production of any and every free action (i.e., is among the antecedents of any and every free action). A libertarian theory that simply assumes, incompatibilistically, that the falsity of determinism is a necessary condition of free action, while failing to integrate this negative necessary condition into the positive, detailed account it gives of how free action actually comes about, makes no serious claim on our attention as a libertarian theory.

So libertarians have to locate an indeterministic occurrence among the antecedents of any free action—and they have to show how its presence helps to make the action free. Assume that a particular action A performed by *a* is truly and fully explicable[9] by reference to a reason-state R made up of desire(s) D and belief(s) B (or by reference to events characterizable in terms of desire and belief), while it also has an indeterministic input X among its antecedents. The question is, where can X be? Clearly

> (1) X cannot somehow intervene between R and A, because then an explanation of A by reference to R alone will not after all be a true full explanation of A. The explanation "A occurred (*a* performed A) because *a* believed B and desired D" will not be true. To make it true, the words "and X occurred," at least, will have to be added. In this case there is, contrary to hypothesis, no true, full rational explanation of A.

It is also clear

> (2) that X cannot be supposed to feature among the antecedents of A in such a way that it is (*a*) simultaneous with R at that stage, S, at which R comes to be such that it is determinative of A,[10] and (*b*) unconnected with R. For if X is unconnected with R and yet has a determining effect on A, then, once again, the explanation of A in terms of R will not be a true, full rational explanation of A, contrary of hypothesis.

It seems, then, that

> (3) X can only come in by occurring prior to S. But once again X cannot be unconnected with R, for reasons just given.

So

> (4) X must come in prior to S in such a way that it has some effect on R's being the way it is. Only in this case can an explanation of A in terms of R be a true, full rational explanation of A while it is also true that X is a determinant of A. How the occurrence

of X can in this case help to make A free is no doubt completely mysterious. That is the libertarians' problem. The present point is just that this their only option for locating indeterministic inputs among the antecedents of action, at least in all those extremely common and for that reason centrally important cases where actions have true, full rational explanations.

This argument could be refined, but I think the idea is clear. The same point can be made much more generally, however, without specific reference to actions that have true, full rational explanations (in the sense defined in *Freedom and Belief,* pp. 33–41) for it is, crucially, *sub specie rationalitatis* that we seek to show our actions to be free; it is specifically *qua* reasons-reflecting, reasons-determined things that actions must be shown to be free. If so, the indeterministic input allegedly necessary for free action cannot possibly be supposed to contribute to freedom either by interfering with or interrupting the determination of actions of reasons[11] or because it is a contributory determining factor that is wholly independent of reasons for actions. So it can play a part only by playing a part in shaping or determining what the agent's reasons for actions are. Libertarianism cannot plausibly locate the indeterministic influence anywhere else.

Will it help to locate an indeterministic influence here? Well, clearly one thing indeterminism can always be invoked to substantiate is the claim that the agent's reasons or reason-states (desires and beliefs) need not have been as they were in fact, in any particular case of action. It seems unclear, however, how this in itself could make a difference to the agent's freedom of action. How could it, in itself? We must ask what more may be thought to be needed.

### 3. *Locating Indeterminism*

It has been argued that the only way in which libertarians can plausibly give indeterminism a positive, freedom-creating role in the process of action production is by holding that indeterminism must affect the agent's reasons or reason-states, and play a part in their being as they are. Libertarians have nowhere else to locate the indeterminism that they must show to enter into the process of action production in such a way as to make actions free. But how can indeterminism do what is expected of it, given that reasons are compounded of beliefs and desires?

That *beliefs* are regularly determined in us by the way the world is is easy to accept, difficult to reject. Their primary business is just to match the way the world is as well as possible. There are other ways in which beliefs are determined in us—by wishful thinking, for example. But we are on the whole concerned simply that our beliefs be true. We do not wish to be undetermined by anything, so far as the formation of our beliefs (and therefore their content) is concerned; nor do we wish to be self-determining with regard to the content of our beliefs; nor do we think we are. (We may of course choose to acquire a lot of beliefs about this or that, but once we are in pursuit of such beliefs we do not wish to be able to choose what their content will be, we just want them to be true.) Rather, we think (and hope) that what we believe is determined by, and as a result reflects, how things are.[12] The topic of the determination of beief is a large one, but no one is likely to want to claim that the freedom of an action stems from the agent's being either (*a*) determined by nothing or (*b*) self-determined with respect to the content of its beliefs, and, in particular, with respect to the content of those of its beliefs that form part of the reasons for which it acts.[13]

That *desires* are determined in us is also easy to accept, in certain contexts of discussion, at least. But if libertarians are to connect indeterminism with free action at all, then it seems that they must show that indeterminism plays some part in the agents having the desires that it does have. For since we ask no more of beliefs than that they be determined in us by the way the world is, according to some reliable process which is such that they generally come out true, it would appear to be far more promising for libertarians to postulate indeterminism in the acquisition or having of desires than in the acquisition or having of beliefs. Prima facie, at least, the Faculty of Desire is a far more promising place to look than the Faculty of Belief when one is seeking a point of entry into the action-producing process of some element which, by being undetermined, can help to introduce freedom into that process.

Apparently, then, a cogent libertarian theory must seek to make its case by rejecting the determination of desires; or at least of some desire or desires implicated in the determination of the occurrence of any particular free action.

## 4. Can Indeterminism Help?

The pursuit of the discussion in these terms is already highly artificial. For it seems obvious that what is required for true responsibility, and hence for freedom, is not merely that the agent be *un*determined in its nature in some respect, but that it be *self*-determined in some respect, and, therefore, undetermined by anything else in that respect. It appears that libertarianism must establish not only that some, at least, of our desires are undetermined, in their occurrence or presence in us, by anything that is external to us, but also that we are able to determine what some, at least, of them are. Given the undeniability of reasons/actions determination[14] we need agent/reasons determination. More particularly, we need self-determination as to desire—since we cannot usefully ask this for beliefs.[15]

Such self-determination as to desire may presumably be only partial, and not cover things like desire for food or drink at particular times. But it would seem that some desire with respect to which the gent is self-determined must be operative in the coming to occur of every free action. The question, then, is how *in*determinism can possibly help to establish any such kind of *self*-determination.

## 5. Evasion: The Notion of Choice

This whole approach may now seem beside the point, for in fact we think of nearly every action as free, even actions which are primarily motivated by desires with respect to which we do not suppose ourselves to be in any way self-determining—like the hunger-derived desire for food. Here we are likely to locate our freedom in our possession of a power to choose whether or not to eat which we have quite independently of having the non-self-determined desire to eat. What we are likely to say is that the fact that we have the desire to eat is not a sufficient explanation of why we do eat, given that we act freely in so doing, because what must also be mentioned is the fact that we *chose* to eat.

But will this do? *a* is hungry. He wants to eat. He decides or chooses to eat. Why does he so decide? "Because I'm hungry, and I want to eat." "But does that want *determine* your action?" "No; I could, if I had so chosen, not have eaten." "Why, then, do you choose to eat?" "Well, I'm hungry, I want to eat, I've no reason not to—no wants that conflict with my want to eat." This banal exchange illustrates the difficulty. For presumably, if *a* had chosen not to eat, it would have been because he had *reason* not to despite his hunger and desire to eat. But then we may ask where and how self-determination and true responsibility are supposed to enter the picture, unless *a* is somehow responsible for his reasons. It seems clear that what *a* does when he acts intentionally is, ultimately, always and necessarily just some more or less complex function of his reasons; and that he cannot therefore be truly self-determining unless he can somehow be self-determining with respect to his reasons and, hence, with respect to his desires. So the question, once again, is how indeterminism can help with this.

This may yet be said: "I just decided to do X, but not because of any reason I had. It was just me, it was just up to me, I just freely decided to. That's the fundamental fact behind freedom." The main reply to this line of thought is given in Section 7. A brief reply is this: it may be that there are intentional actions that are almost entirely undeliberated in their performance, and that are therefore not performed for a reason, where "performed for a reason" is taken to ential some explicit premeditation. Perhaps there may even be supposed to be actions that are not performed for a reason in a stronger sense, according to which there just is no reason at all which can correctly be given for them (though this is an obscure idea). Such cases are, however, of little interest where freedom is in question, because it is above all, even if not exclusively, our most premeditated and fully rationally explicable actions that we hope to show to be free. The "I just decided to" line cannot possibly be supposed to provide a general foundation for the claim that we are free.

Suppose that the introduction of the notion of choice into the simple model of action is now recommended as suitable for the description of *all* free action, and not only for the description of those actions, like eating when hungry, which are such that we cannot even begin to suppose that the primarily motivating desire either is or could be self-determiningly chosen.

Well, such a manner of description is undoubtedly very natural. But it merely shifts the difficulty sideways. We may grant that our having the non-self-determined desire to eat does not of itself determine that we do eat, and that whether or not we do also depends on our decision or choice; but then the decision or choice must itself be shown to be free if the ensuing action is to be. It is for the libertarian *ex hypothesi* not free if determined. But it is no good if it is merely undetermined, or a chance occurrence. The fundamental libertarian thought is (or ought to be) that it must, if it is to be our free choice, issue from us in such a way that we are truly self-determining in making it. But, surely, for this to be the case it must also be the case that we choose to eat because, all things considered, we want (or judge it best or right) so to choose. But then this want (this judging right or best) must enter into the true rational explanation of why we choose as we do, as the crucial determinant of the choice. But then questions arise about this determinant, the same questions as before. Is it determined or undetermined? More importantly, are we, the agents, self-determined with respect to it? If not, then, once again, how can we be said to be truly self-determining, and hence free, in our choice and in our ensuing action?

All this is obvious enough—not to say tiresome. The demand for true self-determination, which is presently being taken to be the fundamental libertarian demand, begins to look slightly (or completely) crackpot in the context of such a mundane example as this, of hunger and eating (the example is useful partly for that reason).[16] And yet it still seems to be, somehow, the right demand, especially when it is from the notion of moral responsibility that one sets out in pursuit of that in which freedom could possibly consist.

It may now be suggested that the reason we are truly self-determining free agents is simply that the process of deliberation (however perfunctory or inexplicit) that leads us to make whatever choice we do finally make is truly *our* deliberation, our doing, ours in such a way that we are truly responsible for whatever we do as a result of it. This is, of course, an attractive idea.[17] It corresponds closely to our natural, prephilosophical, unreflective picture of the basis of freedom-founding self-determination. But it is heir to all the difficulties already discussed. For, briefly, in the end such deliberation comes down to a process of (practical) reasoning that necessarily takes one's desires (values, etc.) and beliefs as starting points. And, given that one does not want to be self-determining either with respect to (simple, factual) belief or with respect to one's canons of reasoning, but simply wants truth in beliefs and validity in reasoning, once again the question arises as to how this process of deliberation can possibly give rise to true self-determination in action. And once again it seems that self-determination with respect to desires is the only possible foundation for true self-determination in action. No doubt it is folly to seek such a foundation. (To force libertarians to think their position through in this way is to provide powerful negative support for compatibilism.) But let us consider the question directly.

## 6. *The Impossibility of Self-Determination as to Desire*

We may presume it to be a fundamental postulate of the libertarian theory presently under consideration that we have at least some of the desires that we do have undeterminedly—desires $1$-$n$, say; and that it is in this manner that the assumption of the truth of indeterminism is introduced into the detailed account of the nature of action production, in the way held to be necessary in Section 2: reference to indeterminism features in the account of action production because it features in the account of the provenance of action-determining desires. This, then, is given as a factual assumption.

But clearly this indeterminism is not in itself enough for true self-determination or freedom. What must also be true, it seems, is that we ourselves are able to govern how we become (in respect of desire) in such a way that we can correctly be said to be truly responsible for how we become (in respect of desire). Just to be as we are undeterminedly from the point of view of physics is obviously not enough; nor is it enough if some of our desires rate as completely undetermined on any true psychological theory about what determines our becoming the way we are—one, for example, that refers to heredity and environment. What must also be true, it seems, is that we have *chosen* to have desires $1$-$n$; that we have, at least partly, chosen to be the way we are.

This leads to the principal difficulty: so to choose, we must have reasons for our choice, prior principles, prior preferences, according to which we choose. Even if we allow that there may be choices made at random, made for no reason, they are of no use here. Even if one could intelligibly be supposed to have made a completely random selection of what desires to have, a choice that was undetermined by anything on all true psychological and physical theories, its mere undeterminedness would do absolutely nothing to make it one's own free choice, whereby one became truly responsible for (certain at least of) one's desires, and, therefore, for one's actions. If one is to be truly responsible for one's actions because one has chosen the desires (values, etc.) which lead one to act as one does, then one must clearly be truly responsible for this choice of desires in turn. And one can be truly responsible for this choice of desires only if one makes it in a reasoned, conscious, intentional fashion. But one cannot do this unless one chooses according to values and preferences one already has in the matter of what desires to have.

But then what about these values and preferences, these principles of choice according to which one chooses? One may be determined by nothing in one's possession of them; but this will not make one the captain of one's soul. For one will need to have chosen these principles as well, in order to be truly responsible for the character-shaping choice of desires which they govern, and which is meant to be such that it makes one truly responsible for one's actions.

This, of course, is a regress we cannot stop. We cannot possibly choose our root principles of choice, our conative base-structure, in the required way. So, if we are truly self-determining as agents, this cannot be because we are truly or ultimately self-determining, self-instituting, self-made, with respect to our desires or values or general character. No amount of postulation or logically possible indeterminism can help with this difficulty, because what is required for its solution is that an infinite regress of choices of principles of choice have a beginning and an end, and that is impossible. No appeal to subatomic indeterminacy can help to provide some sort of way in for the free will, because the impossibility of ultimate self-determination as to desire is a simple conceptual truth. Immaterialists and dualists are as powerless against it as physicalists or materialists.[18]

Russell made the essential point, perhaps, when he said that even if you can act as you please, you can't please as you please.[19] But true self-determination seems a clearly necessary condition of freedom, as freedom is ordinarily conceived. And many thinkers—those who have not either simply avoided the question, or decided that we are not really free at all— have supposed it to be fulfilled. Kant wrote of "man's character, which he himself creates"; Sartre, of "le choix que tout homme fait de sa personnalité"; E. H. Carr asserts that "normal adult human beings are morally responsible for their own personality." It is fairly clear that Aristotle believed both that we are or at least can be responsible for our own characters, and that such responsibility is necessary for freedom.[20] Where this idea is not already explicit in the common moral-metaphysical consciousness, it can easily enough be elicited from its nonexplicit regions by judicious (and noncoercive) Socratic questioning.[21]

Even Hume, having in the *Enquiry* given his classic compatibilist account of 'hypothetical liberty' in line with Hobbes and Locke, goes on to state, indirectly, the real problem about freedom—which he leaves unanswered. (It is curious that he does not in the case of freedom explicitly adopt his characteristic double position: that of inevitable philosophical scepticism about true responsibility on the other hand, and equally inevitable commitment to natural belief in true responsibility on the other hand. It is especially curious because the case for scepticism about true responsibility is essentially stronger than the case for scepticism about, say, the existence of the external world. For in the latter case what philosophy establishes is only that we cannot know that the external world does exist, not that we can know that it does not exist. Whereas in the case of responsibility the stronger conclusion does seem available. The reason Hume does not explicitly adopt the double position in this case is perhaps one of caution—although it is at least as much a desire to indulge in some heavy irony at the expense of theists: for he states the deeper objection to belief in true responsibility in indirect, theological terms, when he could equally well have stated it in terms of godless determinism.)[22]

## 7. Relocating Indeterminism

The plan was to give an account of what conceivable factual conditions could justify a belief in freedom of action understood in the strong, desert-entailing sense—and to do this before asking whether these conditions either were or could be actually satisfied. It had to be a consequence of the resulting theory of freedom that we are free when we act rationally and deliberately in such a way that our actions have true full rational explanations (cf. n. 9). Self-determination as to desire seemed to be necessary—but turned out to be impossible.

It is the indissoluble connection and the notion of freedom with that of reasons for action that forces one to reject any libertarian theory that proposes a different possible point of entry for an undetermined and ipso facto freedom-creating element into the process of action production. Consider now the suggestion that human freedom is based upon some special power to intervene between one's reasons-determined decisions to act[23] and one's initiations of action: one's freedom lies in the possibility of one's making a special interventionary choice or decision to do other than what one has in fact decided to do given one's actual desires and beliefs, a choice that is somehow disengaged from one's necessarily not-self-determined belief-desire (or reason) complex, and is, in particular, undetermined by it, and is for that reason free.

What of this? We are stipulated to be free because capable of these belief-and-desire disengaged choices; it is in so far as they flow from such choices that our actions are free. But then it follows that whenever we are able to give a true full rational explanation of an action, that action, at least, is not free. And this consequence deprives the stipulation of any interest; it does not give us what we want. Even if this supposed independent power to choose to do or not to do something standardly just ratifies (as it were) the decisions put out by one's belief-desire complex, still, so long as one's choice of action is in any way genuinely independent of, and is indeed not a direct result of, one's having the reasons one has, one's resulting 'free' action cannot be a fully rational action, truly explicable just by reference to reasons (so far as mental antecedents are concerned). For now a necessary condition of its being free is that one has made a desire-and-belief-independent choice to perform it. So it is not a rational action at all. The rational explanation we give of it will fit, and will look valid, but it will in fact be false, vitiated by the crucial hiatus introduced by the reason-independent power of choice (or 'choice').

This suggestion, proposing a different possible point of entry for something that could make it true that we are truly self-determining, certainly answers to something that has an important place in the phenomenology of people's experience of the absolute "could-have-done-otherwiseness" of action; but it cannot supply us with what we want, given that free action must in general be rational action. It seems that one may well, if suitably cautious, postulate a postdecision event (a neural event, whatever else it is) of volitional ignition of motor activity.[24] But this, if held to constitute a separate stage in the process of action production, must clearly be conceived to be itself reason-determined and not an intervention on the part of the putative free agent that is radically independent of that agent's state of desire and belief. Otherwise the link between freedom and reason—between free action and action done for a reason—is once again broken, and one's theory is once again condemned to fatuity.

## 8. A 'Leibnizian' View

And yet the phenomenological self-evidence of our power to do otherwise, in a way that makes us free in the strongest sense, remains untouched. Can nothing be done to give belief in such a power a respectable factual or metaphysical grounding? Well, it may now be suggested that the picture of the wholly reasons-independent power of choice proposed in Section 7 is too crude; and that the real reason why one can both be truly free and act rationally, despite the fact that one is necessarily not self-determined with respect to one's reasons, is that one's (necessarily not self-determined) reasons can genuinely *affect* one's decisions about action without its being the case that one is as a rational agent *wholly* determined in one's decisions by the way one's reasons are.

Consider the agent in its mental aspect—the 'agent-self,' as it were. The agent's freedom of action is now held to reside in the fact that, although it cannot be ultimately self-determining with respect to its reasons for action, it has an at least partially reasons-independent power of decision as to action. The necessary link between free action and rational action is maintained, because the agent's decision is, in any particular case of action, affected by, but not wholly determined by, its reasons.

The basic picture may be said to be Leibnizian in character: reasons for action affect agents' decisions, but in so doing only incline them towards, and do not necessitate them in, particular decisions to perform particular actions. But the following question now arises: upon what, exactly, are the agent's decisions about actions now supposed to be based, other than upon its reasons? The agent-self is represented as sitting in detached judgement upon its reasons (desires and beliefs) as they develop and combine in such a way as to become reasons for action. It then decides on an action *in the light of* these reasons for action. And although it cannot be truly self-determining with respect to these reasons for action (Section 6), it is still truly self-determining in action because it is not fully determined in action by these (non-self-determined) reasons for action, but rather decides in the light of them, and so acts both rationally and truly freely.

The trouble with the picture is familiar. If the agent is to be truly self-determining in action this cannot be because it has any *further* desires or principles of choice governing the decisions about how to act that it makes in the light of its *initial* desires or principles of choice. For it could not be truly self-determining with respect to these further desires or principles of choice either, any more than it could be self-determining with respect to its initial desires or principles of choice. But if it does not have any such further desires or principles of choice, then the claim that it exercises some special power of decision or choice becomes useless in the attempt to establish its freedom. For if it has no such desires or principles of choice governing what decisions it makes in the light of its initial reasons for action, then the decisions it makes are rationally speaking random; they are made by an agent-self that is, in its role as decision maker, entirely nonrational in the present vital sense of "rational." It is reasonless, lacking any principles of choice or decision. The agent-self with its putative, freedom-creating power of *partially* reason-independent decision becomes some entirely nonrational (reasons-independent) flip-flop of the soul. And so this theory collapses into fatuity in exactly the same way as the theory discussed in Section 7, which proposed a power of *wholly* reason-independent decision. According to it, no free action is a fully rational action, an action truly and fully explicable by reference to reasons.

The only alternative is to suppose that the agent-self is after all equipped with some extra set of desires or principles of choice. But then the freedom-founding event of decision becomes nothing more than the moment of contact between two distinct but equally non-self-determined[25] reason clusters, and the supposedly crucial power of partially reason-independent decision disappears. The picture is now this: the (putatively only inclining and not necessitating) reasons for action, $R_1$, having achieved summation in provisional decision, come before the agent-self which, given its own further set of reasons for action, $R_2$, decides in the light of these whether to let the first and as it were only prima facie action-prompting reasons $R_1$ actually movtivate its action. The actions are now once again performed for, and are truly explicable just by reference to, reasons. But, by the same token, the original objection regarding the fact that the agent cannot be self-determined with respect to these reasons applies once again with full force.

The fruitlessness of these devices is plain, and it may be objected that the whole current frame of discussion is very unnatural in holding that some type or other of radical self-determination is necessary for freedom. It may be said that there are other intuitively attractive conceptions of free agency that makes no such claim.

This may be so. It is certainly true that the claim that such self-determination is vital for freedom can look very odd. But it is also an extremely natural claim. It is at least as natural as it is odd. The views considered in sections 7 and 8 are not included merely as philosophical decoration—as unrealistic and obviously hopeless proposals. For they represent, albeit in an unusually and designedly vulnerable idiom, two versions of exactly the kind of thing that ordinary people are likely to say when challenged to defend their conviction that true responsibility for actions is possible even if it is true that one cannot be truly self-determining with respect to one's desires or reasons.[26] However implausible or uninteresting these suggestions may look to professional philosophers, they represent natural attempts to substantiate a fundamental view about freedom, according to which one's decisions can be truly free even if one's motives are determined (not self-determined).[27] They are not merely examples of what P. F. Strawson calls the "panicky metaphysics" of theoretical philosophical libertarianism.[28] They are also centrally representative of those vague, ill-formed theories that have a crucial role in structuring our attitude to the notion of freedom. This alone is sufficient reason to set them down. They are important to anyone concerned with the cognitive phenomenology of freedom, and anyone seriously concerned with the philosophical problem of freedom must be concerned with the cognitive phenomenology of freedom.

## Notes

1. H. Sidgwick, *The Methods of Ethics* (Chicago: University of Chicago Press, 1962), p. 66.

2. One could equally well express this requirement as the requirement that one must be a true *originator* of one's actions, but I shall stick to the formulation in terms of self-determination.

3. Just as the qualifier "true" may be used to mark off the ordinary, strong conception of responsibility from any standard compatibilist conception of responsibility, so too it may be used to mark off the strong conception of (true-responsibility-underlying) self-determination from any compatibilist conception of self-determination (e.g., note 1). "Self-determination" will be understood only in this strong sense in what follows, and so it will be possible to bracket or omit the word "true" without risk of ambiguity.

4. Frankfurt's theory of freedom, as expounded in "Freedom of the Will and the Concept of a Person," *Journal of Philosophy* 68 (1971), pp. 5–20, and "Three Concepts of Free Action," *Proceedings of the Aristotelian Society,* supp. 49 (1975), pp. 95–125, is (among other things) an interesting attempt to characterize a notion of self-determination that shows it to be compatible with determinism. As an attempt to define a notion of true-responsibility-entailing freedom, however, it is open to fundamental objection of the sort discussed here.

5. Cf. G. Strawson, *Freedom and Belief* (Oxford: Clarendon Press, 1986), pp. 67–70, 112–13, 167–68.

6. "Action performed for a reason" is the *only* sense of "rational action" tht is of present concern. In this sense one may perform a rational action even if one's reasons for that action are highly irrational from some ordinary point of view.

7. It is true that (*a*) someone can correctly be said to have made a choice without there having been any process of conscious deliberation, or silent "let it be so"; and (*b*) it is perhaps true that there are choices which are in a sense not made for any reason. But the choice mentioned in step 4 as required for true responsibility cannot be of kind (*b*); nor can it be of kind (*a*), I think—though this matters less. In so far as the agent's true responsibility depends on the choice, it must be a conscious, explicit choice.

8. Given these notions, the argument proceeds completely a priori. The issue of the truth or falsity of determinism is not even rasied. Furthermore, no view about the nature or "substantial realization" of the mind is presupposed; the debate about the nature of mind that goes on between identity theorists, dualists, and so on is entirely irrelevant to the basic problem of free will.

9. This notion is defined in Strawson, *Freedom and Belief,* pp. 33–41.

10. That is, R comes to be such that, because of how it then is, the subsequent rational explanation of A in terms of R is a true explanation. (This way of putting it purposely avoids unnecessary inquiry into what exactly this most common sort of occurrence involves.)

11. Remember that this notion of determination is defined in terms of the notion of true explanation.

12. There are some minor qualifications to this claim that are of no present importance (see reference to the lepidopterist in n. 15). On the general topic of determination of belief, see D. Wiggins, "Freedom, Knowledge, Belief and Causality," in G. Vesey, ed., *Knowledge and Necessity* (London: Macmillan, 1970).

13. It is possible that those moral philosophers who hold the view that reasons for actions can consist only of beliefs may want to claim this, with respect to certain beliefs, at least. But if they are libertarians, and are looking for some account of self-determination, this view may only create extra difficulties for them (see n. 15).

14. As noted in Strawson, *Freedom and Belief,* p. 39, the fact that it is natural to say that agents, not their reasons, determine actions provides no grounds for an objection to this way of putting the matter.

15. Libertarians who are trying to show that indeterminism could be a foundation for true self-determination may get into special trouble if they think that reasons for action can consist only of beliefs. For if one cannot plausibly see oneself as self-determining with respect to what one believes (except in the presently irrelevant sense that one can, as an aspiring lepidopterist, set oneself to acquire a great many beliefs about butterflies), then if one acts as one does just because of what beliefs one has, when one acts morally, it would seem that one cannot be self-determining or, therefore, truly responsible or free in so acting.

16. It is precisely in the heat of the pursuit of the notion of radical, determinism-incompatible true responsibility that one naturally takes up elements of the contrary compatibilist idea that liberty of spontaneity—which is, basically, simply freedom to do what you want or choose to do, and which is, as such, entirely compatible with determinism and non-self-determination—is all we could ever really want in the way of freedom. The conflict of intuition that produces this reversal or oscillation of views (the psychological explanation of which is a crucial part of a full account of the problem of freedom) is like a perpetual-motion machine. It promises to provide a source of energy that will keep the free will debate going for as long as human beings can think.

17. For an example of a theory of freedom according to which *a*'s responsibility for his actions consists simply in their being determined by his deliberations, the deliberations themselves not having been determined by anything, see *Time, Action and Necessity,* (London: Duckworth, 1981) by N. Denyer (esp. §§ 45, 73, 76).

18. We can, of course, cultivate tastes, traits, and dispositions, and in that sense we can be said to change and be responsible for how we are. But this is not the sense that matters for true responsibility. If we undertake such self-change at all, we do so for reasons we already have, as remarked in §1, and which we are not responsible for having. A man who sets out to change (reform) his own character, and is judged to have been successful in doing so, is no more truly responsible for how he is and what he subsequently does than anyone else.

19. Perhaps he was echoing Locke, *Essay II,* xxi. 25; the point is an old one.

20. The quotation from Kant is from *Critique of Practical Reason,* L.W. Beck, trans. (Indianapolis: Bobbs-Merrill Co., 1956), p. 101 (*AK.* V. 98). Cf. also

*Religion within the Limits of Reason Alone,* trans. T.M. Greene and H.H. Hudson, (New York: Harper and Row, 1960), p. 40 (*Ak.* VI. 44): "Man *himself* must make or have made himself into whatever, in a moral sense, whether good or evil, he is to become. Either condition must be an effect of his free choice [*Willkür*]; for otherwise he could not be held responsible for it and could therefore be *morally* neither good nor evil." The quotation from E. H. Carr is from *What is History?,* (New York: Vintage Books, 1961), p. 89; it is discussed by I. Berlin, in *Four Essays on Liberty* (New York: Oxford University Press, 1969), pp. xvii ff. Aristotle's views on the subject are in Bk. III, ch. V of the *Nicomachean Ethics* (but perhaps he did not really have in mind what I call true responsibility). For an early version of the opposing view, see Plato, *Timaeus* § 45.

21. Which is not to say that its direct opposite cannot also be elicited, for reasons discussed in ch. 6 of Strawson's *Freedom and Belief.*

22. Compare *Enquiry,* L.A. Selby-Bigge, ed. (Oxford: Clarendon Press, 1902), pp. 99–103. It could be argued that although Hume does not explicitly adopt his double position, it is there in essentials, connected to his moral subjectivism. Hume was surely aware of the sense in which true responsibility is impossible, God or no God. And he was, surely, aware of our deep commitment to belief in true responsibility, for it is built in to our natural disposition to praise and blame and to distinguish vice and virtue in actions, and these distinctions are "founded in the natural sentiments of the human mind [which are] not to be controlled by any philosophical theory or speculation whatsoever" (p. 103). He would have certainly agreed that we cannot give up belief in true responsibility, even if true responsibility is impossible, and not (like the existence of the material objects) just unprovable: "it is a point, which we must take for granted in all our [practical] reasonings," to adapt what he says about belief in material objects (*Treatise* I, iv. 2, p. 187).

23. In its present use, "determined" is *defined* (Strawson, *Freedom and Belief,* pp. 37–38) in terms of true explanation.

24. Cf. D. F. Pears, "The Appropriate Causation of Intentional Basic Action," *Critica* 7 (Oct. 1975), pp. 64–67.

25. It is not meant by this that the reasons are not themselves self-determined, of course, only that the agent whose reasons they are is not self-determined with respect to them.

26. They may well express their grasp of the fact that such self-determination is impossible in terms of the familiar idea that one is the way one is as a result of one's heredity and environment.

27. Cf. Strawson, *Freedom and Belief,* §§ 3.1 and 3.6.

28. Peter Strawson, "Freedom and Resentment," *Proceedings of the British Academy* 48 (1962), p. 25.

# 2

# The Problem
# of Autonomy

## THOMAS NAGEL

. . . Something peculiar happens when we view action from an objective
or external standpoint. Some of its most important features seem to
vanish under the objective gaze. Actions seem no longer assignable to
individual agents as sources, but become instead components of the flux
of events in the world of which the agent is a part. The easiest way to
produce this effect is to think of the possibility that all actions are causally determined, but it is not the only way. The essential source of the
problem is a view of persons and their actions as part of the order of
nature, causally determined or not. That conception, if pressed, leads to
the feeling that we are not agents at all, that we are helpless and not
responsible for what we do. Against this judgment the inner view of the
agent rebels. The question is whether it can stand up to the debilitating
effects of a naturalistic view.

Actually the objective standpoint generates three problems about
action, only one of which I shall take up. . . . The first problem, which I
shall simply describe and put aside, is the general metaphysical problem
of the nature of agency. It belongs to the philosophy of mind.

The question "What is action?" is much broader than the problem of
free will, for it applies even to the activity of spiders and to the periph-
eral, unconscious, or subintentional movements of human beings in the
course of more deliberate activity.[1] It applies to any movement that is
not involuntary. The question is connected with our theme because *my*

*doing* of an act—or the doing of an act by someone else—seems to disappear when we think of the world objectively. There seems no room for agency in a world of neural impulses, chemical reactions, and bone and muscle movements. Even if we add sensations, perceptions, and feelings we don't get action, or doing—there is only what happens.

. . . I think the only solution is to regard action as a basic mental or more acurately psychophysical category—reducible neither to physical nor to other mental terms. I cannot improve on Brian O'Shaughnessy's exhaustive defense of this position. Action has its own irreducibly internal aspect as do other psychological phenomena—there is a characteristic mental asymmetry between awareness of one's own actions and awareness of the actions of others—but action isn't anything else, alone or in combination with a physical movement: not a sensation, not a feeling, not a belief, not an intention or desire. If we restrict our palette to such things plus physical events, agency will be omitted from our picture of the world.

But even if we add it as an irreducible feature, making subjects of experience also (and as O'Shaughnessy argues, inevitably) subjects of action, the problem of free action remains. We may act without being free, and we may doubt the freedom of others without doubting that they act. What undermines the sense of freedom doesn't automatically undermine agency.[2] I shall leave the general problem of agency aside in what follows, and simply assume that there is such a thing.

What I shall discuss concerns the problem of free will. [There are two aspects to this problem,] corresponding to the two ways in which objectivity threatens ordinary assumptions about human freedom. I call one the problem of autonomy and the other the problem of responsibility; the first presents itself initially as a problem about our own freedom and the second as a problem about the freedom of others.[3] An objective view of actions as events in the natural order (determined or not) produces a sense of impotence and futility with respect to what we do ourselves. It also undermines certain basic attitudes toward all agents—those reactive attitudes[4] that are conditional on the attribution of responsibility. It is the second of these effects that is usually referred to as the problem of free will. But the threat to our conception of our own actions—the sense that we are being carried along by the universe like small pieces of flotsam—is equally important and equally deserving of the title. [It is this form of the problem that I shall discuss here.] . . .

Like other basic philosophical problems, the problem of free will is not in the first instance verbal. It is not a problem about what we are to *say* about action, responsibility, what someone could or could not have done, and so forth. It is rather a bafflement of our feelings and attitudes—a loss of confidence, conviction, or equilibrium. Just as the basic problem of epistemology is not whether we can be *said to know* things, but lies rather in the loss of belief and the invasion of doubt, so the problem of free will lies in the erosion of interpersonal attitudes and of the sense of autonomy. Questions about what we are to say about action and responsibility merely attempt after the fact to express those feelings—feelings of impotence, of imbalance, and of affective detachment from other people.

These forms of unease are familiar once we have encountered the problem of free will through the hypothesis of determinism. We are undermined but at the same time ambivalent, because the unstrung attitudes don't disappear; they keep forcing themselves into consciousness despite their loss of support. A philosophical treatment of the problem must deal with such disturbances of the spirit, and not just with their verbal expression.

I change my mind about the problem of free will every time I think about it, and therefore cannot offer any view with even moderate confidence; but my present opinion is that nothing that might be a solution has yet been described. This is not a case where there are several possible candidate solutions and we don't know which is correct. It is a case where nothing believable has (to my knowledge) been proposed by anyone in the extensive public discussion of the subject.

The difficulty, as I shall try to explain, is that while we can easily evoke disturbing effects by taking up an external view of our own actions and the actions of others, it is impossible to give a coherent account of the internal view of action which is under threat. When we try to explain what we believe which seems to be undermined by a conception of actions as events in the world—determined or not—we end up with something that is either incomprehensible or clearly inadequate.

This naturally suggests that the threat is unreal, and that an account of freedom can be given which is compatible with the objective view, and perhaps even with determinism. But I believe this is not the case. All such accounts fail to allay the feeling that, looked at from far enough outside, agents are helpless and not responsible. Compatibilist accounts of freedom tend to be even less plausible than libertarian ones. Nor is it possible simply to dissolve our unanalyzed sense of autonomy and responsibility. It is something we can't get rid of, either in relation to ourselves or in relation to others. We are apparently condemned to want something impossible.

[How, then, does the problem of autonomy arise?] In acting we occupy the internal perspective, and we can occupy it sympathetically with regard to the actions of others. But when we move away from our individual point of view, and consider our own actions and those of others simply as part of the course of events in a world that contains us among other creatures and things, it begins to look as though we never really contribute anything.

From the inside, when we act, alternative possibilities seem to lie open before us: to turn right or left, to order this dish or that, to vote for one candidate or the other—and one of the possibilities is made actual by what we do. The same applies to our internal consideration of the actions of others. But from an external perspective, things look different. That perspective takes in not only the circumstances of action as they present themselves to the agent, but also the conditions and influences lying behind the action, including the complete nature of the agent himself. While we cannot fully occupy this perspective toward ourselves while acting, it seems possible that many of the alternatives that appear to lie open when viewed from an internal perspective would seem closed from this outer point of view, if we could take it up. And even if some of them are left open, given a complete specification of the condition of the agent and the circumstances of action, it is not clear how this would leave anything further for the agent to contribute to the outcome—anything that he could contribute as source, rather than merely as the scene of the outcome—the person whose act it is. If they are left open given everything about him, what doe he have to do with the result?

From an external perspective, then, the agent and everything about him seems to be swallowed up by the circumstances of action; nothing of him is left to intervene in those circumstances. This happens whether or not the relation between action and its antecedent conditions is conceived as deterministic. In either case we cease to face the world and instead become parts of it; we and our lives are seen as products and manifestations of the world as a whole. Everything I do or that anyone else does is part of a larger course of events that no one "does," but that happens, with or without explanation. Everything I do is part of something I don't do, because I am a part of the world. We may elaborate this external picture by reference to biological, psychological, and social factors in the formation of ourselves and other agents. But the picture doesn't have to be complete in order to be threatening. It is enough to form the idea of the possibility of a picture of this kind. Even if we can't attain it, an observer literally outside us might.

Why is this threatening, and what does it threaten? Why are we not content to regard the internal perspective of agency as a form of clouded subjective appearance, based as it inevitably must be on an incomplete view of the circumstances? The alternatives are alternatives only relative to what we know, and our choices result from influences of which we are only partly aware. The external perspective would then provide a more complete view, superior to the internal. We accept a parallel subordination of subjective appearance to objective reality in other areas.

The reason we cannot accept it here, at least not as a general solution, is that action is too ambitious. We aspire in some of our actions to a kind of autonomy that is not a mere subjective appearance—not merely ignorance of their sources—and we have the same view of others like us. The sense that we are the authors of our own actions is not just a feeling but a belief, and we can't come to regard it as a pure appearance without giving it up altogether. But what belief is it?

I have already said that I suspect it is no intelligible belief at all; but that has to be shown. What I am about to say is highly controversial, but let me just describe what I take to be our ordinary conception of autonomy. It presents itself initially as the belief that antecedent circumstances, including the condition of the agent, leave some of the things we will do undetermined: they are determined only by our choices, which are motivationally explicable but not themselves causally determined. Although many of the external and internal conditions of choice are inevitably fixed by the world and not under my control, some range of open possibilities is generally presented to me on an occasion of action—and when by acting I make one of those possibilities actual, the final explanation of this (once the background which defines the possibilities has been taken into account) is given by the intentional explanation of my action, which is comprehensible only through my point of view. My reasons for doing it is the *whole* reason why it happened, and no further explanation is either necessary or possible. (My doing it for no particular reason is a limiting case of this kind of explanation.)

The objective view seems to wipe out such autonomy because it admits only one kind of explanation of why something happened—causal explanation—and equates its absence with the absence of any explanation at all. It may be able to admit causal explanations that are probabilistic, but the basic idea which it finds congenial is that the explanation of an occurrence must show how that occurrence, or a range of possibilities within which it falls, was necessitated by prior conditions and events. (I shall not say anything about the large question of how this notion of necessity is to be interpreted.) To the extent that no such necessity exists, the occurrence is unexplained. There is no room in an objective picture of the world for a type of explanation of action that is not causal. The defense of freedom requires the acknowledgment of a different kind of explanation essentially connected to the agent's point of view.

Though it would be contested, I believe we have such an idea of autonomy. Many philosophers have defended some version of this position as the truth about freedom: for example Farrer, Anscombe, and Wiggins. (The metaphysical theories of agent-causation espoused by Chisholm and Taylor are different, because they try to force autonomy into the objective causal order—giving a name to a mystery.) But whatever version one picks, the trouble is that while it may give a correct surface description of our prereflective sense of our own autonomy, when we look at the idea closely, it collapses. The alternative form of explanation doesn't really explain the action at all.

The intuitive idea of autonomy includes conflicting elements, which imply that it both is and is not a way of explaining why an action was done. A free action should not be determined by antecedent conditions, and should be fully explained only intentionally, in terms of justifying reasons and purposes. When someone makes an autonomous choice such as whether to accept a job, and there are reasons on both sides of the issue, we are supposed to be able to explain what he did by pointing to his reasons for accepting it. But we could equally have explained his refusing the job, if he had refused, by referring to the reasons on the other side—and he could have refused for those other reasons: that is the essential claim of autonomy. It applies even if one choice is significantly more reasonable than the other. Bad reasons are reasons too.[5]

Intentional explanation, if there is such a thing, can explain either choice in terms of the appropriate reasons, since either choice would be intelligible if it occurred. But for this very reason it cannot explain why the person accepted the job for the reasons in favor instead of refusing it for the reasons against. It cannot explain on grounds of intelligibility why one of two intelligible courses of action, both of which were possible, occurred. And even where it can account for this in terms of further reasons, there will be a point at which the explanation gives out. We say that someone's character and values are revealed by the choices he makes in such circumstances, but if these are indeed independent conditions, they too must either have or lack an explanation.

If autonomy requires that the central element of choice be explained in a way that does not take us outside the point of view of the agent (leaving aside the explanation of what faces him with the choice), then intentional explanations must simply come to an end when all available reasons have been given, and nothing else can take over where they leave off. But this seems to mean that an autonomous intentional explanation cannot explain precisely what it is supposed to explain, namely *why I did what I did rather than the alternative that was causally open to me.* It says I did it for certain reasons, but does not explain why I didn't decide not to do it for other reasons. It may render the action subjectively intelligible, but it does not explain why this rather than another equally possible and comparably intelligible action was done. That seems to be something for which there is no explanation, either intentional or causal.

Of course there is a trivial intentional explanation: my reasons for doing it are also my reasons against not doing it for other reasons. But since the same could be said if I had done the opposite, this amounts to explaining what happened by saying it happened. It does not stave off the question why these reasons rather than the others were the ones that motivated me. At some point this question will either have no answer or it will have an answer that takes us outside of the domain of subjective normative reasons and into the domain of formative causes of my character or personality.[6]

So I am at a loss to account for what we believe in believing that we are autonomous—what intelligible belief is undermined by the external view. That is, I cannot say what would, if it were true, support our sense that our free actions originate with us. Yet the sense of an internal explanation persists—an explanation insulated from the external view which is complete in itself and renders illegitimate all further requests for explanation of my action as an event in the world.

As a last resort the libertarian might claim that anyone who does not accept an account of what I was up to as a basic explanation of action is the victim of a very limited conception of what an explanation is—a conception locked into the objective standpoint which therefore begs the question against the concept of autonomy. But he needs a better reply than this. Why aren't these autonomous subjective explanations really just descriptions of how it seemed to the agent—before, during, and after—to do what he did; why are they something more than impressions? Of course they are at least impressions, but we take them to be impressions *of* something, something whose reality is not guaranteed by the impression. Not being able to say what that something is, and at the same time finding the possibility of its absence very disturbing, I am at a dead end.

I have to conclude that what we want is something impossible, and that the desire for it is evoked precisely by the objective view of ourselves that reveals it to be impossible. At the moment when we see ourselves from outside as bits of the world, two things happen: we are no longer satisfied in actioon with anything less than intervention in the world from outside; and we see clearly that this makes no sense. The very capacity that is the source of the trouble—our capacity to view ourselves from outside—encourages our aspirations of autonomy by giving us the sense that we ought to be able to encompass ourselves completely, and thus become the absolute source of what we do. At any rate we become dissatisfied with anything less.

When we act we are not cut off from the knowledge of ourselves that is revealed from the external standpoint, so far as we can occupy it. It is, after all, *our* standpoint as much as the internal one is, and if we take it up, we can't help trying to include anything it reveals to us in a new, expanded basis of action. We act, if possible, on the basis of the most complete view of the circumstances of action that we can attain, and this includes as complete a view as we can attain of ourselves. Not that we want to be paralyzed by self-consciousness. But we can't regard ourselves, in action, as subordinate to an external view of ourselves, because we automatically subordinate the external view to the purposes of our actions. We feel that in acting we ought to be able to determine not only our choices but the inner conditions of those choices, provided we step far enough outside ourselves.

So the external standpoint at once holds out the hope of genuine autonomy, and snatches it away. By increasing our objectivity and self-awareness, we seem to acquire increased control over what will influence our actions, and thus to take our lives into our own hands. Yet the logical goal of these ambitions is incoherent, for to be really free we would have to act from a standpoint completely outside ourselves, choosing everything about ourselves, including all our principles of choice—creating ourselves from nothing, so to speak.

This is self-contradictory. In order to do anything we must already be something. However much material we incorporate from the external view into the grounds of action and choice, this same external view assures us that we remain parts of the world and products, determined or not, of its history. Here as elsewhere the objective standpoint creates an appetite which it shows to be insatiable.

The problem of freedom and the problem of epistemological skepticism are alike in this respect. In belief, as in action, rational beings aspire to autonomy. They wish to form their beliefs on the basis of principles and methods of reasoning and confirmation that they themselves can judge to be correct, rather than on the basis of influences that they do not understand, of which they are unaware, or which they cannot assess. That is the aim of knowledge. But taken to its logical limit, the aim is incoherent. We cannot assess and revise or confirm our entire system of thought and judgment from outside, for we would have nothing to do it with. We remain, as pursuers of knowledge, creatures inside the world who have not created ourselves, and some of whose processes of thought have simply been given to us.

In the formation of belief, as in action, we belong to a world we have not created and of which we are the products; it is the external view which both reveals this and makes us wish for more. However objective a standpoint we succeed in making part of the basis of our actions and beliefs, we continue to be threatened by the idea of a still more external and comprehensive view of ourselves that we cannot incorporate, but that would reveal the unchosen sources of our most autonomous efforts. The objectivity that seems to offer greater control also reveals the ultimate givenness of the self.

Can we proceed part way along the inviting path of objectivity without ending up in the abyss, where the pursuit of objectivity undermines itself and everything else? In practice, outside of philosophy we find certain natural stopping places along the route, and do not worry about how things would look if we went further. In this respect too the situation resembles that in epistemology, where justification and criticism come fairly peacefully to an end in everyday life. The trouble is that our complacency seems unwarranted as soon as we reflect on what would be revealed to a still more external view, and it is not clear how we can reestablish these natural stopping places on a new footing once they are put in doubt.

It would require some alternative to the literally unintelligible ambition of intervening in the world from outside (an ambition expressed by Kant in the unintelligible idea of the noumenal self which is outside time and causality). This ambition arises by a natural extension or continuation of the pursuit of freedom in everyday life. I wish to act not only in light of the external circumstances facing me and the possibilities that they leave open, but in light of the internal circumstances as well: my desires, beliefs, feelings, and impulses. I wish to be able to subject my motives, principles, and habits to critical examination, so that nothing moves me to action without my agreeing to it. In this way, the setting against which I act is gradually enlarged and extended inward, till it includes more and more of myself, considered as one of the contents of the world.

In its earlier stages the process does genuinely seem to increase freedom, by making self-knowledge and objectivity part of the basis of action. But the danger is obvious. The more completely the self is swallowed up in the circumstances of action, the less I have to act with. I cannot get completely outside myself. The process that starts as a means to the enlargement of freedom seems to lead to its destruction. When I contemplate the world as a whole I see my actions, even at their empirically most "free," as part of the course of nature, and this is not my doing or anyone else's. The objective self is not in a position to pull the strings of my life from outside any more than [Thomas Nagel] is.

At the end of the path that seems to lead to freedom and knowledge lie skepticism and helplessness. We can act only from inside the world, but when we see ourselves from outside, the autonomy we experience from inside appears as an illusion, and we who are looking from outside cannot act at all.

## Notes

1. See H. Frankfurt, "The Problem of Free Action," *American Philosophical Quarterly* 15 (April 1978), pp. 157–62.

2. Here I agree with Taylor, *Action and Purpose* (Englewood Cliffs, N.J.: Prentice Hall, 1966), p. 140.

3. Jonathan Bennett makes this distinction, calling them the problems of agency and accountability, respectively. (*Kant's Dialectic* [Cambridge University Press, 1974], ch. 10).

4. P. Strawson, "Freedom and Resentment," *Proceedings of the British Academy* 48 (1962), pp. 1–25.

5. Some would hold that we have all the autonomy we should want if our choice is determined by compelling reasons. Hampshire, for example, attributes to Spinoza the position that "a man is most free, . . . and also feels himself to be most free, when he cannot help drawing a certain conclusion, and cannot help embarking on a certain course of action in view of the evidently compelling reasons in favor of it. . . . The issue is decided for him when the arguments in support of a theoretical conclusion are conclusive arguments" ("Spinoza and the Idea of Freedoom," in his *Freedom of Mind* [Princeton: Princeton University Press, 1974], p. 198). And Wolf proposes as the condition of freedom that the agent "could have done otherwise if there had been good and sufficient reason" ("Asymmetrical Freedom," *Journal of Philosophy* 77 [1980], p. 159)—which means that if there wasn't a good reason to act differently, the free agent needn't have been able to act differently.

Something like this has more plausibility with respect to thought, I believe, than it has with respect to action. In forming beliefs we may hope for nothing more than to be determined by the truth (see D. Wiggins, "Freedom, Knowledge, Belief and Causality," in G. Vesey, ed., *Knowledge and Necessity* [London: Macmillan, 1970], pp. 145–48), but in action our initial assumption is different. Even when we feel rationally compelled to act, this does not mean we are causally determined. When Luther says he *can* do nothing else, he is referring to the normative irresistibility of his reasons, not to their causal power, and I believe that even in such a case causal determination is not compatible with autonomy.

6. Lucas notices this but is not, I think, sufficiently discouraged by it: "There remains a tension between the programme of complete explicability and the requirements of freedom. If men have free will, then no complete explanation of their actions can be given, except by reference to themselves. We can give their reasons. But we cannot explain why their reasons were reasons for them. . . . Asked why I acted, I give my reasons: asked why I chose to accept them as reasons, I can only say 'I just did' " (*The Freedom of the Will* [Oxford: Clarendon Press, 1970], pp. 171–72).

# 3

## On Giving Libertarians What They Say They Want

### DANIEL DENNETT

Why is the free will problem so persistent? Partly, I suspect, because it is called *the* free will problem. Hilliard, the great card magician, used to fool even his professional colleagues with a trick he called the tuned deck. Twenty times in a row he'd confound the quidnuncs, as he put it, with the same trick, a bit of prestidigitation that resisted all the diagnostic hypotheses of his fellow magicians. The trick, as he eventually revealed, was a masterpiece of subtle misdirection; it consisted entirely of the *name*, "the tuned deck," plus a peculiar but obviously nonfunctional bit of ritual. It was, you see, *many* tricks, however many different but familiar tricks Hilliard had to perform in order to stay one jump ahead of the solvers. As soon as their experiments and subtle arguments had conclusively eliminated one way of doing the trick, that was the way he would do the trick on future trials. This would have been obvious to his sophisticated onlookers had they not been so intent on finding *the* solution to *the* trick.

The so called free will problem is in fact many not very closely related problems tied together by a name and lots of attendant anxiety. Most people can be brought by reflection to care very much what the truth is on these matters, for each problem poses a threat—to our self-esteem, to our conviction that we are not living deluded lives, to our conviction that we may justifiably trust our grasp of such utterly familiar notions as possibility, opportunity, and ability.[1] There is no very good reason to suppose that an acceptable solution to *one* of the problems will be, or even point to, an acceptable solution to the others, and we may be misled by residual unallayed worries into rejecting or undervaluing partial solutions, in the misguided hope that we might allay all the doubts with one overarching doctrine or theory. But we don't have any good theories. Since the case for determinism is persuasive and since we all want to believe we have free will, *compatibilism* is the strategic favorite, but we must admit that no compatibilism free of problems while full of the traditional flavors of responsibility has yet been devised.

The alternatives to compatibilism are anything but popular. Both the libertarian and the hard determinist believe that free will and determinism are incompatible. The hard determinist says: "So much of the worse for free will." The libertarian says: "So much the worse for determinism," at least with regard to human action. Both alternatives have been roundly and routinely dismissed as at best obscure, at worst incoherent. But alas for the compatibilist, neither view will oblige us by fading away. Their persistence, like Hilliard's success, probably has many explanations. I hope to diagnose just one of them.

In a recent paper, David Wiggins has urged us to look with more sympathy at the program of libertarianism.[2] Wiggins first points out that a familiar argument often presumed to demolish libertarianism begs the question. The first premise of this argument is that every event is either causally determined or random. Then since the libertarian insists that human actions cannot be both free and determined, the libertarian must be supposing that any and all free actions are random. But one would hardly hold oneself responsible for an action that merely happened at random, so libertarianism, far from securing a necessary condition for responsible action, has unwittingly secured a condition that would defeat responsibility altogether. Wiggins points out that the first premise, that every event is either causally determined or random, is not the innocent logical truth it appears to be. The innocent logical truth is that every event is either causally determined or nor causally determined. There may be an established sense of the word "random" that is unproblematically synonymous with "not causally determined," but the word "random" in common parlance has further connotations of pointlessness or arbitrariness, and it is these very connotations that ground our acquiescence in the further premise that one would not hold oneself responsible for one's random actions. It may be the case that whatever is random in the sense of being causally undetermined, is random in the sense connoting utter meaninglessness, but that is just what the libertarian wishes to deny. This standard objection to libertarianism, then, assumes what it must prove; it fails to show that undetermined action would be random action, and hence action for which we would not be held responsible.

But is there in fact any reasonable hope that the libertarian can find some defensible ground between the absurdity of "blind chance" on the one hand and on the other what Wiggins calls the cosmic unfairness of the determinist's view of these matters? Wiggins thinks there is. He draws our attention to a speculation of Russell's: "It might be that without infringing the laws of physics, intelligence could make improbable things happen, as Maxwell's demon would have defeated the second law of thermodynamics by opening the trap door to fast-moving particles and closing it to slow-moving particles.'[3] Wiggins sees many problems with the speculation, but he does, nevertheless, draw a glimmer of an idea from it.

> For indeterminism maybe all we really need to imagine or conceive is a world in which (a) there is some macroscopic indeterminacy founded in microscopic indeterminacy, and (b) an appreciable number of the free actions or policies or deliberations of individual agents, although they are not even in principle hypothetico-deductively derivable from antecedent conditions, can be such as to persuade us to fit them into meaningful sequences. We need not trace free actions back to volitions construed as little pushes aimed from outside the physical world. What we must find instead are patterns which are coherent and intelligible in the low level terms of practical deliberation, even though they are not amenable to the kind of generalization or necessity which is the stuff of rigorous theory. (p. 52)

The "low level terms of practical deliberation" are, I take it, the familiar terms of intentional or reason-giving explanation. We typically render actions intelligible by citing their reasons, the beliefs and desires of the agent that render the actions at least marginally reasonable under the circumstances. Wiggins is suggesting then that if we could somehow *make sense* of human actions at the level of intentional explanation, then in spite of the fact that those actions might be physically undetermined, they would not be random. Wiggins invites us to take this possibility seriously, but he has little further to say in elaboration or defense of this. He has said enough, however, to suggest to me a number of ways in which we could give libertarians what they seem to want.

Wiggins asks only that human actions be seen to be *intelligible* in the low-level terms of practical deliberation. Surely if human actions were *predictable* in the low-level terms of practical deliberation, they would be intelligible in those terms. So I propose first to demonstrate that there is a way in which human behavior could be strictly undetermined from the physicist's point of view while at the same time accurately predictable from the intentional level. This demonstration, alas, will be very disappointing, for it relies on a cheap trick and what it establishes can be immediately seen to be quite extraneous to the libertarian's interests. But it is a necessary preamble to what I hope will be a more welcome contribution to the libertarian's cause. So let us get the disappointing preamble behind us.

Here is how a bit of human behavior could be undetermined from the physicist's point of view, but quite clearly predictable by the intentionalist. Suppose we were to build an electronic gadget that I will call an answer box. The answer box is designed to record a person's answers to simple questions. It has two buttons, a Yes button, and a No button, and two foot pedals, a Yes pedal, and a No pedal, all clearly marked. It also has a little display screen divided in half, and on one side it says "use the buttons" and on the other side it says "use the pedals". We design this bit of apparatus so that only one half of this display screen is illuminated at any one time. Once a minute, a radium randomizer determines, in an entirely undetermined way of course, whether the display screen says "use the buttons" or "use the pedals." I now propose the following experiment. First, we draw up a list of ten very simple questions that have Yes or No answers, questions of the order of difficulty of "Do fish swim?" and "Is Texas bigger than Rhode Island?" We seat a subject at the answer box and announce that a handsome reward will be given to those who correctly follow all the experimental instructions, and a bonus will be given to those who answer all our questions correctly.

Now, can the physicist in principle predict the subject's behavior? Let us suppose the subject is in fact a physically deterministic system, and let us suppose further that the physicist has perfect knowledge of the subject's initial state, all the relevant deterministic laws, and all the interactions within the closed situation of the experimental situation. Still, the unpredictable behavior of the answer box will infect the subject on a macroscopic scale with its own indeterminacy on at least ten occasions during the period the physicist must predict. So the best the physicist can do is issue a multiple disjunctive or multiple conditional prediction. Can the intentionalist do any better? Yes, of course. The intentionalist, having read the instructions given to the subject and having sized up the suject as a person of roughly normal intelligence and motivation, and having seen that all the odd numbered questions have Yes answers and the even numbered questions have No answers, confidently predicts that the subject will behave as follows: "The subject will give Yes answers to questions *1, 3, 5, 7,* and *9,* and the subject will answer the rest of the questions in the negative." There are no *if's, or's,* or *maybe's* in those predictions. They are categorical and precise—precise enough, for instance, to appear in a binding contract or satisfy a court of law.

This is, of course, the cheap trick I warned you about. There is no real difference in the predictive power of the two predictors. The intentionalist, for instance, is no more in a position to predict whether the subject will move finger or foot than the physicist is, and the physicist may well be able to give predictions that are tantamount to the intentionalist's. The physicist may, for instance, be able to make this prediction: "When question 6 is presented, if the illuminated sign on the box reads 'use the pedals', the subject's right foot will move at velocity $k$ until it depresses the No pedal $n$ inches, and if the illuminated sign says 'use the buttons', the subject's right index finger will trace a trajectory terminating on the No button." Such a prediction is, if anything, more detailed than the intentionalist's simple prediction of the negative answer to question 6, and it might in fact be more reliable and better grounded as well. But so what? What we are normally interested in, what we are normally interested in *predicting*, moreover, is not the skeletal motion of human beings but their actions, and the intentionalist can predict the actions of the subject (at least insofar as most of us would take any interest in them) without the elaborate rigmarole and calculations of the physicist. The possibility of indeterminancy in the environment of the kind introduced here, and hence the possibility of indeterminacy in the subject's reaction to that environment, is something with regard to which the intentionalistic predictive power is quite neutral. Still, we could not expect the libertarian to be interested in this variety of undetermined human behavior, behavior that is undetermined simply because the behavior of the answer box, something entirely external to the agent, is undetermined.

Suppose then we move something like the answer box inside the agent. It is a commonplace of action theory that virtually all human actions can be accomplished or realized in a wide variety of ways. There are, for instance, indefinitely many ways of insulting your neighbor, or even of asserting that snow is white. And we are often not much interested, nor should we be, in exactly which particular physical motion accomplishes the act we intend. So let us suppose that our nervous system is so constructed and designed that whenever in the implementation of an intention, our countrol system is faced with two or more options with regard to which we are nonpartisan, a purely undetermined tie-breaking "choice" is made. There you are at the supermarket, wanting a can of Campbell's Tomato Soup, and faced with an array of several hundred identical cans of Campbell's Tomato Soup, all roughly equidistant from your hands. What to do? Before you even waste time and energy pondering this trivial problem, let us suppose, a perfectly random factor determines which can your hand reaches out for. This is, of course, simply a variation on the ancient theme of Buridan's ass, that unfortunate beast who, finding himself hungry, thirsty, and equidistant between food and water, perished for lack of the divine nudge that in a human being accomplishes a truly free choice. This has never been a promising vision of the free choice of responsible agents, if only because it seems to secure freedom for such a small and trivial class of our choices. What does it avail me if I am free to choose *this* can of soup, but

not free to choose between buying and stealing it? But however unprom-
ising the idea is as a centerpiece for an account of free will, we must not
underestimate its possible scope of application. Such trivial choice points
seldom obtrude in our conscious deliberation, no doubt, but they are
quite possibly ubiquitous nonetheless at an unconscious level. Whenever we choose to perform an action of a certain sort, there are no doubt
slight variations in timing, style, and skeletal implementation of those
actions that are within our power but beneath our concern. For all we
know, which variation occurs is *undetermined.* That is, the implementation of any one of our intentional actions may encounter undetermined
*choice points* in many places in the causal chain. The resulting behavior
would not be distinguishable to our everyday eyes, or from the point of
view of our everyday interests, from behavior that was rigidly determined. What we are mainly interested in, as I said before, are actions,
not motions, and what we are normally interested in predicting are
actions.

It is worth noting that not only can we typically predict actions from
the intentional stance without paying heed to possibly undetermined
variations of implementation of these actions, but we can even put
together chains of intentional predictions that are relatively immune to
such variation. In the summer of 1974 many people were confidently
predicting that Nixon would resign. As the day and hour approached,
the prediction grew more certain and more specific as to time and place;
Nixon would resign not just in the near future, but in the next hour, and
in the White House, and in the presence of television cameramen, and so
forth. Still, it was not plausible to claim to know just how he would
resign, whether he would resign with grace, or dignity, or with an attack
on his critics, whether he would enunciate clearly or mumble or trem-
ble. These details were not readily predictable, but most of the further
dependent predictions we were interested in making did not hinge on
these subtle variations. However Nixon resigned, we could predict that
Goldwater would publicly approve of it, Cronkite would report that
Goldwater had so approved of it, Sevareid would comment on it, Ro-
dino would terminate the proceedings of the Judiciary Committee, and
Gerald Ford would be sworn in as Nixon's successor. Of course, some
predictions we might have made at the time would have hinged crucially on particular details of the precise manner of Nixon's resignation,
and if these details happened to be undetermined both by Nixon's intentions and by any other feature of the moment, then some human actions
of perhaps great importance would be infected by the indeterminancy of
Nixon's manner at the moment just as our exemplary subject's behavior
was infected by the indeterminacy of the answer box. That would not,
however, make these actions any the less intelligible to us as actions.

This result is not just what the libertarian is looking for, but it is a useful result nevertheless. It shows that we can indeed install inde-terminism in the internal causal chains affecting human behavior *at the macroscopic level* while preserving the intelligibility of practical delibera-tion that the libertarian requires. We may have good reasons from other quarters for embracing determinism, but we need not fear that macro-scopic indeterminism in human behavior would of necessity rob our lives of intelligibility by producing chaos. Thus, philosophers such as Ayer and Hobart,[4] who argue that free will requires determinism, must be wrong. There are *some* ways our world could be macroscopically indeterministic, without that fact remotely threatening the coherence of the intentionalistic conceptual scheme of action description presupposed by claims of moral responsibility.

Still, it seems that all we have done is install indeterminism in a *harmless* place by installing it in an *irrelevant* place. The libertarian would not be relieved to learn that although his decision to murder his neigh-bor was quite determined, the style and trajectory of the death blow was not. Clearly, what the libertarian has in mind is indeterminism at some earlier point, prior to the ultimate decision or formation of intention, and unless we can provide that, we will not aid the libertarian's cause. But perhaps we can provide that as well.

Let us return, then, to Russell's speculation that intelligence might make improbable things happen. Is there any way that something like this could be accomplished? The idea of intelligence exploiting ran-domness is not unfamiliar. The poet, Paul Valéry, nicely captures the basic idea:

> It takes two to invent anything. The one makes up combinations; the other one chooses, recognizes what he wishes and what is important to him in the mass of the things which the former has imparted to him. What we call genius is much less the work of the first one than the readiness of the second one to grasp the value of what has been laid before him and to choose it.[5]

Here we have the suggestion of an intelligent *selection* from what may be a partially arbitrary or chaotic or random *production,* and what we need is the outline of a model for such a process in human decision making.

An interesting feature of most important human decision making is that it is made under time pressure. Even if there are, on occasion, algorithmic decision procedures giving guaranteed optimal solutions to our problems, and even if these decision procedures are in principle available to us, we may not have time or energy to utilize them. We are rushed, but moreover, we are all more or less lazy, even about terribly critical decisions that will affect our lives—our own lives, to say nothing of the lives of others. We invariably settle for a *heuristic* decision proce-dure; we *satisfice,*[6] we poke around hoping for inspiration; we do our best to think about the problem in a more or less directed way until we must finally stop mulling, summarize our results as best we can, and act. A realistic model of such decision making just *might* have the following feature: when someone is faced with an important decision, something in him generates a variety of more or less relevant considerations bearing on the decision. Some of these considerations, we may suppose, are determined to be generated, but others may be nondeterministically generated. For instance, Jones, who is finishing her dissertation on Aristotle and the practical syllogism, must decide within a week whether to accept the assistant professorship at the University of Chicago or the assistant professorship at Swarthmore. She considers the difference in salaries, the probable quality of the students, the quality of her colleagues, the teaching load, the location of the schools, and so forth. Let us suppose that considerations *A, B, C, D, E,* and *F* occur to her and that those are the only considerations that occur to her, and that on the basis of those, she decides to accept the job at Swarthmore. She does this *knowing* of course that she could devote more time and energy to this deliberation, could cast about for other relevant considerations, could perhaps dismiss some of *A–F* as being relatively unimportant and so forth, but being no more meticulous, no more obsessive, than the rest of us about such matters, she settles for the considerations that have occurred to her and makes her decision.

Let us suppose though, that after sealing her fate with a phone call, consideration *G* occurs to her, and she says to herself: "If only *G* had occurred to me before, I would cetainly have chosen the University of Chicago instead, but *G* didn't occur to me." Now it just might be the case that *exactly* which considerations occur to one in such circumstances is to some degree strictly undetermined. If that were the case, then even the intentionalist, knowing everything knowable about Jones' settled beliefs and preferences and desires, might nevertheless be unable to predict her decision, except perhaps conditionally. The intentionalist might be able to argue as follows: "If considerations *A–F* occur to Jones, then she will go Swarthmore," and this would be a prediction that would be grounded on a rational argument based on considerations *A–F* according to which Swarthmore was the best place to go. The intentionalist might go on to add, however, that if consideration *G* also occurs to Jones (which is strictly unpredicatable unless we interfere and draw Jones's attention to *G*), Jones will choose the University of Chicago instead. Notice that although we are supposing that the decision is in this way strictly unpredictable except conditionally by the intentionalist, whichever choice Jones makes is retrospectively intelligible. There will be a rationale for the decision in either case; in the former case a rational argument in favor of Swarthmore based on *A–F,* and in the latter case, a rational argument in favor of Chicago based on *A–G.* (There may, of course be yet another rational argument based on *A–H,* or *I,* or *J,* in favor of Swarthmore, or in favor of going on welfare, or in favor of suicide.) Even if *in principle* we couldn't predict which of many rationales could ultimately be correctly cited in justification or retrospective explanation of the choice made by Jones, we could be confident that there would be some sincere, authentic, and not unintelligible rationale to discover.

The model of decision making I am proposing has the following feature: when we are faced with an important decision, a consideration generator whose output is to some degree undetermined produces a series of considerations, some of which may of course be immediately rejected as irrelevant by the agent (consciously or unconsciously). Those considerations that are selected by the agent as having a more than negligible bearing on the decision then figure in a reasoning process, and if the agent is in the main reasonable, those considerations ultimately serve as predictors and explicators of the agent's final decision. What can be said in favor of such a model, bearing in mind that there are many possible substantive variations on the basic theme?

First, I think it captures what Russell was looking for. The intelligent selection, rejection, and weighting of the considerations that do occur to the subject is a matter of intelligence making the difference. Intelligence makes the difference here because an intelligent selection and assessment procedure determines which microscopic indeterminacies get amplified, as it were, into important macroscopic determiners of ultimate behavior.

Second, I think it installs indeterminism in the right place for the libertarian, if there is a right place at all. The libertarian could not have wanted to place the indeterminism *at the end* of the agent's assessment and deliberation. It would be insane to hope that, after all, rational deliberation had terminated with an assessment of the best available course of action, indeterminism would then intervene to flip the coin before action. It is a familiar theme in discussions of free will that the important claim that one could have done otherwise under the circumstances is not plausibly construed as the claim that one could have done otherwise given *exactly* the set of convictions and desires that prevailed at the end of rational deliberation. So if there is to be a crucial undetermined nexus, it had better be prior to the final assessment of the considerations on the stage, which is right where we have located it.

Third, I think that the model is recommended by considerations that have little or nothing to do with the free will problem. It may well turn out to be that from the point of view of biological engineering, it is just more efficient and in the end more rational that decision making should occur in this way. Time rushes on, and people must act, and there may not be time for a person to canvass all his beliefs, conduct all the investigations and experiments that he would see were relevant, assess every preference in his stock before acting, and it may be that the best way to prevent the inertia of Hamlet from overtaking us is for our decision-making processes to be expedited by a process of partially random generation and test. Even in the rare circumstances where we know there is, say, a decision procedure for determining the optimal solution to a decision problem, it is often more reasonable to proceed swiftly and by heuristic methods, and this strategic principle may in fact be incorporated as a design principle at a fairly fundamental level of cognitive-conative organization.

A fourth observation in favor of the model is that it permits moral education to make a difference, without making all of the difference. A familiar argument against the libertarian is that if our moral decisions were not in fact determined by our moral upbringing, or our moral education, there would be no point in providing such an education for the young. The libertarian who adopted our model could answer that a moral education, while not completely determining the generation of considerations and moral decision making, can nevertheless have a prior selective effect on the sorts of considerations that will occur. A moral education, like mutual discussion and persuasion generally, could adjust the boundaries and probabilities of the generator without rendering it deterministic.

Fifth—and I think this is perhaps the most important thing to be said in favor of this model—it provides some account of our important intuition that we are the authors of our moral decisions. The unreflective compatibilist is apt to view decision making on the model of a simple balance or scale on which the pros and cons of action are piled. What gets put on the scale is determined by one's nature and one's nurture, and once all the weights are placed, gravity as it were determines which way the scale will tip, and hence determines which way we will act. On such a view, the agent does not seem in any sense to be the author of the decisions, but at best merely the locus at which the environmental and genetic factors bearing on him interact to produce a decision. It all looks terribly mechanical and inevitable, and seems to leave no room for creativity or genius. The model proposed, however, holds out the promise of a distinction between authorship and mere implication in a causal chain.[7]

Consider in this light the difference between completing a lengthy exercise in long division and constructing a proof in, say, Euclidean geometry. There is a sense in which I can be the author of a particular bit of long division, and can take credit if it turns out to be correct, and can take pride in it as well, but there is a stronger sense in which I can claim authorship of a proof in geometry, even if thousands of school children before me have produced the very same proof. There is a sense in which this is something original that I have created. To take pride in one's *computational accuracy* is one thing, and to take pride in one's *inventiveness* is another, and as Valéry claimed, the essence of invention is the intelligent selection from among randomly generated candidates. I think that the sense in which we wish to claim authorship of our moral decisions, and hence claim responsibility for them, requires that we view them as products of intelligent invention and not merely the results of an assiduous application of formulas. I don't want to overstate this case; certainly many of the decisions we make are so obvious, so black and white, that no one would dream of claiming any special creativity in having made them and yet would still claim complete responsibility for the decisions thus rendered. But if we viewed all our decision making on those lines, I think our sense of our dignity as moral agents would be considerably impoverished.

Finally, the model I propose points to the multiplicity of decisions that encircle our moral decisions and suggests that in many cases our ultimate decision as to which way to act is less important phenomenologically as a contributor to our sense of free will than the prior decisions affecting our deliberation process itself: the decision, for instance, not to consider any further, to terminate deliberation; or the decision to ignore certain lines of inquiry.

These prior and subsidiary decisions contribute, I think, to our sense of ourselves as responsible free agents, roughly in the following way: I am faced with an important decision to make, and after a certain amount of deliberation, I say to myself: "That's enough. I've considered this matter enough and now I'm going to act," in the full knowledge that I could have considered further, in the full knowledge that the eventualities may prove that I decided in error, but with the acceptance of responsibility in any case.

I have recounted six recommendations for the suggestion that human decision making involves a nondeterministic generate-and-test procedure. First, it captures whatever is compelling in Russell's hunch. Second, it installs determinism in the only plausible locus for libertarianism (something we have established by a process of elimination). Third, it makes sense from the point of view of strategies of biological engineering. Fourth, it provides a flexible justification of moral education. Fifth, it accounts at least in part for our sense of authorship of our decisions. Sixth, it acknowledges and explains the importance of decisions internal to the deliberation process. It is embarrassing to note, however, that the very feature of the model that inspired its promulgation is *apparently* either gratuitous or misdescribed or both, and that is the causal indeterminacy of the generator. We have been supposing, for the sake of the libertarian, that the process that generates considerations for our assessment generates them at least in part by a physically or causally undetermined or random process. But here we seem to be trading on yet another imprecision or ambiguity in the word "random." When a system designer or programmer relies on a "random" generation process, it is not a *physically undetermined* process that is required, but simply a *patternless* process. Computers are typically equipped with a random number generator, but the process that generates the sequence is a perfectly deterministic and determinate process. If it is a good random number generator (and designing one is extraordinarily difficult, it turns out) the sequence will be locally and globally patternless. There will be a complete absence of regularities on which to base predictions about unexamined portions of the sequence.

Isn't it the case that the new, improved proposed model for human deliberation can do as well with a random-but-deterministic generation process as with a causally undetermined process? Suppose that to the extent that the considerations that occur to me are unpredictable, they are unpredictable simply because they are fortuitously determined by some arbitrary and irrelevant factors, such as the location of the planets or what I had for breakfast. It appears that this alternative supposition diminishes not one whit the plausibility or utility of the model that I have proposed. Have we, in fact, given the libertarians what they really want without giving them indeterminism? Perhaps. We have given the libertarians the materials out of which to construct an account of personal authorship of moral decisions, and this is something that the compatibilistic views have never handled well. But something else has emerged as well. Just as the presence or absence of macroscopic indeterminism in the implementation style of intentional actions turned out to be something essentially undetectable from the vantage point of our *Lebenswelt,* a feature with no significant repercussions in the "manifest image," to use Sellars' term, so the rival descriptions of the consideration generator, as random-but-causally-deterministic *versus* random-and-causally-*in*deterministic, will have no clearly testable and contrary implications at the level of micro-neurophysiology, even if we succeed beyond our most optimistic fantasies in mapping deliberation processes onto neural activity.

That fact does not refute libertarianism, or even discredit the motivation behind it, for what it shows once again is that we need not fear that causal indeterminism would make our lives unintelligible. There may not be compelling grounds from *this* quarter for favoring an indeterministic vision of the springs of our action, but if considerations from other quarters favor indeterminism, we can at least be fairly sanguine about the prospects of incorporating indeterminism into our picture of deliberation, even if we cannot yet see what point such an incorporation would have. Wiggins speaks of the cosmic unfairness of determinism, and I do not think the considerations raised here do much to allay our worries about *that.* Even if one embraces the sort of view I have outlined, the deterministic view of the unbranching and inexorable history of the universe can inspire terror or despair, and perhaps the libertarian is right that there is no way to allay these feelings short of a brute denial of determinism. Perhaps such a denial, and only such a denial, would permit us to make sense of the notion that our actual lives are created by us over time out of possibilities that exist in virtue of our earlier decisions; that we trace a path through a branching maze that both defines who we are, and why, to some extent (if we are fortunate enough to maintain against all vicissitudes the integrity of our deliberational machinery) we are *responsible* for being who we are. That prospect deserves an investigation of its own. All I hope to have shown here is that it is a prospect we can and should take seriously.

## Notes

1. An incomplete list of the very different questions composing the free will problem: (1) How can a material thing (a mechanism?) be correctly said to reason, to have reasons, to act on reasons? (a question I attempt to answer in chap. 12 of my *Brainstorms* [Cambridge, MA: Bradford Books, 1978]). (2) How can the unique four dimensional nonbranching world-worm that comprises all that has happened and will happen admit of a notion of possibilities that are not actualities? What does an *opportunity* look like when the world is viewed *sub specie aeternitatis*? (3) How can a person be an author of decisions, and not merely the locus of causal summation for external influences? (4) How can we make sense of the intuition that an agent can only be responsible if he could have done otherwise? (5) How can we intelligibly describe the relevant mental history of the truly culpable agent, the villain or rational cheat with no excuses? As Socrates asked, can a person knowingly commit evil?

2. D. Wiggins, "Towards a Reasonable Libertarianism," in T. Honderich, ed., *Essays on Freedom of Action* (London: Routledge & Kegan Paul, 1973).

3. Bertrand Russell, "The Physiology of Sensation and Volition," in *Human Knowledge; Its Scope and Limits* (New York: Simon and Schuster, 1948), p. 54.

4. A. J. Ayer, "Freedom and Necessity," in *Philosophical Essays* (London: Macmillan, 1954); R. B. Hobart, "Free Will as Involving Determination and Inconceivable Without It," *Mind* 43 (1934), pp. 1–27.

5. Quoted by Jacques Hadamard in *The Psychology of Invention in the Mathematical Field* (Princeton, NJ: Princeton University Press, 1949), p. 30. I discuss the implications of Valéry's claim in chapter 5 of *Brainstorms*.

6. The term is Herbert Simon's. See his *The Sciences of the Artificial* (Cambridge, MA: MIT Press, 1969) for a review of the concept.

7. Compare the suggestive discussion of genius in Kant's *Critique of Judgment*, sections 46, 47.

# 4

## Libertarianism and Rationality

RICHARD DOUBLE

The argument that libertarian style free will would be destructive to the rationality of human decisions is not new. Despite the antiquity of this compatibilist theme two important recent defenses of libertarianism, Peter van Inwagen's *An Essay on Free Will* and Robert Kane's *Free Will and Values,* are not daunted by this objection. In this paper I argue that these accounts leave little or no room for the reasonability of libertarian free choices. I begin with the accounts of van Inwagen and Kane and then show how the compatibilist theme counts against each.

Van Inwagen expresses his primary worry with compatibilism this way:

> If determinism is true, then our acts are the consequences of the laws of nature and events in the remote past. But it is not up to us what went on before we were born, and neither is it up to us what the laws of nature are. Therefore, the consequences of these things (including our present acts) are not up to us.[1]

Kane faults determinism because it takes away our ultimate responsibility for our actions, which is illustrated by the fact that determinism is compatible with the existence of a "covert non-constraining controller" who is the ultimate cause behind our decisions:

> [W]hat determinism takes away is a certain sense of the importance of oneself as an individual. If I am ultimately responsible for certain

occurrences in the universe, if the only explanation for their occurring rather than not is to be found in my rational will, then my choices and my life take on an importance that is missing if I do not have such responsibility.[2]

The solutions to these worries adopted by van Inwagen and Kane have our decisions determine our actions, but make our decisions themselves indeterminate with respect to what has gone before. Regarding van Inwagen's worry, if some of our decisions are not the products of previous events given the laws of nature, then these decisions at least have a chance of being "up to us." Concerning the second worry, as Kane notes, indeterministic decisions would be a sure way to foil the control of an aspiring covert controller as well as giving us a sense of ultimate responsibility (Kane, pp. 35–37).

The exact placement of the indeterminacy is a vital question for the libertarian, since the indeterminacy may be located at the moment of the choice while keeping all previous psychological factors the same or earlier in the deliberative process. Libertarians like van Inwagen who opt for the former seem naturally drawn towards a nonevent metaphysics of free will ("non-occurrent cause theories" according to Kane), such as those held by Kant, Taylor, and Chisholm. Those such as Kane, who locate the indeterminacy in the psychological states that precede the choice, may be called "Valerian libertarians" after Dennett's citing of Paul Valery's claim that the invention is selection among choices that occur to one randomly.[3]

Consider van Inwagen's account of free will:

> When I say of a man that he "has free will" I mean that very often, if not always, when he has to choose between two or more mutually incompatible courses of action—that is, courses of action that it is impossible for him to carry out more than one of—each of these courses of action is such that he can, or is able to, or has it within his power to carry it out. (van Inwagen, p. 8)

Van Inwagen provides an example of what it would be like to manifest libertarian free will. Sometimes while stealing money a thief remembers the face of his dying mother as he promised her he would lead an honest life. Just once when this happens the thief decides not to complete the crime and "this decision was undetermined." By this van Inwagen means

> there are possible worlds in which things were absolutely identical in every respect with the way they are in the actual world up to the momment at which our repentant thief made his decision—worlds in which, moreover, the laws of nature are just what they are in the actual world—and in which he takes the money. (van Inwagen, p. 128)

Kane, who exemplifies the Valerian approach, defines "freedom of the will" in this way:

> A rational agent . . . S is (was) free at time t with respect to a choice or decision J, if and only if, S has (had) the power at t to make J at t and S has (had) the power at t to do otherwise at t . . . (Kane, p. 21)

Kane's dual *desiderata* of rational indeterminacy enter his account in his requirement that free agents satisfy the Condition of Ultimate Dominion (CUD):

> An agent's power (or control) over a choice at a time t satisfies the condition of sole or ultimate dominion if and only if (i) the agent's making the choice rather than doing otherwise (or vice versa, i.e., doing otherwise rather than making the choice) can be explained by saying that the agent rationally willed at t to do so, and (ii) no further explanation can be given for the agent's choosing rather than doing otherwise (or vice versa), or of the agent's rationally willing at t to do so, that is an explanation in terms of conditions whose existence cannot be explained by the agent's choosing or rationally willing something at t. (Kane, p. 46)

Although CUD is Kane's principle rather than van Inwagen's, I am going to treat it as a requirement that any satisfactory libertarian view must meet. The second, indeterminacy, condition is one any libertarian should wish to satisfy; the first, rational explanation, condition must be met if the libertarian is to avoid the familiar charge that indeterminate will destroys the rational agency of free agents. I shall argue that van Inwagen's account clearly violates CUD, while Kane's account, though ingeniously designed not to violate CUD, avoids doing so at the expense of producing a theory that is weak on its rationality commitment without enjoying the incompatibilist advantages of van Inwagen's view.

I begin by citing Kane's lucid analysis of the problem that libertarian free will has with rationality:

> If the agent might either make a choice or do otherwise, given all the same past circumstances, and the past circumstances include the entire psychological history of the agent, it would seem that no explanation in terms of the agent's psychological history, including prior character, motives and deliberation, could account for the actual occurrence of one outcome *rather than* the other, i.e., for the choosing rather than doing otherwise, or vice versa . . . the outcome may be different . . . though the psychological history is the same. (P. 53)

> . . . what I cannot understand is how I could have reasonably chosen to do otherwise, how I could have reasonably chosen B, *given exactly the same prior deliberation* that led me to choose A, the same information deployed, the same consequences considered, the same assessments made, and so on. (P. 57)

I shall try to develop Kane's point by showing that depending on what the non-Valerian libertarian counts as an explanation, CUD either will not be satisfied or will be so weak that it credits clearly unfree persons with ultimate dominion over their decisions. Thus, non-Valerian free will either violates CUD's rationality requirement, or, if it is argued that such freedom produces ultimate control, then that control is at one with the control enjoyed by paradigmatically unfree persons.

Consider the second horn of the dilemma. The first, and most natural, interpretation of CUD's first condition that the agent's choice "can be explained by saying the agent rationally willed at t to do so" would be to treat it as elliptical for "can be explained *truly*" or "can be *adequately* explained." If the first condition does not mean this, then CUD could be satisfied by persons whose indeterministic choices are entirely unconstrained by reasons provided that there is some confabulated explanation of that person's choice in terms of rational willing. Thus, CUD would entail that schizophrenics exercise ultimate control provided their choices satisfy condition (ii), since we can always make up rational explanations for their choices via post facto attributions of beliefs and desires.

So, I think that condition (i) of CUD must be understood to require true or adequate explanations. The question of what constitutes an adequate explanation is, of course, one of the foremost debates in the philosophy of science, the disputants being advocates of the deductive-nomological model (e.g., Hempel) vs. those who believe that not all adequate explanations must make the *explanandum* a logical consequence of the *explanans* (e.g., Dray, Haugeland). There is a minimal principle, however, that I believe is so weak that both sides to the debate would accept it. I call it "the Principle of Rational Explanation (PRE)":

> Citing a person's reasoning process *R* rationally explains a choice *C* only if the probability of *C* given *R* is greater than the probability of not *C* given *R*.

For example, if citing Smith's deliberative process concerning smoking is to truly explain Smith's decision to smoke a cigarette, then a very minimal condition needs to be met, viz., that the deliberative process made it more likely that Smith decide to smoke than decide not to.

PRE is not committed to any particular view of the logical form that rational explanations must take, nor to the type of *explanans* (causal, teleological, functional laws) permitted. PRE does not even claim that a good rational explanation must make the *explanandum* highly probable, but only more likely than its negation. To see how innocuous PRE is, imagine what one would have to say to reject it. Let 'P' designate the entire psychological state of a subject prior to a particular choice C. Suppose that the occurrence of P makes C no more likely than not C. PRE is false only if P explains C. But under the stipulated condition, it is difficult to see how P *explains* C; instead it seems that the occurrence of P was irrelevant to explaining why the choice was C rather than not C. The temptation to believe that P is explanatory owes, I think, to the fact that in a 'normal,' that is, nonlibertarian, scenario we *would* count P as a viable candidate for being an adequate explanation. But we should be careful not to let our commonsense acceptance of rational explanation, which I think is at least broadly deterministic, spill over into a case where, *ex hypothesi,* the *explanans* is debarred from making the *explanandum* more likely than not.

Having argued for PRE, we are now ready to consider whether on non-Valerian accounts of free will our total psychological states make our free decisions more probable than their contradictories. For van Inwagen, at least, the answer appears to be negative. In the thief example, van Inwagen imagines the thief's total psychological state to include two conflicting pairs of beliefs and desires: (a) the desire to keep his promise to his mother not to steal, (b) the belief that the best way to keep his promise is to refrain from robbing the poor-box, (c) the desire for money, and (d) the belief that the best way to get money is to rob the poor-box. Van Inwagen suggests that if God were to "reset" the world to its identical state at the moment of the thief's decision thousands of times, then "on about half these occasions" (a) and (b) would produce the thief's decision to refrain while "on the other occasions" (c) and (d) would produce the decision to rob (pp. 140–41). So, it seems that the argument below is directly applicable to van Inwagen:

(i) If we have libertarian free will, then our deliberations do not make our decisions more than .5 probable.
(ii) If PRE is true, then if our deliberations do not make our decisions more than .5 probable then our deliberations do not explain our decisions.
(iii) PRE is true.
(iv) Therefore, if we have libertarian free will, then our deliberations do not explain our decisions.

Let me try to illustrate this objection by comparing two scenarios. In both cases I am a student trying to learn the inference rules of sentence logic. My task is to identify the rule that was used to produce a certain line in a proof, a common exercise in elementary logic books. Alternatively, my task can be described as deciding which rule I think was used or deciding what answer to give. In Case 1 we make the following stipulations. My deliberative process will proceed through consciously accessible states for which I produce a completely accurate protocol. For instance, a transcription of my 'thinking out loud' reads "Well, the previous line was a conditional. What rules of inference use conditionals?

*Modus ponens* does, but . . ." Although I may or may not decide on the correct answer, because I am subject to determinism each subsidiary decision I make en route to my final choice is a causal product of my previous deliberative states.

In Case 2 I am faced with the same problem, but here I exercise non-Valerian free will. My reasoning process has delimited my choice of an answer to either *modus ponens* or *modus tollens,* but my continued reflections do not uniquely determine which rule I shall select. That is, I can adduce reasons for thinking that the rule is each, but my will is not determined in either direction by my reasoning. In an instant I select *modus ponens* owing to an indeterministic emission of a beta particle from an atom in my brain.[4] Had the particle been emitted a nanosecond before or later I would have selected *modus tollens.* Moreover, in van Inwagen's words, "there are possible worlds in which things were absolutely identical . . . with the way they are in the actual world" up until the decision and yet the decision was *modus tollens.*

The first question I wish to ask about these cases is: *In which case do I display more rationality in reaching the final answer?* In Case 1 my reasoning process is rational if the causal sequence of inferences is itself logically well-founded and otherwise not. The fact that my deliberations were related between themselves causally neither establishes their rationality nor counts against the rationality of the deliberations. This is not true of Case 2. By hypothesis, since my choice between the two inference rules was not caused by some logically salient reason, my choice cannot be reasonable. This obvious fact might tend to be obscured by the possibility that afterwards I might ardently defend the rationality of my decision by citing my reasons for selecting *modus ponens.* To all observers (including myself) my selection seems reasonable; after all, I did have my reasons. But, in response to this, we must note that the stipulation that my choice owed to quantum indeterminacy rather than my reasoning process demonstrates that such *post facto* rationalization is worthless. Even in nonstipulated cases, there is abundant evidence from social psychology that we should be extremely wary of individuals' attributions of the causes of the behavior of themselves and others.[5] The moral is that the fact that the subject's choice in Case 2 *seemed* reasonable to the subject provides no evidence that it was.

The libertarian might adopt a fall-back position here, pointing out that the decision in Case 2 was *pretty* reasonable because it was *circumscribed by,* if not caused by, our reasoning. This reply is unacceptable because it takes a perspective that is too narrow. We may grant that if I have narrowed my choice to *modus ponens* or *modus tollens* I have done something commendable—at least it is better than having no clue as to which inference rule to select. But if each of the subsidiary decisions I made en route to limiting my final selection to one of these two had manifested libertarian free will, then there is no reason to believe that I would have reached that penultimate position with any more probability than I would have reached any other mathematically possible position. That is, if in every step along the way my subordinate decision had been indeterministically free of the control of my reasoning process, then who knows where I would have ended up. My decision process would be an exercise in anarchy. So, when one cites the partial reasonability of my final choice between *modus ponens* and *modus tollens,* the reasonability that brought us to the final choice was the rational determinism of the previous decisions. The final indeterministic choice merits no "credit" for the rationality of the prior decisions: instead, with respect to rationality, the final choice is a "freeloader" on the previous determinism decisions that delimited the range of the final choice.

The second question: *In which case, if either, do I deserve credit for getting right answers or criticism for wrong answers?* There are familiar arguments that moral responsibility is impossible in a deterministic world and equally familiar ones that moral responsibility is impossible in a libertarian world.[6] Rather than address *that* issue, let us concern ourselves with what might be called "epistemic credit" and "epistemic criticism" rather than moral responsibility. It seems that one deserves epistemic credit for getting the right answer only if one knows, or at least justifiably believes, the right answer, and it seems that any plausible acount of these notions excludes one's arriving at the answer "just by luck."[7] Regarding epistemic criticism, it seems it is applicable only if appropriate epistemic criteria are not invoked and if this failure was under the control of the agent. The second part of this necessary condition implies that one is not subject to epistemic criticism if failure to meet appropriate epistemic criteria was simply a matter of luck.

If the above claims about the necessary conditions for epistemic credit and criticism are correct, then in Case 1 I am at least in principle subject to both credit and criticism. Determinism *per se* counts against neither possibility. Our conditions do count against the possibility of credit and criticism in Case 2. Now, it might be objected that if libertarianism is true then I am criticizable for making decisions under conditions of inappropriate evidence. A good epistemic agent in the Case 2 situation where one has equal reasons for *modus ponens* and *modus tollens* would suspend judgment rather than opt for either. But this point is confused. In Case 2 I did not decide to choose arbitrarily between the two equally attractive alternatives. Instead, my deliberations took me up to the point of equilibrium between *modus ponens* and *modus tollens* and then "chance intervened"—the next thing I knew I had chosen the former. Thus, I should not be criticized for *deciding* on inadequate evidence any more than I should be criticized for reaching the actual wrong answer in the libertarian mode.

As far as I can tell (since his book is rich and intricate, I do not claim certainty), Kane would reply that whatever the merits of this argument against non-Valerian libertarianism, it does not touch his argument since on his view our deliberations do make our decisions more than .5 probable. Briefly, for Kane free practical choices result from the rational deliberations performed on options, beliefs, desires, and so on, some of which indeterminately occur to one during the deliberation process. So, e.g., given that remembrance A comes to mind randomly, I may rationally elect to do X, while had remembrance B come to mind I would have equally rationally elected to do y. Thus, our deliberations *do* explain our decisions relative to our preceding psychological states; it is just that there are different physically possible worlds where the preceding psychological states could have been otherwise, thereby producing different decisions.

There are three criticisms to make of this Valerian way of avoiding the previous argument. First, recall Dennett's original motivation outlining Valerian libertarianism: this sort of indeterminacy seems no better than determinism for the purposes of human freedom and responsibility (Dennett, 1978, 297–98). What does it matter whether the random considerations that come to a deliberator are truly indeterminate or simply unexpected, though determined? So, at the very least, actual indeterminacy cannot *help* the rationality of the choice.

Second, the best part of our decision making is the deterministic part, *e.g.*, our consideration of the pros and cons of various options, strategies, and so forth. As Kane notes, the indeterministic "popping into" one's head of thoughts makes no contribution to one's deliberations unless we interpret these thoughts (Kane, p. 105). For instance, my random remembrance of feature *A* has no weight for or against any choice unless I assign a value to *A*. Worse still, the indeterminate thoughts are parasitic upon the determinate thought processes that give them value. As we noted in scenario two, had indeterminate ideas just continually "popped" into the deliberator's head there is no telling which direction the final choice would have taken. (It is worth mentioning that a nonreason-governed, *deterministic*, popping of reasons into one's head would be destructive to the deliberative process as run-a-way indeterministic mental states. Nonrational determinism is no more constitutive of the efficacy of the agent than is indeterminacy.) In terms of control, one is victim to any considerations that simply come to one (indeterminately or deterministically) until one can rationally reflect on and evaluate these deterministically.

The third criticism of Valerian free will is that it does not provide categorical contracausal freedom, which I take to be a crucial incompatibilist *desideratum*. For Kane, once the indeterminate psychological item occurs to the agent, decision is reached in a deterministic way. This means that the agent does not possess the categorical ability to do otherwise, given the exact circumstances the agent was in at the instant of choice. For Kane, the agent could have chosen otherwise—provided a different indeterminate state had occurred. But this represents a hypothetical ability to choose otherwise, no less than the determinist who says one could have chosen otherwise had one wanted. So, for the purposes of moral responsibility, Kane's Valerian theory does no better at accommodating the incompatibilist intuition that moral responsibility requires actual, categorical ability to choose otherwise than do deterministic theories. As Kane shrewdly observes in his book, neither libertarians nor compatibilists are likely to be entirely satisfied with his theory.

I conclude that the non-Valerian libertarianism of van Inwagen has insuperable difficulties with the rationality of choices and Kane's view, though somewhat less troubled by that objection, diminishes the rationality of choices just to the extent that Valerian processes occur, while losing its claim to provide an alternative to soft deterministic theories of free will.[8]

## Notes

1. *An Essay on Free Will* (Oxford: Oxford University Press, 1983), p. 56.
2. *Free Will and Values* (Albany: SUNY Press, 1985), p. 178.
3. *Brainstorms* (Cambridge, MA: Bradford Books, 1978), p. 297.
4. Kane suggests that quantum indeterminacy in the brain is the most likely physiological vehicle through which indeterminism might enter into human decisions. See especially chapter 9, "Factual Issues and Incompatibility Revisited," in *Free Will and Values*.
5. R. Nisbett and L. Ross, *Human Inferences: Strategies and Shortcomings of Social Judgment* (Englewood Cliffs, NJ: Prentice-Hall, 1980).
6. P. Strawson, "Freedom and Resentment," reprinted in G. Watson, ed., *Free Will* (Oxford: Oxford University Press, 1982).
7. It is easy to see how indeterminacy makes knowledge impossible according to causal accounts of knowledge, but this is also true for the justified true belief account of knowledge once we distinguish between reasons that actually justify our beliefs and reasons that one has (and can confabulate *ex post facto*) for one's beliefs. See R. Audi, "Foundationism, Epistemic Dependence, and Defeasibility," *Synthese* 55 (1983), pp. 119–39.
8. I wish to thank Robert Kane and anonymous referee of *The Southern Journal of Philosophy* for helpful comments on an earlier draft of this paper.

# II

# Indeterminism and Free Will: Contemporary Proposals

# 5

# Reasons Explanation of Action: An Incompatibilist Account

## CARL GINET

Incompatibilism is the thesis that any free action must be an undetermined event. By a *free* action I mean one such that until the time of its occurrence the agent had it in her power to perform some alternative action (or to be inactive) instead. By an *undetermined* event I mean one that was *not* nomically necessitated by the antecedent state of the world. (Hence, a determined event is one that *was* nomically necessitated by its antecedents.) By saying of an event that it was *nomically necessitated* by the antecedent state of the world, I mean that the antecedent state together with the laws of nature determined that that event, rather than some alternative, would occur.

I believe that a compelling argument for incompatibilism can be given but I will not undertake to give it here.[1] I want rather to rebut two arguments *against* incompatibilism that have been put forward from time to time. One of these, to which I will give by far the larger response, combines the consideration that a free action can be influenced by the agent's intentions, desires, and beliefs—can have an explanation in terms of reasons for which the agent did it—with the assumption that only a determined event can have such an explanation.[2] My response to this will be to counter the assumption by offering an adeterministic or *anomic* account of such explanations. The other argument does not assume that reasons explanations are deterministic (nor does it assume the contradictory) but simply claims that where we have an undetermined action we do not have an agent in control of (determining) what her action is to be: we do not have an action that the agent chooses, freely or otherwise.

*I*

Let me first dispose of this latter argument. It is contained (though mingled with and not clearly distinguished from the other argument) in the following remarks of Frithjof Bergmann:

> Would indeterminacy, even if its existence could be demonstrated, really vouchsafe freedom, or would it not fulfill this expectation? . . . Where or when would [the indeterminacy] have to occur to provide us with freedom? . . . Imagine Raskolnikov walking up the steps to the old pawnbroker woman's room and assume that his mind still vacillates, that with every tread he climbs his thinking alternates from one side to the other. . . . he mounts the staircase thinking "I shall kill her," "no, I shall not." This continues till he stands right before her door. Now let us hypothesize that his last thought just as he pushes the door open is "no, I shall not do it" and that the sought-for indeterminacy occurs right after these words crossed his mind. The thinking of this thought is the last link in a causal chain, but now there is a gap between this and the next event, which is his bringing the axe down on her head.
>
> What would this mean? Would the occurrence of a disjuncture in this place render Raskolnikov's act more free; would it provide him with a power or a control that he lacks otherwise? . . . The implication, if anything, would be the reverse. If his last thought really is "no, I shall not do it" and this thought is somehow disconnected from the next event so that it has no causal influence on it and he then kills her, then one could only say that the indeterminacy has rendered his will ineffectual, that instead of giving him greater power or control the causal gap *decreased* it.
>
> . . . one could envision two alternatives: either something other than his own last thought "influences" him so that he does commit the murder, or the last reversal was quite strictly not effected by anything whatever and occurred entirely "by chance." . . . in either case it was not *he* that made the decision, and *he* certainly did not exercise his freedom. We therefore can conclude that the occurrence of a causal gap in this particular location—between his last thought and his action— would not furnish him with freedom, but on the contrary would undermine the agent and make him a victim.[3]

Bergmann is suggesting that there is an absurdity in the thought that positing a break in the causal necessitation just before Raskolnikov's action helps to make it one that *he* chooses. In fact, he suggests, it would do just the opposite: it would go against its being the case that

Raskolnikov determines whether or not he delivers the murdering blow. And if Raskolnikov does not determine that, then surely his delivering the blow is not his freely chosen action for which he can be held morally responsible.

Why exactly is the indeterminacy just before the action supposed to deprive the agent of control over his action? One reason, Bergmann seems to suggest, is that (as he thinks) if the action is undetermined then it is in no way influenced by his antecedent intentions or thoughts, and its being influenced by them is essential to its being controlled by the agent. But his words, particularly the last few sentences quoted, also invite the thought that the implication is more direct and does not depend on taking a deterministic view of how motives influence actions or on taking any particular view as to what agent control consists in: it is, one may think, just obvious that if an action is undetermined then the agent does not control (determine) it, has no say in whether or not it occurs.

We also find this latter idea in the argument that van Inwagen (1983) refers to as "the third strand of the *Mind* Argument" for compatibilism. The premise of that argument, as van Inwagen phrases it (p. 144), is "the principle that no one has any choice about the occurrence of an undetermined event." I believe we adequately capture the idea here if we express it as follows:

(1) For any time t and any undetermined event occurring at t: it is not possible for it to have been in anyone's power to determine whether that event or some alternative (undetermined) event instead would occur at t.

From this premise we can in two short steps derive a conclusion severely damaging to incompatibilism:

(2) Therefore, for any time t and undetermined action occurring at t: it is not possible for it to have been in the agent's power to determine whether that action or some alternative (undetermined) action instead would occur at t.

(3) Therefore, it is not possible for a free action to be undetermined.

It is impossible for the conclusion (3) and incompatibilism both to be true *if* it is also true that free action is at least possible (whether or not actual). The metaphysical possibility of free action is something that most incompatibilists assume, myself included, as of course do most compatibilists. That assumption conjoined with (3) does entail that incompatibilism is false. Since the argument is obviously valid, if free action is possible, either incompatibilism or the argument's premise is wrong. A little reflection will show us that the latter is the problem.

Whatever plausibility this premise has derives, I think, from ambiguity in sentences of the following form when they are about events that are actions.

(A)  It was in S's power to determine whether undetermined event E or some alternative undetermined event instead would occur at t.

When the event E is *not an action of S's* a natural reading of this sentence does make it express a plainly impossible proposition:

(A1)  It was in S's power so to act that S's action (in concert with other circumstances at the time) would have nomically necessitated that E would occur at t and have been undetermined; and it was in S's power so to act that S's action would have nomically necessitated that some alternative instead of E would occur at t and have been undetermined.

Here each conjunct is impossible, for it implies that it was in S's power to make the case something that is impossible, namely, that an event at t would have been both determined and undetermined. On this inconsistent reading of (A) the premiss of the argument, (1) above, obviously holds.

But when the event E is an action of S's, another reading of (A) is possible, one that is perfectly consistent:

(A2)  It was in S's power to act in a certain way at t without being nomically necessitated to do so; and it was in S's power to act in some alternative way at t without being nomically necessitated to do so.

Here each conjunct attributes to S the power to make the case something that in itself is perfectly possible, namely, S's performing an undetermined action. If an undetermined action is possible then there is no reason to say that an undetermined action cannot be in the agent's power to perform.

To determine an event is to act in such a way that one's action makes it the case that the event occurs. Let us grant (for the sake of this discussion) that if the event is *not* one's own action then this requires that the event be causally necessitated by one's action (in concert with other circumstances) and thus that it not be an undetermined event. But if the event *is* one's own action then one's determining it requires only that one perform it; and one's performing it, which is just the action's occurring, is compatible with the action's being undetermined, not causally necessitated by antecedents.

Suppose that S's raising her arm at t did occur as an undetermined action: S raised her arm at t without being nomically necessitated to do so. In that case, it was open to S, in S's power, up to t to raise her arm at t without being nomically necessitated to do so. There is no reason to doubt it. Nor is there any reason to be puzzled as to how this can be so. But van Inwagen (in uncomfortable company with some compatibilists) seems to find a mystery here. He says:

> I must reject the following proposition:
>> If an agent's act was caused but not determined by his prior inner state, and if nothing besides that inner state was causally relevant to the agent's act, then that agent had no choice about whether that inner state was followed by that act.
>
> I must admit that I find it puzzling that this proposition should be false . . .
>
> Now I wish I knew *how it could be* that, for example, our thief had a choice about whether to repent [or instead rob the poor box], given that his repenting was caused, but not determined, by his prior inner states, and given that no other prior state "had anything to do with"—save negatively: in virtue of its non-interference with—his act. I have no theory of free action or choice that would explain how this could be.[4]

As I understand him, what puzzles van Inwagen is how an agent could have a choice about whether or not his action occurred, i.e., could determine that it occurred rather than something else instead, *if* the only antecedent things causally relevant to its occurrence, the agents motives for it (his "prior inner state"), left it undetermined, nomically unnecessitated. How, by what means, van Inwagen seems to want to ask, did the thief ensure that that action (rather than some alternative) occurred? The answer is: by no *means*, by nothing distinct from and productive of the action, but simply by performing the action itself. If an event is S's action then S (but, of course, no one else) can ensure its occurrence, determine *that* it occurs and thus *whether or not* it occurs, just by performing it.

So I attribute the puzzlement van Inwagen feels here to failure to distinguish the two very different readings sentences of form (A) can have when E is one of S's own actions. He wants to say that (A) can be true in such a case but he wonders *how* it can be. His feeling that (A) can be true is traceable to the (A2) interpretation, which gives a proposition whose possibility is clear and straightforward. His conflicting feeling that there is no way (A) can be true in such a case is traceable to the (A1) interpretation, which gives an inconsistent proposition.

## II

Let us turn now to the other argument against incompatibilism I mentioned earlier. This one crucially assumes that if an action is not a purely chance or random event, if it is influenced by or has an explanation in terms of the agent's reasons or motives for doing it, then it is *ipso facto* determined. A. J. Ayer (1946), for instance, says

> Either it is an accident that I choose to act as I do or it is not. If it is an accident, then it is merely a matter of chance that I did not choose otherwise; and if it is merely a matter of chance that I did not choose otherwise, it is surely irrational to hold me morally responsible for choosing as I did. But if it is not an accident that I choose to do one thing rather than another, then presumably there is some causal explanation of my choice: and in that case we are led back to determinism.[5]

J. J. C. Smart (1968) argues that

> the question of pure chance or determinism is irrelevant to the question of free will, though, so far from free will and determinism being incompatible with one another, a close approximation to determinism on the macro-level is required for free will.
>
> Some philosophers would . . . say that in free choice we act from reasons, not from causes, and they would say that acting from reasons is neither caused nor a matter of pure chance. I find this unintelligible.
>
> [T]he free choice is supposed to be not deterministic and not a matter of pure chance. It is supposed to be pure chance in the sense of "not being determined" but the suggestion is that it is also not merely random and is "acting from reasons." The previous paragraph [not quoted here; see n. 16 for a description of its content] suggests, however, that acting from reasons is not merely random precisely because it is also acting from causes.[6]

We can formulate the argument these authors make as follows:

(1) Incompatibilism entails that an action cannot be both free and determined by an antecedent state of the world.
(2) If an action is not determined by an antecedent state of the world then it has no explanation in terms of its antecedents.
(3) But some free actions do have explanations in terms of their antecedents.
(4) Therefore, incompatibilism is wrong.

Premise (1) is true by the definition of incompatibilism. Premise (3) is obviously undeniable. We frequently give explanations of our own actions, and accept explanations of others' actions, like the following:

> S opened the window in order to let the smoke out.
> S wanted to get out of the country quickly and realized it would take days unless she gave the official a bribe, so she handed him all her rubles.

These are explanations of actions because they answer the question "Why did S do that?" The first explains why S opened the window. The second explains why S handed the official all her rubles. These examples illustrate a category of explanations that apply only to actions: they are explanations that give us the agent's reasons for acting as she did. For most of our actions, or most that we have occasion to reflect on, we believe that they have such reasons explanations. Very often some of the intentions, desires, or beliefs that we bring into such an explanation are antecedents of the action. It would be preposterous to suggest that free actions can never have such explanations, to deny premise (3).

Some philosophers seem to think that premise (3) would be acceptable even if it were stronger and said that an action *must* have an explanation in terms of its antecedents, or that this must be true of *responsible* actions or of ones that the agent *chooses*, ones that are truly the agent's actions. Bergmann, for example, seems to suggest this in the remarks quoted above (p. 2). But I can see no reason to accept these much stronger claims. When I cross my legs while listening to a lecture, that action (usually) has no explanation in terms of reasons for doing it that I had antecedently. I just spontaneously do it. A spontaneous action, not arising from any antecedent motive, can even be undertaken with a further intention that begins to exist just when the action does. For example, a bird catches a person's eye and, without having antecedently formed the intention to keep watching it, she moves her head when the bird moves, in order to keep her eyes on it.

But premise (3) itself is obviously true. As I said, it would be absurd to suppose that a free action could not have an explanation in terms of the agent's antecedent reasons for doing it. It is premise (2), that an action has no explanation in terms of its antecedents if it is not determined by them, that is the substantive and deniable premise in the argument. Ayer clearly assumes that there are only two alternatives: either an action is determined or it is a purely chance event. He says, "if it is not an accident that I choose to do one thing rather than another, then presumably there is some causal explanation of my choice: and in that case we are led back to determinism." Smart finds unintelligible the suggestion that there is a third alternative, "that acting from reasons is neither caused [determined] nor a matter of pure chance."

To assume premise (2) is to assume that *all* explanations of events must be law-governed or *nomic*. That is to assume that an explanation can be true only if laws of nature guarantee that the explaining factors plus other circumstances are accompanied by the explained event. Applied specifically to reasons explanations of actions, this means the following:

(B) A reasons explanation can be true only if laws of nature guarantee that the agent's reasons for performing the action plus other circumstances are accompanied by the explained action.

This bold, bald assumption is false.

## III

Some philosophers have thought that the laws of nature that govern reasons explanations in the way required by assumption (B) are fairly obvious. J. S. Mill, for example, in his *Examination of Sir William Hamilton's Philosophy* says that "Necessitarians," of whom he counts himself one,

> affirm, as a truth of experience, that volitions do, in point of fact, follow determinate moral antecedents with the same uniformity, and (when we have sufficient knowledge of the circumstances) with the same certainty, as physical effects follow their physical causes. These moral antecedents are desires, aversions, habits, and dispositions, combined with outward circumstances suited to call those internal incentives into action. . . . A volition is a moral effect, which follows the corresponding moral causes as certainly and invariably as physical effects follow their physical causes.[7]

One may object that, in point of fact, the same volition or action does not invariably follow the same set of "moral" antecedents and this is particularly clear in cases (which are common) where the moral antecedents include the agent's having two or more desires that conflict, so the agent can satisfy at most one of these desires. For example, on a Saturday afternoon I have a desire to spend the rest of the afternoon doing some philosophical work and also a desire to spend it watching a football game on television. Suppose this same set of conflicting motives recurs on several Saturday afternoons. Can't I choose to satisfy one of the motives on some of these occasions and the other on others of them, without there being any relevant difference in the antecedents on these several occasions? Mill says no.

> When we think of ourselves hypothetically as having acted otherwise than we did, we always suppose a difference in the antecedents: we picture ourselves as having known something that we did not know, or not known something that we did know; which is a difference in the external inducements; or as having desired something, or disliked something, more or less than we did; which is a difference in the internal inducements.[8]

It is already clear to Mill what the general law must be in such cases of conflict of motives: the chosen action will be the one that satisfies whichever of the conflicting motives is stronger than all the others: the strongest motive prevails.[9]

Thomas Reid (writing more than sixty years before Mill) makes the following remarks about this way of dealing with conflict-of-motives cases.

When it is said, that of contrary motives the strongest always prevails, this can neither be affirmed nor denied with understanding, until we know distinctly what is meant by the strongest motive . . . when the motives are of different kinds, as money and fame, duty and worldly interest, health and strength, riches and honor, by what rule shall we judge which is the strongest motive? Either we measure the strength of motives, merely by their prevalence, or by some other standard distinct from their prevalence. If we measure their strength merely by their prevalence, and by the strongest motive mean only the motive that prevails, it will be true indeed that the strongest motive prevails; but the proposition will be identical, and mean no more than that the strongest motive is the strongest motive. From this surely no conclusion can be drawn. . . . We are therefore brought to this issue, that unless some measure of the strength of motives can be found distinct from their prevalence, it cannot be determined, whether the strongest motive always prevails or not. If such a measure can be found and applied, we may be able to judge of the truth of this maxim, but not otherwise.[10]

This suggests that one can secure confidence in Mill's law only by making it true by definition: "the strongest motive" *means* the motive that prevails. If this term is defined by some logically independent criterion, so that the proposed law will be a nontrivial proposition, then it is an open question whether the facts would give us reason for confidence in it. Reid presents Mill with a dilemma: either the strongest motive law is true by definition, in which case it is not the law of nature that was wanted, or some independent test of the strongest motive is to be found, in which case we do not know yet whether the proposed law holds.

Mill attempts to reply to this line of thought. He says there are two flaws in the argument that "I only know the strength of motives in relation to the will by the test of ultimate prevalence; so that this means no more than that the prevailing motive prevails."

First, those who say that the will follows the strongest motive, do not mean the motive which is strongest in relation to the will, or in other words, that the will follows what it does follow. They mean the motive which is strongest in relation to pain and pleasure; since a motive, being a desire or aversion, is proportional to the pleasantness, as conceived by us, of the thing desired, or the painfulness of the thing shunned. . . . The second [flaw] is, that even supposing there were no test of the strenth of motives but their effect on the will, the proposition that the will follows the strongest motive would not . . . be identical and unmeaning. We say, without absurdity, that if two weights are placed in opposite scales, the heavier will lift the other up; yet we mean nothing by the heavier, except the weight which will lift up the other. The proposition, nevertheless, is not unmeaning, for it signifies that in many or most cases there *is* a heavier, and that this is always the same

one, not one or the other as it may happen. In like manner, even if the
strongest motive meant only the motive which prevails, yet if there is a
prevailing motive—if, all other antecedents being the same, the motive
which prevails today will prevail tomorrow and every subsequent
day—Sir W. Hamilton was acute enough to see that the free-will theory
is not saved.[11]

This fails to wriggle out of the dilemma. Mill's proposed independent
criterion of motive strength is the degree of pain and pleasure antici-
pated. On any ordinary understanding of this, the facts will not support
the proposed law: people sometimes choose an alternative they believe
will be more painful or less pleasant than another alternative they believe open to them, in order to keep a promise, for example. In his
second point Mill seems to give the game away, apparently without
quite realizing it. He says that, even if there were no other test of strongest motive but the one that prevails, this would make the strongest
motive law no more absurd and unmeaning than "the heaviest weight
always lifts the other up". To this Reid should reply: Exactly so. No more
unmeaning *and no less tautologous.*

Mill goes on to claim that the proposition, "The heavier weight lifts
the other up," "signifies that in many or most cases there is a heavier *and
this is always the same one,* not one or the other as it may happen"
(emphasis added). He implies that the corresponding proposition, "The
strongest motive prevails," implies a corresponding thing, that the prevailing motive in recurrences of the same set of conflicting motives is
always the same one. But, of course, neither tautology can have the
implication claimed for it. It is a contingent proposition, and therefore
compatible with "the heavier weight lifts the other up," that two objects
should change over time with respect to which is the heavier of the two.
Likewise it is contingent, and therefore compatible with the tautological
interpretation of "the strongest motive prevails," that when the same set
of conflicting motives recurs a different one prevails from the one that
prevailed earlier. And, more important, this is not only a logical possibility but actually happens, often. Sometimes when my desire to work
conflicts with my desire to watch football the first motive prevails, and
sometimes the other prevails. Sometimes when my desire to get an early
start on the day conflicts with my desire to sleep a bit more the first
desire prevails, and sometimes the other does. If there are laws of nature
that explain why the prevailing motive does prevail in such cases, that
explain this in terms of antecedents of the action, it is far from obvious
what the contents of those laws are and it seems unlikely that they deal
entirely in terms of "moral" antecedents (i.e., the agent's antecedent
reasons or motives), for it seems that we already know all the relevant
facts about them: the agent had the conflicting motives and it seemed a
tossup which to satisfy.

There is another sort of case, noted by Reid, where the strongest motive law cannot apply at all, even on its tautological interpretation, because there is no motive that distinguishes the chosen alternative from another one.[12] On my computer's keyboard there are two keys such that if I press either of them the result is that an asterisk appears on the screen. I know this about these keys and I want to produce an asterisk, so I have a motive or reason for pressing one of them. Now suppose further that I have no desire such that pressing one but not the other of these two keys satisfies it. I have no motive for pressing one of them that is not also equally a motive for pressing the other. I am utterly indifferent between these two equally good means to my end of putting an asterisk on the screen. So I arbitrarily choose to press one of them. Here we cannot say that my pressing one rather than the other signified the prevailing of one over another of two conflicting motives I had. There *were no* conflicting motives such that one motive favored the one key and the other motive favored the other key. Yet I did press the key I pressed for a reason, namely, in order to produce an asterisk. The answer to "Why did he press that key?" is "Because he wanted to produce an asterisk."

Of course, I did not have a reason for pressing that key *rather than the other.* There is no answer to "Why did he press that key rather than this other one?", at least no answer that is a reasons explanation. I chose to press that key for a certain reason, but it is not the case that I had a reason for *not* pressing this other one instead. A similar thing holds in a conflict-of-motives case where it seems to the agent a tossup which motive to satisfy. The answer to "Why did he get out of bed just then?" is "Because he wanted to get an early start on his day." But to the question "Why did he get out of bed rather than stay in it for a while longer?" there may be no answer, because there may be no answer to "Why did he choose to get an early start rather than to get more sleep?".

In this case it is plausible to suppose that, *if* there is a *nomic* explanation of why he got out of bed rather than remaining in it, his desire to get an early start will figure in it, since it was a reason for that action but not a reason for the alternative. Of course it cannot be the only relevant antecedent in a nomic explanation here and the available reasons explanation affords little clue as to what might be the other antecedents that would subsume the case under laws of nature. In the indifferent means case, however, we have no good reason to suppose that, if there is a nomic explanation of why I pressed that key rather than the other one, my motive for pressing that key will figure in it, since it was an equally good motive for the other alternative. It seems that here the available reasons explanation for my action gives little hint as to what any of the antecedents of this nomic explanation might be if there is one.

So, contrary to what Mill appears to suggest, our reasons explanations for our actions do not always show us, or even give us much of a clue to, what the laws are (if any) that govern the determination of our actions by their antecedents.

## IV

But to show that we do not know any causal laws governing our reasons explanations is not to show that no such laws obtain[13] or that their obtaining would be incompatible with the reasons explanations. Some philosophers have tried to make this latter claim of incompatibility,[14] but their arguments do not succeed, as Davidson (1963), among others, has shown.[15] But that issue is not relevant here, for assumption (B) makes a much stronger claim than that a reasons explanation of an action is *compatible* with the action's being nomically necessitated by its antecedents. Assumption (B) is that reasons explanations *require* such necessitation. That is something that Davidson (1963) does *not* argue for but simply assumes. Neither does Ayer or Smart argue for this requirement. Smart writes as if he has done so when he says, "The previous paragraph suggests . . . that acting from reasons is not merely random precisely because it is also acting from causes," but in the paragraph he refers to he argues only that reasons explanations *can* be nomic.[16] That is not the same thing. The possibility of nomic reasons explanations does not imply the impossibility of anomic reasons explanations.

There are arguments that might be given for assumption (B). It might be said, for instance, that in giving a reasons explanation we are giving *causes* of the action—we do frequently use the word "because" in giving reasons explanations—and where there are causes there must be nomic necessitation. But this last premise amounts to just another way of stating assumption (B). A more worthy argument is this: in any explanation of an event in terms of its antecedents there must be some relation between explanans and explanandum in virtue of which the one explains the other. What else could this explanatory connection be if it is not that the explanans plus other antecedent circumstances nomically necessitates the explanandum?

That is a fair question. We can show that the right answer is *not* "There is nothing else it could be" by showing that for paradigm reasons explanations there are conditions that

> are obviously sufficient for their truth,
> obviously do not entail that there is any true law covering the case (any nomic explanation of the action),
> but do involve another sort of obviously explanatory connection between the explained action and its explanans.

Any condition satisfying these criteria I will call an *anomic* sufficient condition for a reasons explanation. It is not difficult to specify such conditions.

Consider first a very simple sort of reasons explanation, the sort expressed in a sentence of one of the following forms:[17]

(1) a. S V-ed in order (thereby) to U.
　 b. By V-ing S intended to U.
　 c. S V-ed with the intention of (thereby) U-ing.

I take these different forms to give us different ways of saying the same thing.[18] Some instances of these forms:

> S rubbed her hands together in order to warm them up.
> By flipping the switch S intended to turn on the light.
> S opened the window with the intention of letting out the smoke.

A statement of any of the forms (1a–c) is an answer to the question, "Why did S V?"; it offers an explanation of S's V-ing. It says that S's reason for V-ing was that she believed and intended that by V-ing she would U. Actually, "believed and intended" is redundant. S's intending that by V-ing she would U implies that S believes that by V-ing she has enough chance of U-ing to make V-ing worth the effort, and that is all the belief that the explanation requires. So we can say that such an explanation says that S's reason (or at least one of S's reasons) for V-ing was her intention thereby to U.

The only thing *required* for the truth of a reasons explanation of this sort, besides the occurrence of the explained action, is that the action have been *accompanied* by an intention with the right sort of content. Specifically, given that S did V, it will suffice for the truth of "S V-ed in order to U" if the following condition obtains.

(C1) Concurrently with her action of V-ing, S intended by *that* action to U (S intended *of* that action that by it she would U).

If from its inception S intended of her action of opening the window that by performing it she would let in fresh air (from its inception she had the intention that she could express with the sentence "I am undertaking this opening of the window to let in fresh air") then ipso facto it was her purpose in that action to let in fresh air, she did it in order to let in fresh air.

This is so even in the possible case where there is also true some independent explanation of the action, in terms other than the agent's reasons. Imagine that by direct electronic manipulation of neural events in S (through, say, electrodes planted in the part of S's brain that controls voluntary bodily exertion) someone else caused S voluntarily to open a window. Now the (C1) condition (where "V" is "open the window" and "U" is "let in fresh air") could also be true in such a case. The accompanying intention required by (C1) is at least conceptually compatible with the direct manipulation of S's voluntary exertions by another. Indeed, there appears to be nothing incoherent in the supposition that the controllers of the implanted electrodes might arrange to produce both S's voluntary exertion and the accompanying intention about it. If the (C1) condition were also true then it would be the case that S intended by her opening the window to let in fresh air. So it would be the case that S opened the window because of the other's manipulation of S's brain events *and* S opened the window in order to let in fresh air. There is no reason to think that the truth of either explanation must preclude the truth of the other.

Note that the content of the intention specified in (C1) refers *directly* to the action it is an intention about. That is, it does not refer to that particular action via a description of it but rather, as it were, demonstratively. The content of the intention is not the proposition, "There is now exactly one action of V-ing by me and by it I shall U," but rather the proposition, "By *this* V-ing (of which I am now aware) I shall U."[19] It is owing to this direct reference that the intention is about, and thus explanatory of, *that particular* action. Such an intention, which is directly about a particular action, could not begin before the particular action does. In general, whether the propositional attitude be intending or believing or desiring or any other, for the proposition involved to contain direct or demonstrative reference to a particular requires that the particular have an appropriate sort of role in causing whatever constitutes the reference to it, a relation that is precluded if the reference comes before the particular begins to exist. (It is enough if the particular has begun to exist, even if it is an event: one can demonstratively refer to a particular event by demonstratively referring to a part of it.) This means that we have a factor, the agent's concurrently intending something of the action, that is sufficient to verify a reasons explanation of the action and that not only does not but could not be antecedent to the action. We have a sufficient condition that entails nothing about what happened before the action that is relevant to explaining it. We have a reasons explanation that is entirely in terms of a concurrent state or process and not at all in terms of any antecedent one.

Usually, some explanatory antecedent is in the background of this sort of reasons explanation, "S V-ed in order to U." Usually, the intention concurrent with S's V-ing is the outcome of an antecedent intention, or at least desire, to U in the very near future. Usually, maybe even always, when an agent opens a window in order to let in fresh air, or pushes on a door in order to open it, she has already formed the intention to perform such an action for such an end and the action is under-taken in order to carry out that antecedently formed intention, or at least she antecedently possessed a desire for that end and the action is under-taken in order to satisfy that antecedently existing desire. But, however common it may be, there is no necessity that it be so: one can quite spontaneously do such things with such intentions.

So we see that our sufficient condition for explanations of sort (1), in terms of a concurrent intention regarding the particular action, does not entail that the action has a nomic explanation in terms of its anteced-ents. We should also see that it does not entail that the action has a nomic explanation in terms of concurrent conditions. Of course the following generalization is true of such cases: for any agent S and time t, if S intends of her V-ing at t that she thereby U then S Vs at t. But this is logically necessary and not a law of nature. It may be, of course, that when S has an intention directly about a current action of hers, intends of *this* V-ing that by it she U, there is a mental state of S that is necessary for her having this intention but is compatible with the nonoccurrence of the action of V-ing, a mental state that needs to be supplemented only by the right relation to the action for the whole to be her intending something *of* that action. But it will not be plausible to suppose that it is a law of nature that whenever an agent has this sort of mental state— ingredient in intending something of a concurrent V-ing but compatible with there being no V-ing—she does concurrently V. Her belief of her concurrent action that it is a V-ing could be false. Even if that belief could not be false (as might plausibly be held for the case where V-ing is a mental act of volition), there is no case for saying that our sufficient condition entails a nomic connection. Either there is an ingredient of the agent's direct intention about her V-ing that is compatible with her not V-ing or there is no such ingredient. If the latter, then the intention does not give us the nonentailing condition necessary for a nomic explana-tion. If the former then, although this aspect *could* be part of a nomically necessitating factor, there is nothing in the condition itself that entails that it must be so. There is, we have noted, a causal connection between the action and the intention required for the latter to refer directly to the former. But even if this must involve a nomic connection—and it is by no means clear that it must—the causation goes in the wrong direction, opposite to that from explaining intention to explained action. (In gen-eral, when one's thought contains a direct reference to a particular, it is in virtue of the particular's producing something in the thought, not vice versa.)

If the explanatory connection between the explaining intention and the explained action is not nomic necessitation then what is it? Well, it stares one in the face. In reasons explanations of sort (1) the concurrent intention explains the action simply in virtue of being an intention of that action that by or in it the agent will do a certain thing, in virtue, that is, of being that sort of propositional attitude (an intention) whose content has that feature (its being that by or in that action a certain thing will be done). That is all there is to it. It is simple but for the purpose of explaining the action it is sufficient. Aside from the relation required for the direct reference, this is an *internal* relation between the explaining factor and the explained action. It follows from the direct reference plus *intrinsic* properties of the relata, namely, the property of one that it is an action of S's and the property of the other that it is an intention of S's with a certain sort of content, namely, that the item to which it directly refers be an action with such-and-such properties. The explanatory connection is made, not by laws of nature, but by the direct reference and the internal relation.

Are reasons explanations of sort (1) *causal* explanations? They are if all one means by "causal" is that the explanation can be expressed with a "because" linking the explanation and the explanans. ("She opened the window because she intended thereby to let out the smoke.") If, on the other hand, one requires that a cause, properly so called, precede its effect, then these are not causal explanations. And it perhaps sounds odd to speak of a *concurrent* intention about an action as *causing* or *producing* or *resulting in* or *leading to* the action.

None of these expressions sounds odd, however, when speaking of a motive or reason the agent had prior to the action. One case where the explaining factor is antecedent to the action is the case where we explain the action as the carrying out of a decision the agent had made, an intention she had formed. One class of such explanations are expressible by sentences of the following form:

(2) a. S V-ed then in order to carry out her intention to V when F.
    b. S V-ed then because she had intended to V when F and she believed it was then F.

Here (2b) simply spells out more fully what (2a) implies. Some examples of this sort of explanation:

> S opened the window in order to carry out her intention to open the window when people started smoking.
> S raised her hand in order to carry out her intention to raise it as soon as the Chair called for the votes in favor of the motion.

What is an anomic sufficient condition for the truth of such an explanation? The wording of (2a) suggests that it should include, besides the explained action and the antecedent intention, an intention concurrent with the action to the effect that the action be a carrying out of the prior intention. This will make it the case that S performed the action *in order to* carry out that prior intention, performed it, that is, with the intention of carrying out that prior intention. So we can say that an explanation of sort (2) is true if (C2) is true.

(C2) (a) Prior to this V-ing S had an intention to V when F, and (b) concurrently with this V-ing S remembered that prior intention and its content and intended of this V-ing that it carry out that prior intention (be a V-ing when F).

Note that S cannot have the concurrent intention specified in (C2b) without believing that F now obtains; so it guarantees the second conjunct of (2b).

It is obvious that this sufficient condition is anomic. That is, it is obviously compatible with the truth of (C2) in a particular case of S's V-ing that there should be another case (involving S or some other agent) that is exactly similar in everything antecedent to the action (including other circumstances as well as the agent's intention to V) but lacks the agent's V-ing. Thus (C2) could hold even if there were no nomic explanation of S's V-ing in terms of the prior intention plus other antecedent circumstances. What then makes the explanatory connection here, if it is not nomic connection? Well, in the concurrent intention required by (C2) S intends of her current action that it be of just the sort specified in the content of the required prior intention (to which the content of the concurrent intention must refer), namely, a V-ing when F. It is this internal and referential relation between the contents of the prior and the concurrent intention, together with the explanatory relation of the concurrent intention to the action, which we have already discussed, that makes the explanatory connection between the prior intention and the action. The connection has two links, from prior to concurrent intention and from concurrent intention to action.

Following the model of (C2) for explanations of sort (2), it is not difficult to work out anomic sufficient conditions for other forms of reasons explanations in terms of antecedent states of the agent. Consider, for example, the sort expressed by sentences of the following form:

(3) a. S V-ed in order to carry out her (antecedent) intention to U.
b. S V-ed because she had intended to U and believed that by V-ing she would (might) U.

Here (3b) spells out more fully what is implied by (3a). Some examples of instances of this form of explanation:

> S shouted in order to carry out her (antecedent) intention to frighten away any bears there might be in the vicinity.
> S uttered, "They're gone," because she had intended to let R know when they had gone and believed that by such an utterance she would do so.

The following is an anomic sufficient condition for the truth of explanations of sort (3).

(C3) (a) Prior to V-ing S had the intention to U and (b) concurrently with V-ing S remembered that prior intention and intended that by this V-ing she would carry it out.

S's having the concurrent intention specified in (C3b) requires that S believe that by this V-ing she would or might U, and thus it entails the second conjunct of (3b).

Still another sort of reasons explanation in terms of antecedents is expressible in sentences of the following form.

(4) S V-ed because she had desired that p and believed that by V-ing she would (might) make it the case that p (or contribute to doing so).

Examples of this sort of explanation:

S opened the window because she had a desire for fresher air in the room and believed that opening the window would let in fresher air.

S voted for the motion because she wanted it to pass and believed that her vote would help it to do so.

The following gives an anomic sufficient condition for explanations of this sort.

(C4) (a) Prior to V-ing S had a desire that p and (b) concurrently with V-ing S remembered that prior desire and intended of this V-ing that it satisfy (or contribute to satisfying) that desire.

Our anomic sufficient conditions for explanations of actions in terms of antecedent reasons, (C2)–(C4), require S to remember the prior mental state (of intention or desire) while engaged in the action that that prior state explains. This will be a feature of any anomic sufficent condition for a reasons explanation of an action in terms of a prior state of the agent. If at the time the agent begins the action she has no memory at all of the prior desire or intention, then it can hardly be a factor motivating that action. Now it is not necessary in order for (C4), for example, to be an anomic sufficient condition for the truth of (4) that this memory connection be anomic as well. Even if it were true that there is remembering of the prior desire only if there is a nomic connection between the prior state (plus its circumstances) and some current state, it would not follow from this and (C4) that there must be a nomic connection between the prior desire (plus its circumstances) and the action for which, given the truth of (C4), it provides a reasons explanation. But it is interesting to note, incidentally, that it is possible to specify an anomic sufficient condition for remembering, for the connection between an earlier state of mind and a later one that makes the latter a memory of the former. S's seeming to remember a prior intention to do such-and-such will be a memory of a particular prior intention *if* S had such a prior intention and nothing independent of that prior intention has happened sufficient to produce S's seeming to remember such an intention. More generally, one's having had prior experience of a certain sort is the *default* explanation of one's later seeming to remember having had such experience, in the sense that it is the explanation *unless* this role is preempted by something else, independent of it, that was sufficient to cause the memory impression.[20]

Like those in terms of concurrent intentions, our anomic sufficient conditions for reasons explanations in terms of antecedent motives are compatible with the truth of independent explanations in terms other than the agent's reasons. Consider again our example of S's voluntarily opening a window *both* as a result of another's manipulation of events in S's brain *and* in order to let in fresh air. Add to it that S had earlier formed a desire for fresher air in the room and concurrently with her opening the window remembered that desire and intended of that action that it satisfy that desire, making true the appropriate instance of (C4). Then you have a case where S opened the window both because of the signals sent to the volitional part of her brain and in order to satisfy her antecedent desire. Again there is no reason to think that the truth of either explanation excludes the truth of the other.

A noteworthy fact about (C4), the anomic sufficient condition for an explanation of the form "S V-ed because she had desired that p and believed that by V-ing she would satisfy that desire," is that it suggests a way of distinguishing between (i) a desire that was a reason for which the agent acted as she did and (ii) a desire that was *not* a reason for which the agent acted as she did although it was a reason for so acting that the agent was aware of having at the time. A desire of the agent's fits description (i) if the agent acts with the intention that that action satisfy that desire; and a desire of the agent's fits description (ii) if, and only if, the agent has no such intention concurrent with the action despite being aware of the desire and of the fact that it is a reason for acting as she did (given her beliefs).

One may wonder, however, if and how there *could* be cases that fit description (ii). Our account does not answer this question, but only turns it into the question whether it could be that an agent at the time of acting believes that her action will satisfy a certain desire she has without intending of the action that it satisfy that desire. Suppose S urgently needs her glasses which she left in R's room where R is now sleeping. S has some desire to wake R, because she would then have R's company, but also some desire *not* to wake R, because she knows that R needs the sleep. S decides to enter R's room in order to get her reading glasses, knowing as she does so that her action will satisfy her desire to wake R. Could it nevertheless be true that S did not intend of her action that it wake R? Bratman (1987) offers an illuminating account of how this could be so.[21] It seems right to say that S did not intend to wake R if S was so disposed that, had it turned out that her entering the room did not wake R, S would not have felt that her plan had failed to be completely realized and she must then either wake R in some other way or decide to abandon part of her plan. And S's being thus *uncommitted* to waking R is quite compatible with S's expecting and desiring to wake R.

## V

The anomic sufficient conditions we have given for explanations of actions in terms of antecedent reasons allow the possibility that the very same antecedent state of the world could afford a reasons explanation for either of two or more different alternative actions. Suppose, for example, that there have been two different occasions when I have formed the intention to produce an asterisk on my computer screen and have known that either of two keys will do the job. If on one of those occasions I pressed one of those keys, my action can be explained by saying that I pressed that key in order to produce an asterisk; and if on the other occasion I pressed the other key, that action can be explained by saying that I pressed *that* key in order to produce an asterisk. The only differences we need to suppose in the two situations are in the action explained (my pressing the one key rather than the other) and its concurrent intention (which I could have expressed, "By this pressing of *this* key I intend to produce an asterisk"). We need suppose no differences at all in the relevant *antecedent* intention. On both occasions it was just an intention to produce an asterisk.

In that example the agent was indifferent between alternative means to an intended end. In another sort of example the agent chooses arbitrarily between incompatible desired ends. Suppose S desires the motion to pass and at the same time desires to avoid offending her friend who opposes the motion. Whether she votes for the motion or votes against it, the explanation can be that S did it in order to satisfy the relevant prior desire. Again, the only differences in the two alternative situations that we need to suppose, in order to make the alternative explanations hold in them, are differences in the actions and their concurrent accompaniments. We need suppose no difference in the antecedents.

Here we have a striking difference between the anomic explanatory connection we have found in explanations of actions in terms of antecedent reasons and the nomic explanatory connection in deterministic explanations of events. The nomic, deterministic connection, by its very nature, can go from a given antecedent state of the world to just one subsequent development. If the antecedent state of the world explains a subsequent development via general laws of nature then that same antecedent state could not likewise explain any alternative development. Given fixed laws of nature, a given antecedent situation has the potential to explain nomically and deterministically at most one subsequent alternative development. But the same antecedent state can explain in the anomic, reasons way any of several alternative possible subsequent actions. If the antecedent situation contains the agent's having desires for two or more incompatible ends or her being indifferent between alternative means to an intended end, then it has the potential to explain in the reasons way whichever of the alternative actions occurs. The one that occurs needs only to have the right sort of accompanying memory and intention.[22]

It is true, as we noted earlier, that when an agent chooses arbitrarily between incompatible ends or between alternative means to an intended end we do not have an explanation of why the agent acted as she did *rather than* in one of the other ways. Nevertheless, we do have an explanation of why the agent acted as she did: she so acted in order to carry out the intention or to satisfy the relevant desire. The truth of that explanation is not undermined by the agent's not having any reason for, there not being any explanation of, her not doing one of the other things instead.

But now one may wonder about cases where the antecedents explain an action in the reasons sort of way but do *not* have the potential to explain alternative actions equally well, where the antecedents give the agent's reason for acting as she did and also explain why she did not act in any alternative way instead. If such explanations must be nomic, must imply that sufficiently similar antecedents will (as a matter of the laws of nature) always lead to the same sort of action rather than to any alternative, then incompatibilism is still in serious trouble. For it would be absurd to say that any such reasons explanation of an action renders it unfree.

Incompatibilists need not worry. Such explanations need not be nomic either. Consider again reasons explanations of sort (3).

(3) S V-ed in order to carry out her intention to U.

Our anomic sufficient condition for such an explanation was (C3).

(C3) (a) Prior to V-ing S had the intention to U and (b) concurrently with V-ing S remembered her prior intention and its content and intended that by this V-ing she would carry it out.

What sort of enriched condition will be sufficient for the truth of a similar explanation of why S V-ed *and* did not do something else instead (either some other sort of action or being inactive)? A commonly occurring condition that accomplishes this is the following.

(C3*) (a) Just before V-ing the agent intended to U at once and preferred V-ing then to any alternative means to U-ing then that occurred to her that she thought she could then perform, and (b) concurrently with V-ing she remembered her prior intention and intended by this V-ing to carry it out and she continued to prefer V-ing to any alternative means of U-ing that occurred to her that she thought she could then perform.

It is obvious that (C3*) is sufficient for the truth of a reasons explanation of the sort under consideration, one of the form:

(3*) S V-ed then rather than doing something else or being inactive instead because she intended to U at once and she preferred V-ing to any other means of U-ing that occurred to her that she thought she could then perform.

It should be equally obvious that (C3*) does not entail that S's V-ing was nomically necessitated by its antecedents. There certainly is no plausibility in the proposition that the antecedents given in (C3*a) must always issue in S's V-ing. Often enough such antecedents are followed by S's doing something else instead, owing to some new alternative occurring to S at the last minute, or to S's changing her mind about what alternatives are open to her, or to S's suddenly abandoning (perhaps even forgetting) her intention to U at once, or to S's weakness of will (though S believed that V-ing was definitely the best means to U-ing and therefore intended to take that means, there was in some other means a temptation that she was in the end unable to resist). As with the antecedents that explain why S V-ed (those given in (C3a)), the antecedents that explain why not any other alternative instead (added in (C3*a)) do so completely only in conjunction with conditions concurrent with and not antecedent to the action explained (specified in (C3*b)). To suppose that there occurs another case where the antecedents are exactly the same but S does not V but is inactive or does something else instead is not to suppose anything incompatible with the truth of the explanation entailed by (C3*).

## VI

I hope to have made it clear that incompatibilism does not entail certain absurdities it has been alleged to entail. The thesis that a free action cannot be nomically determined by its antecedents does not entail that an agent cannot determine which free action she performs or that an agent cannot perform a free action for reasons. When one sees how easy it is to give *a*nomic sufficient conditions for reasons explanations of actions, one may find it surprising that many philosophers should have subscribed to the assumption that such explanations must be nomic. (Even some incompatibilists have been guilty of this assumption; they have typically also been "hard" determinists, denying that we in fact have free will.[23]) Perhaps the error is less surprising if we see it as a case of overgeneralizing a well-understood and highly respected paradigm, in this case the explanatory paradigm of the natural sciences where laws of nature are what make explanatory connections. Fascination with this paradigm can, it seems, blind one to the fact that the explanatory paradigm of our ordinary reasons explanations of action is quite different. There an internal and referential relation is sufficient to make the explanatory connection and has no need of a nomic connection. Neither does it rule out a nomic connection. Reasons explanations are not *in*deterministic, only *a*deterministic; but that is all that the defense of incompatibilism requires.

## Notes

1. Versions of the argument that are substantially adequate though flawed in minor ways can be found, among other places, in C. Ginet "Might We Have No Choice?" (in Keith Lehrer, ed., *Freedom and Determinism* [New York: Random House, 1966]); P. van Inwagen "The Incompatibility of Free Will and Determinism," (*Philosophical Studies* 27 [1975], pp. 185–99); Ginet "The Conditional Analysis of Freedom," (in P. van Inwagen, ed., *Time and Cause: Essays Presented to Richard Taylor* [Dordrecht: Reidel, 1980]); Ginet "In Defense of Incompatibilism" (*Philosophical Studies* 44 (1983), pp. 391–400); and van Inwagen, *An Essay on Free Will* (Oxford: Clarendon Press, 1983).

2. The earliest appearance of this argument, or one closely akin to it, that I know of is in Hume's *Treatise*, Bk. II, Pt. III, Sec. 2.

3. Frithjof Bergmann, *On Being Free* (Notre Dame, IN: University of Notre Dame Press, 1977), pp. 234–35. This is the central argument in an appendix titled "Freedom and Determinism."

4. Van Inwagen, *An Essay on Free Will*, pp. 149–50.

5. A. J. Ayer, "Freedom and Necessity," reprinted in A. J. Ayer, *Philosophical Essays* (London: Macmillan, 1959), p. 275.

6. J. J. C. Smart, *Between Science and Philosophy* (New York: Random House, 1968), pp. 300–301.

7. J. S. Mill, *An Examination of Sir William Hamilton's Philosophy* (Toronto: University of Toronto Press, 1979 [1872], J. B. Robson, ed.), pp. 449–50.

8. Mill, *An Examination*, p. 451.

9. See Mill, *An Examination*, pp. 451–53.

10. Thomas Reid, *The Works of Thomas Reid*, vols. III–IV (Charlestown, MA: Samuel Etheridge, Jr., 1815), quoted from G. Dworkin, ed., *Determinism, Free Will, and Moral Responsibility* (Englewood Cliffs, NJ: Prentice-Hall, 1970), pp. 88–89.

11. Mill, *An Examination*, pp. 468–69.

12. See Dworkin, *Determinism*, p. 87, excerpted from Reid (1815).

13. As Donald Davidson points out in "Actions, Reasons, and Causes" (*Journal of Philosophy* 60 [1963], pp. 685–700; reprinted in Davidson, *Essays on Actions and Events* [Oxford: Clarendon Press, 1980]).

14. For example, A. I. Melden, *Free Action* (London: Routledge & Kegan Paul, 1961) and Norman Malcolm, "The Conceivability of Mechanism" (*Philosophical Review* 77 [1968], pp. 45–72).

15. See Alvin Goldman, "The Compatibility of Mechanism and Purpose" (*Philosophical Review* 78 [1969], pp. 468–82), which focuses on Malcolm, "The Conceivability of Mechanism."

16. He argues (Smart, *Between Science and Philosophy*, p. 300) that a computer programmed to select items from a set according to certain criteria can be said to have been "programmed to act in accordance with what we would call 'good reasons'."

17. In these forms "V-ed" is a variable ranging over past-tense singular forms of action verb phrases (for example, "opened the door"), "to U" ranges over infinitive forms ("to open the door"), and "V-ing" ranges over progressive forms minus their auxiliaries ("opening the door").

18. Certainly (1b) and (1c) are equivalent and each implies (1a), and in normal sorts of cases where (1a) is true (1b–c) will be true also. Michael Bratman (*Intentions, Plans, and Practical Reason* [Cambridge, MA: Harvard University Press, 1987], ch. 8) describes unusual sorts of cases where it seems right to say that (1a) is true but (1b–c) are not, given the plausible assumption that, if one believes that ends E1 and E2 cannot both be achieved, one cannot (without being criticizably irrational) intend to achieve both, but one can both undertake action A1 in order to achieve (aiming at achieving) E1 and undertake action A2 in order to achieve E2.

19. George Wilson, *The Intentionality of Human Action* (Amsterdam: North Holland, 1980), chapter 5, calls attention to such directly referring intentions. He calls them "act-relational" intentions and contrasts them with "future action" intentions. To be exact, it is the statements attributing these two kinds of intentions, rather than the intentions themselves, that he calls "act-relational" and "future action". An act-relational statement attributes, as he puts it, an intention *with which* the agent acts, an intention the agent has *in* the action.

20. I have argued this point more fully in Ginet, *Knowledge, Perception, and Memory* (Dordrecht: D. Reidel, 1975), pp. 160–65.

21. See Bratman, *Intentions*, pp. 155–60. The example he discusses differs from mine in that the agent in his example believes that the expected but unintended effect (the "side" effect) will help to achieve the same end that his intended means is intended to achieve, whereas in my example S does not believe this but desires the expected side effect, waking R, for reasons independent of her intended end, getting her glasses. But this difference seems immaterial to Bratman's account of how the side effect can, though expected and even desired (or believed to promote desired ends), can still be unintended.

22. We have here a solution to another puzzle of van Inwagen's, concerning how an agent can have a choice about—can have it in her power to

determine—which of competing antecedent motives will cause her action, be the reason for which she acts. He expresses this puzzle in a footnote appended to his remarks I quoted at the end of Section I:

> Alvin Plantinga has suggested to me that the thief may have had a choice about whether to repent owing to his having had a choice about whether, on the one hand, DB [a certain complex of desire and belief in the thief] caused R [the thief's repenting], or, on the other, his desire for money and his belief that the poor-box contained money (DB*) jointly caused the event *his robbing the poor-box* (R*). We should note that the two desire-belief pairs, DB and DB*, both actually obtained; according to the theory Plantinga has proposed, what the thief had a choice about was which of these two potential causes became the actual cause of an effect appropriate to it. This may for all I know to be the correct account of the "inner state" of a deliberating agent who has a choice about how he is going to act. But if this account is correct, then there are two events *its coming to pass that DB causes R* and *its coming to pass that DB* causes R** such that, though one of them must happen, it's causally undetermined which will happen; and it will have to be the case that the thief has a choice about which of them will happen. If this were so, I should find it very puzzling and I should be at a loss to give an account of it. (van Inwagen, *An Essay*, p. 239, n. 34)

The proper account seems to me straightforward. The thief determines which of the antecedent motives he acts out of simply by acting in the way recommended by one of them while concurrently remembering the motive and intending his action to satisfy it. His doing so is obviously compatible with his action's being nomically undetermined by the antecedent state of the world.

23. For example: Paul Henri Thiry, baron d'Holbach, *Systeme de la Nature* (*System of Nature or The Laws of the Moral and Physical World*) (London [Philadelphia], 1770 [1808]), ch. XI–XII; Paul Ree *Die Illusion der Willens Freiheit* (Berlin, 1885), ch. I–II (an English translation of the major parts of ch. 1–2, by Stefan Bauer-Mengelberg, is published in P. Edwards and A. Pap, eds., *A Modern Introduction to Philosophy* Third Edition [New York: Free Press, 1973] under the title, "Determinism and the Illusion of Moral Responsibility"); and Clarence Darrow, *Crime, Its Cause and Treatment* (New York: Crowell, 1922).

# 6

# Agents, Causes, and Events: The Problem of Free Will

## RODERICK M. CHISHOLM

In earlier writings on this topic, I had contrasted *agent causation* with *event causation* and had suggested that "causation by agents" could not be reduced to "causation by events." I now believe that that suggestion was a mistake. What I had called agent causation is a *subspecies* of event causation. My concern in the present study is to note the specific differences by reference to which agent causation can be distinguished from other types of event causation.

We cannot hope to succeed in this task unless we try to cope with the very difficult concept of *causation*—event causation. And this means, in turn, that we should have a clear conception of the ontological status of *events* and, in particular, of their relation to attributes or properties and of their relation to individual things.

We begin with the ontological question.

### The Nature of States

Events are here construed as being a subspecies of states. The concept of a *state* is taken as undefined, but it can be clarified in several different ways.

Suppose that you are reading. Then the following entities are involved: (1) that *contingent substance* which is yourself; (2) that *noncontingent thing*, which is *the property of reading;* and (3) that contingent *state* which is *you reading*. It will be useful to say that you are the *substrate* of that state and that the property of reading is the *content*.

We introduce the following twofold definitional abbreviation:

> D1  x is the substrate of the state y, and z is the content of the state y
>     = Df. y is that state which is x-exemplifying-the-property z.

We may now formulate a general principle, telling us that every state is necessarily such that it has the substrate that it has.

> A1  For every x, if there exists the state, x-being-F, then x-being-F is
>     necessarily such that it is a state of x.

From the fact that that *state*, which is you reading something, is necessarily such that it is a state of you, it does *not* follow, of course, that *you* are necessarily such that you are reading something.

### Higher Order States and the Concept of an Event

We have assumed that, for every x there is the state x-being-F, if and only if x is F. Our assumptions imply, therefore, that there are infinitely many states. They also imply that there is an infinite hierarchy of states. The hierarchy may be illustrated this way:

> (1)  x-being-F
> (2)  (x-being-F)-being-G
> (3)  [(x-being-F)-being-G]-being-H

An instance of (1) would be Jones walking. An instance of (2) would be (Jones walking) being strenuous. And an instance of (3) would be (Jones walking being strenuous) contributing causally to (Jones being tired).

We could say that a *first-order state is a state that has a non-state as its substrate. Second-order* states will have first-order states as *their* substrates. Second-order states are illustrated by those states that consist of one first-order state contributing causally to another first-order state.

In order to say what an event is, we refer to the concepts of a first-order state and of a second-order state:

> D2  x is a *first-order state* = Df. x is a state of a substance.
> D3  x is a *second-order state* = Df. x is a state of a first-order state.

We are now in a position to characterize the concept of an event.

> D4  x is an *event* = Df. x is either a first-order state or a second-order state.

In some of his earlier writings on the concept of an event, Jaegwon Kim suggests a theory according to which all events would be *first-order* states.[1] Such a restriction provides no place for those paradigmatic events that consist of one event *contributing causally* to the occurrence of another event. Examples are the striking of a match contributing causally to the burning of a piece of paper; the treatment of a patient contributing causally to the patient being cured; and the rush of the sea contributing causally to the destruction of the pier. Here we have second-order events that relate first-order events.

## Events and the Concept of Causation

*Causation* cannot be analyzed by reference to the "constant conjunction" of events. Most investigators agree that the concept of causation is *nomological.*[2] It presupposes the concept of physical necessity, a concept that is usually expressed by reference to "laws of nature."

How are we to interpret "It is a *law of nature* that if A occurs then B occurs"? Speaking somewhat loosely, we may say that the reference to "a law of nature" is intended to call attention to two types of necessity: that imposed "by logic" and that imposed "by nature." How, then, might one distinguish "laws of logic" from "laws of nature"?

If it is "a law of logic that if A then B," then conceivably a rational being could know a priori, just by reflection, that it must be the case that if A occurs, then B occurs. Some philosophers would say: "Every possible world is such that, if A occurs in that world, then B also occurs in that world." But rational reflection does not suffice to tell us what the laws of nature are.

It is possible that there occurs a conjunction of events A that taken together will constitute a sufficient causal condition of B without logically implying B. The states that would make up such a conjunction are *"partial causes,"* or *"contributing causes,"* of B. One of the most common errors to which discussions of freedom and causation are subject is that of confusing partial or contributing causes with sufficient causal conditions. The contributing causes that make up a sufficient causal condition of an event B need not themselves be sufficient causal conditions of B.

Let us consider an example.

We will define the concept of a *sufficient causal condition,* not by reference to a set of states or events, but by reference to those properties we have called the *contents* of the states or events. Thus we may have:

> D5  S is a sufficient causal condition of E = Df. S is a set of properties such that the conjunction of its members does not logically imply E; and it is law of nature that, if all the members of S are exemplified by the same thing at the same time, then E will be exemplified either at that time or later.

In referring in the definition to the properties of the thing that undergoes the effect, we do not thereby exclude the properties of other things that happen to be in the environment of the thing that undergoes the effect. The piece of wood burns in part because of the presence of oxygen in the environment. But in that case one of the properties of the piece of wood is that it happens to *be* in an environment in which oxygen is present.

The realistic view of properties, here presupposed, implies that, for any two properties, P and Q, there is also the property, P-and-Q. It also implies that, for any two properties, there is also the property of *having* those two properties.

Why say that the effect of the sufficient causal conditions must be exemplified either *at the same time as* or *later than* the members of that condition? To say this is simply to say that the effect not precede its cause. The effect, in other words, will not be exemplified *before* the members of any sufficient causal condition of that effect are exemplified.

We next single out the concept of a *minimal* sufficient causal condition:

> D6   C is a minimal sufficient causal condition of E = Df. C is a sufficient causal condition of E; and no subset of C is a sufficient causal condition of E.

We may speak of a "subset" of a sufficient causal condition, since such a condition, according to our previous definition, is a set of properties.

If your action is a part or member of a minimal sufficient causal condition of an event, then, clearly, the action contributes causally to that event. It is a *partial cause* of the event (which is not to say, of course, that it is *the cause* of that event).

> D7   That state which is x-being-C contributes causally to that state which is y-being-E = Df. C is a member of a set S of properties that are all exemplified by x at the same time, and S is a minimal sufficient causal condition of E.

What of those situations where the effect is overdetermined? Two marksmen shoot at the victim; they are each successful and the two shots do their work at precisely the same time. Given the one shot, the other shot was not needed to bring about the effect. *Both* shots, therefore, would not be a part of a minimal sufficient causal condition; yet each contributed. We need not, therefore, revise the definition of a minimal sufficient causal condition.

### Freedom and Indeterminism

The concept of *being able to undertake* is somewhat more broad than that of *being free to undertake*. It is only when you "could have done otherwise" that your undertaking may be said to be free.

I have not used the expression "free will," for the question of freedom, as John Locke said, is not the question "whether the will be free"; it is the question "whether a man be free."[3] The question is whether the agent is free to undertake any of those things he does *not* undertake and whether he is free not to undertake any of those things he *does* undertake.

Consider the question: Is the person free to bring about what it is that he or she undertakes to bring about? This is *not* the question with which we have been concerned. But many would have us *think* that it is. Many philosophers and theologians whose views may seem unduly to curtail our freedom have tried to soften this consequence by redefining the problem of freedom. Thus Jonathan Edwards, using the the verb "to will" where I have used "to undertake," would have us think that the question is this: Is the person free to do what it is that he wills to do? *This* question is not difficult to deal with. We may answer it affirmatively by pointing out that on occasion people do do the things that they will to do; that is to say, they do bring about what it is that they undertake to bring about.[4] Those who put this question are asking about what Thomas Aquinas called the *actus voluntatis imperatus.* They are simply asking: Do we ever bring about the things we intend to bring about? But our question might be put by asking: Are we free to will the things that we do will? Thus they have tried to bypass the more fundamental question of the freedom of the *actus voluntatis elicitus.*[5]

Objection: "An undertaking that has no sufficient causal condition is completely arbitrary; it is simply a random event for which the agent has no responsibility at all. Hence your proposal implies that we are really not responsible for anything that we do."

From the fact that an undertaking has no sufficient causal condition, it does not at all follow that it is "completely arbitrary" or "random." Nor does it follow that the person has no responsibility for that undertaking. For even if the undertaking has no sufficient causal condition, there are several ways in which other events may contribute causally to that undertaking.

Suppose you are in the middle of a room that has many exits and you hear someone screaming "Fire!" Your hearing the scream may complete a sufficient causal condition for your undertaking to leave the room. But, so far as each particular exit is concerned, there may be no sufficient causal condition for your undertaking to leave by *that* exit rather than by any of the others. Suppose, then, that you undertake to leave by the exit that is north of you and that you succeed. In this case, *your undertaking to leave* may have a sufficient causal condition but *your undertaking to leave by the northern exit* may not. The latter event, although it has no sufficient causal condition, was such that the shout of "Fire!" contributed causally to it.

And there are other ways of contributing causally to an event that has no sufficient causal condition.

An automobile driver with a long trip ahead of him interrupts the trip to get something to eat. Of the two available restaurants, he chooses the one that serves alcoholic beverages, not with the intention of getting a drink, but because he thinks the food is better there. He knows full well, however, that he could easily succumb to the temptation to have a drink. Suppose now that he *does* succumb to that temptation and endeavors to have a drink. Even if this endeavor has no sufficient causal condition, the driver's beliefs, motives, and desires contributed causally to its occurrence. And if the results of that endeavor should be still more drinks and a subsequent serious accident, then one would be completely justified in holding him responsible for that free endeavor and for everything to which it led.

If an agent's undertaking contributes causally to a certain event, then *he,* the agent, may also be said to contribute causally to that event. Agent causation need not be construed as an *alternative* to event causation; we may think of it as a *subspecies* of event causation. For "*Agent S* contributed causally to so-and-so" may be construed as: "There was a certain thing that agent S undertook and his undertaking that thing contributed causally to the occurrence of so-and-so."

## Notes

1. See his "Events as Property Exemplifications," in Myles Brand and D. Walton, eds., *Action Theory* (Dordrecht: Reidel, 1976), pp. 159–77.

2. Compare the article "Causality" by Edward Madden, in Hans Burkhardt and Barry Smith, eds., *Handbook of Metaphysics and Ontology* (Munich: Philosophia Verlag, 1992), vol. I, pp. 133–36.

3. *Essay Concerning Human Understanding,* Book II, Chapter xxi.

4. See Edward's *Freedom of the Will* (1754), passim.

5. The classic statement of this distinction is in the *Summa Theologica,* First Part of the Second Part, Question I, Article 1 ("Whether it Belongs to Man to Act for an End").

# 7

## Choice and Indeterminism

ROBERT NOZICK

### I. Weigh(t)ing Reasons

Making some choices feels like this. There are various reasons for and against doing each of the alternative actions or courses of action one is considering, and it seems and feels as if one could do any one of them. In considering the reasons, mulling them over, one arrives at a view of which reasons are more important, which ones have more weight. One decides which reasons to act on; or one may decide to act on none of them but to seek instead a new alternative since none previously considered was satisfactory.[1]

After the choice, however, others will say we were caused to act by the considerations which were (or turned out to be) more weighty. And it is not just others. We too, in looking back at our past actions, will see which reasons swayed us and will view (accepting) those considerations as having caused us to act as we did. Had we done the other act, though, acting on the opposing considerations, we (along with the others) would have described those considerations as causing us to do that other act. Whichever act we do, the (different) background considerations exist which can be raised to causal status. Which considerations will be so raised depends upon which act we do. Does the act merely show which of the considerations was the weightier cause, or does the decision make one of them weightier?

The reasons do not come with previously given precisely specified weights; the decision process is not one of discovering such precise weights but of assigning them. The process not only weighs reasons, it (also) weights them.[2] At least, so it sometimes feels. This process of weighting may focus narrowly, or involve considering or deciding what sort of person one wishes to be, what sort of life one wishes to lead.

What picture of choice emerges if we take seriously the feeling that the (precise) weights to be assigned to reasons is "up to us"? It is causally undetermined (by prior factors) which of the acts we will decide to do. It may be causally determined that certain reasons are reasons (in the one direction or the other), but there is no prior causal determination of the precise weight each reason will have in competition with others. Thus, we need not hold that every possible reason is available to every person at every time or historical period. Historians and anthropologists delineate how certain ideas and considerations can be outside the purview of some societies, some of whose reasons would not count as reasons for us. (Yet, there does remain the question of whether an innovator couldn't have recognized as a reason something outside the purview of others in his society.) Psychology, sociobiology, and the various social sciences, on this view, will offer causal explanations of why something is or is not a reason for a person (in a situation). They will not always be able to explain why the reasons get the precise weights they do. Compare the way art historians treat style; not every style is equally available to every artist in every period, yet within a style creative choices are made, and some artistic revolutions introduce new stylistic possibilities.

It is neither necessary nor appropriate, on this view, to say the person's action is uncaused. As the person is deciding, mulling over reasons $R_A$ which are reasons for doing act A and over $R_B$ which are reasons for doing act B, it is undetermined which act he will do. In that very situation, he could do A and he could do B. He decides, let us suppose, to do act A. It then will be true that he was caused to do act A by (accepting) $R_A$. However, had he decided to do act B, it then would have been $R_B$ that caused him to do B. Whichever he decides upon, A or B, there will be a cause of his doing it, namely $R_A$ or $R_B$. His action is not (causally) determined, for in that very situation he could have decided differently; if the history of the world had been replayed up until that point, it could have continued with a different action. With regard to his action the person has what has been termed contracausal freedom—we might better term it contradeterministic.[3]

Thus, we draw a distinction between an action's being caused, and its being causally determined. Some philosophers would deny this distinction, maintaining that whenever one event causes another, there holds a general law in accordance with which it does so: some specification of the first event (along with other conditions which hold) always is and would be followed by an event of the same type as the second. It is a metaphysical thesis that the root notion of causality, producing or making something happen, can operate only through such lawlike universality. If this were correct, and if a law could not hold only at that (moment of) time, then causality necessarily would involve causal determination: under exactly the same conditions repeated, exactly the same thing would have (again) to happen. According to the view that distinguishes causality from causal determination, an act can be done because of something and have a cause even though in exactly the same conditions another act could have been done. It is common, in retrospect, to see what caused us to act as we did. Although we can retrospectively identify a cause, this does not mean our action was causally determined; had we acted differently in that situation (as we could have) we retrospectively would have identified a different cause—$R_B$ instead of $R_A$.

The weights of reasons are inchoate until the decision. The decision need not bestow exact quantities, though, only make some reasons come to outweigh others. A decision establishes inequalities in weight, even if not precise weights.[4]

These bestowed weights (or comparative weightings of reasons) are not so evanescent as to disappear immediately after the very decision that bestows them. They set up a framework within which we make future decisions, not eternal but one we tentatively are committed to. The process of decision fixes the weights reasons are to have. The situation resembles that of precedents within a legal system; an earlier decision is not simply ignored though it may be overturned for reason, the decision represents a tentative commitment to make future decisions in accordance with the weights it establishes, and so on.[5]

The claim that we always do what we most prefer or always act from the strongest motive is sometimes said to be empty of content, since the preference or the strength of motive is identified by what the person does. If the claim is to have empirical content, it must sometimes be possible to discover what a person's preference or strongest motive is via some other situation, to independently identify it in order then to check in this situation whether the person is doing what he most prefers or has the strongest motive to do.[6] Defenders of the claim do point out other situations (of choice or answering questions) where the relevant preference or motive can be identified; so the truth of the claim in this decision situation is testable, given the assumption that the preference or motive is stable from the one situation to the other.[7] However, if our conception of the bestowal of weights (with a commitment that lingers) holds true, then these independent "tests" are to be interpreted differently. We do not always act on what was a preexistingly strongest preference or motive; it can become strongest in the process of making the decision, thereafter having greater weight (in other future decisions) than the reasons it vanquished. The prior independent test of a preference therefore need not discover one that existed; it may establish a preference which then consistently carries over into a new decision situation. The testing procedure cannot show that we always act on a preexistingly strongest preference or motive.[8]

Only when there are opposed reasons for different actions is it necessary to arrive at a weighting; otherwise, one can just do what all the reasons favor. However, neither group of these opposed reasons need be moral; decisions that involve a conflict of duty or other moral motives with (nonmoral) desires are only a subclass of the free decisions.[9] Shall we say, though, that every free decision involves a conflict of some sort, with reasons pulling in different directions? The reasons in conflict need not then have indeterminate weight, for a free decision may "act out" an earlier weighting decision as precedent. (But is there always present a reason of indeterminate weight to reexamine and overturn an earlier precedent, which reason itself must be given a determinate lesser weight in the decision to follow the precedent?) Even though it will include no interesting cases we especially want to judge, still, we may formulate the theory to avoid the uncomfortable consequence that actions in the face of no contrary reasons are not free ones.

In this conception of decision as bestowing weights coherent? It may help to compare it to the currently orthodox interpretation of quantum mechanics. The purpose of this comparison is not to derive free will from quantum mechanics or to use physical theory to prove free will exists, or even to say that nondeterminism at the quantum level leaves room for free will. Rather, we wish to see whether quantum theory provides an analogue, whether it presents structural possibilities which if instanced at the macrolevel of action—this is not implied by microquantum theory— would fit the situation we have described. According to the currently orthodox quantum mechanical theory of measurement, as specified by John von Neumann, a quantum mechanical system is in a superposition of states, a probability mixture of states, which changes continuously in accordance with the quantum mechanical equations of motion, and which changes discontinuously via a measurement or observation. Such a measurement "collapses the wave packet," reducing the superposition to a particular state; which state the superposition will reduce to is not predictable.[10] Analogously, a person before decision has reasons without fixed weights; he is in a superposition of (precise) weights, perhaps within certain limits, or a mixed state (which need not be a superposition with fixed probabilities). The process of decision reduces the superposition to one state (or to a set of states corresponding to a comparative ranking of reasons), but it is not predictable or determined to which state of the weights the decision (analogous to a measurement) will reduce the superposition. (Let us leave aside von Neumann's subtle analysis, in ch. 6, of how any placing of the "cut" between observer and observed is consistent with his account.) Our point is not to endorse the orthodox account as a correct account of quantum mechanics, only to draw upon its theoretical structure to show our conception of decision is a coherent one. Decision fixes the weights of reasons; it reduces the previously obtaining mixed state or superposition. However, it does not do so at random.

## II. Nonrandom Weighting

Granting the coherence of the conception wherein the process of decision bestows weights, still, is that free will? An action's being non-determined is not sufficient for it to be free—it might just be a random act. If we acted in the way uranium 238 emits alpha particles, determinism would be false but (unless we are greatly mistaken about uranium 238) we would not thereby have free will. What makes the bestowal of weights on reasons any different? If that too is a random act, then is acting on those weights in that very decision other than random? Acting on those same weights later will not be random, but is it better than any other determined act if it traces its history back not to causes before birth but to a recent random weighting of reasons?

How can the giving of weights be other than random? Since (by hypothesis) there is no cause for giving or bestowing these particular weights on reasons rather than other weights, must it be merely a random act when these are bestowed? (Let us leave aside for the moment the distinction between 'caused' and 'causally determined'.) If the absence of causation entailed randomness, then the denial of (contra-causal) free will would follow immediately. However, 'uncaused' does not entail 'random'. To be sure, the theorist of free will still has to explain wherein the act not causally determined is nonrandom, but at least there is room for this task.

In what way is the bestowal of weights not simply random? There may be causes limiting the reasons on which (nonzero) weight can be bestowed, and the interval within which these weights fall may similarly be limited. However, although it is not a random matter that the weights bestowed fall within this range, neither is that decided by the person. The question remains: how is her decision among the alternatives causally open to her (the alternatives it is not causally determined she won't choose) not simply a random matter?

First, the decision may be self-subsuming; the weights it bestows may fix general principles that mandate not only the relevant act but also the bestowing of those (or similar) weights. The bestowal of weights yields both the action and (as a subsumption, not a repetition) that very bestowal. For example, consider the policy of choosing so as to track bestness: if the act weren't best you wouldn't do it, while if it were best you would. The decision to follow this policy may itself be an instance of it, subsumed under it.

Another issue shows how an act of decision can refer to itself. In contrast to optimizing models of decision, which see the agent as maximizing some objective function, Herbert Simon has presented a *satisficing* model of decision (to use his term): an agent will do an action that is "good enough," but failing to find one among his alternatives he will search for still others; repeated failure to find a suitable one will change his view of what is good enough, lowering his level of aspiration. It is natural to try to embed these considerations within an optimizing model that includes the costs of searching for new alternatives, gathering further information, as well as estimates of the probability of finding a new better alternative. The optimizing model would view "searching for another alternative," or "searching for more information about the other alternatives" as (always) among the actions or options already available. It therefore sees the choice among these available alternatives as involving maximization (under risk or uncertainty).[11] This faces the following difficulty, however. In making that choice among those alternatives on the basis of that information, was the structuring of that choice situation based on a previous optimizing decision or upon a satisficing decision that the structuring was "good enough"? Whichever, is not a decision made, at some point, which includes estimates of the costs and benefits of gathering some information in *that very* choice situation? Won't there be some decision, whether optimizing or satisficing, whose scope covers all costs including its own?[12]

Consider a self-subsuming decision that bestows weights to reasons on the basis of a then chosen conception of oneself and one's appropriate life, a conception that includes bestowing those weights and choosing that conception (where the weights also yield choosing that self-conception). Such a self-subsuming decision will not be a random brute fact; it will be explained as an instance of the very conception and weights chosen. (I do not say that all of one's choices or all that bestow weights are self-subsuming in this way; however, the other ones that are based on weights previously given in such decisions, revokable weights, will inherit autonomy.) It will no more be a random brute fact than is the holding of a fundamental deep explanatory law that subsumes and thereby explains itself. A self-subsuming decision does not happen inexplicably, it is not random in the sense of being connected to no weighted reasons (including the self-subsuming ones then chosen). But although it doesn't happen just randomly, still, there are different and conflicting self-subsuming decisions that could be made; just as there are different fundamental, self-subsuming laws that could hold true, could have held true. Is it not arbitrary then that one self-subsuming decision is made rather than another? Won't it be left inexplicable why this one was made (rather than another one)?

### III. Understanding and Explaining Free Choices

First, a word about explanation and intelligibility. When deductive explanations subsume an event under a covering law, then we understand why that event occurred rather than any other. (It is another question why that covering law held rather than another; given that it did, we understand why the particular event occurred.) The situation is different with statistical explanations. Suppose a fundamental law states that the probability that anything has property Q given that it has property P is .95; if we wish to explain why some entity has property Q, we cannot deduce this fact from the entity's having property P plus the probabilistic law. Nevertheless, many have thought the statistical law does enable us to explain why the entity has property Q. Hempel has held that high probability events are explained by subsuming them under probabilistic laws; the high-probability probabilistic explanation is an approximation to a deduction.[13] What of the low probability event, though; when we encounter an entity that is P but isn't Q, can we explain why it is not Q? There is no way to do this on Hempel's view. True, if many P's are observed, then it can be very likely that one or another of them will not have property Q; we expect (as our best estimate) only 95 percent of the P's to have property Q, so there is a high probability that one of the very many P's we encounter will lack Q. When this one lacks Q, isn't the explanation simply that some (small) percentage of the P's will lack Q, and this is simply one of the ones that do? Strictly, on Hempel's view we have only an explanation that some P or other will lack Q, for that fact has a high probability; but we do not have an explanation of why, for example, this entity E lacks Q even though it has P. But even though we cannot deduce or yield with a high probability that it, entity E, will lack property Q, still, when we encounter it don't we know the explanation of why it does? We know there exists a system, a chance mechanism or whatever, that generates some P's that are not Q's, and we explain why this P is non-Q, by its being one of the things spewed forth by the operation of the chance mechanism.[14] The alternative (if there are some fundamental probabilistic laws) is to say these low probability events are unexplainable.

The moral I wish to draw is this: we can have an explanation and understanding of why something occurred even when we do not know of any reason why it, rather than something else, occurred that time, in that instance. Even when the event is random, its occurrence need not be inexplicable; it can be seen as an event, one of a type to be expected, arising from a mechanism or system that, in a way we may have better or worse understanding of, yields such events among others.

I am not suggesting that free decisions are random happenings from a chance mechanism with a well-defined probability distribution (whether flat or otherwise) over the various alternative actions. The process of choice among alternative actions is different; there are not fixed factual probabilities for each action, there is no such dispositional propensity or limit of long-run frequencies or whatever. Rather, there is a process operating wherein each alternative action could be yielded, and one of them was. This time, the process gave rise to that particular alternative. (Compare: this time the random system yielded that particular event.)

To be sure, we do not want to say simply that there is a process which could give rise to any of the alternative actions—we want to know more about the process, we want to delineate and understand it, we want to know how it works.

According to the view currently fashionable, we adequately understand a psychological process only if we can simulate that process on a digital computer. To understand a psychological notion is to know a set of quadruples that would place a Turing machine under the notion. Any process of choosing an action that could be understood in this sense would appear not to be a process of free choice. Suppose that this is so. Does the fact that we cannot, in this sense, understand what a free choice is, indicate some defect in the notion of a free choice or rather is the defect in the view that this mode of understanding is the sole mode? Is the result, that we cannot understand what a free choice is, an *artifact* of this method of understanding?[15]

In what other way, if not simulation by a Turing machine, can we understand the process of making free choices? By making them, perhaps. We might interpret those theorists who pointed to our choices not as trying to prove that we made free choices but as ostensively explaining the notion, showing its intelligibility. Were they saying that we understand free choice and agency by virtue of making free choices as agents? To accept a (restricted) form of knowledge by self-acquaintance, encompassing knowledge of a mode of action and of ourselves, runs afoul of views that we know something only when (and to the extent that) we know the laws it obeys.[16] However, even if such views are rejected, the nature of this other mode of knowledge, by self-acquaintance, is unclear;[17] an adequate theory, showing how it is possible, would take us into issues far removed from our present concern without helping us especially with the topic of free will. Our problem is that we are puzzled about the nature of free choices, so any inside knowledge we may have of such choices due to and in making them obviously hasn't served to clear up our puzzles about their nature. It is tempting to say our puzzlement stems from supposing we must be able discursively to say or describe what a free choice is like, yet the fact that we cannot, when we are directly acquainted with them, doesn't interfere with understanding them. But too many ineffabilities spoil the philosophical broth. Since I do not myself have even the feeling of understanding, I will continue the (discursive) attempts at explanation.

We can explain an action as an intentional doing arising out of a process of choice among alternatives, if we can illuminate this process; however, we need not offer a Turing machine model, a computer simulation of the process of decision that matches which alternative the person chooses. We have said already that the decision process (sometimes) bestows weights on the reasons for and against the various alternatives, and that this bestowal of weights is self-subsuming and so to that extent not random. Still, there can be different self-subsuming bestowals of weight. Although after one occurs we will be able retrospectively to give a reason as the cause (though without causal determination), can anything be said about why that one self-subsuming decision is made rather than another? No, the weights are bestowed in virtue of weights that come into effect in the very act of bestowal. This is the translation into this context of the notion of reflexivity: the phenomenon, such as reference or a law's holding, has an "inside" character when it holds or occurs in virtue of a feature bestowed by its holding or occurring.

The free decision is reflexive; it holds in virtue of weights bestowed by its holding. An explanation of why the act was chosen will have to refer to its being chosen. However, not every act you do is a minor miracle of reflexive self-subsumption, only the ones involving choice of fundamental principles and self-conception. (Yet since such a choice is revokable, do later choices reaffirm it, and so also involve reflexive self-subsumption?)

Suppose a process of decision can have these features, bestowing weights in a self-subsuming fashion which is reflexive. The decision then does not simply dangle there at random—we can see the many ties and connections it has (including internal ones); the particular decision is not inexplicable—we see it as something that could arise from a process of this sort.

More might be demanded, however; it might be demanded that the theorist of free will show how the decision is causally determined. Otherwise, it will be said, the character and nature of the decision will remain mysterious. But clearing up any mystery in that way would come at the cost of the act's contracausal freedom. No adequate condition on explanation or understanding necessitates either causal explanation or Turing machine delineation. Free will is to be explained differently, by delineating a decision process that can give rise to various acts in a nonrandom nonarbitrary way; whichever it gives rise to—and it could give rise to any one of several—will happen nonarbitrarily. These remarks are independent of the particular process we have delineated here, involving the bestowal of weights, reflexive self-subsumption, and so on. What is inappropriate is to demand that a free choice be explained in a way that shows it is unfree.

The theme of the bestowal of weights to reasons, in a situation of no preexistingly determinate weights, seems to me phenomenologically accurate[18] and proper to emphasize. I have more worries about terming this bestowal nonarbitrary and nonrandom because it is self-subsuming and reflexive. This position has too much the flavor of applying shiny new tools and ideas everywhere, as a magic key— except that some of the applications depend, perhaps, upon these ideas being not so well understood, not so shiny. So we should be somewhat wary of this use of the themes of self-subsumption and reflexiveness to delineate the nonarbitrary nature of a free choice. They do have the right flavor, though. For example, consider all the talk (in the literature) of "stepping back" to reconsider any previous commitment of self-conception. Is this merely the analogue of Peirce's point in epistemology that anything can be doubted but not everything at once—any motive or reason can be examined though not every one simultaneously? To where do we step back? In the case of a free choice, it seems appropriate that it be to somewhere such that (the act of) stepping to there is an instance of being there, which you are in virtue of a feature of your being there. "Stepping back," at least sometimes, is not like moving up to different levels in a type theory hierarchy; rather, it is self-subsuming and reflexive.

There are other issues that need to be explored, but will not be here: how the later (possible) revocation of bestowed weights works; whether there is causal leeway not only in bestowing weights on reasons, but also in the generation of alternative actions;[19] how the later less fundamental choices, which spin out the previously bestowed weightings, inherit autonomy. One further word can be said about the commitment involved in the bestowal of weights. Acting later on those weights anchors your later choices to them, and them to the later choices. Part of this nonrandom character of the weighting is shown by the life built upon them; perhaps it not merely is exhibited there but exists there.[20] If this is too strong, at least we may see the later adherence to weights as an indication of their nonrandom character; if the choice of these weights was simply random and arbitrary, would they win continued adherence?

## IV.  *Could One Have Bestowed Otherwise?*

Elsewhere[21] I have shown how, within a closest-continuer framework for personal identity, the self weights dimensions to yield a measure of closeness for itself, in accordance with its own self-conception, and how this weighting, including of plans, desires, and values, can be an important component in reflexive self-synthesis. Another way in which bestowal of weight upon reasons can be nonarbitrary is that the self can synthesize itself around this bestowing: "I value things in this way." If in that reflexive self-reference, the I synthesizes itself (in part) around the act of bestowing weight on reasons, then it will not be arbitrary or random that *that* self bestowed those weights.[22]

The process of decision can yield the intentional doing of different actions, and it would have if different weights had been assigned, which could have happened. But does it follow that the person could have done otherwise, that it was within the person's power to bestow different weights, as opposed to that merely happening? In what way could the person have *done* otherwise, not merely been the arena in which otherwise happened?

It would be fruitless to embark upon the theoretical regress wherein a different intentional action of bestowing weights occurs with its own separate weights which have to be bestowed by a still separate act.[23] And why is it asked only if another bestowal could have been done; why is it not similarly asked whether the bestowal that did occur was a doing or merely a happening? Maybe it is possible for weights somehow to just happen to get bestowed on reasons; however, when the bestowal is anchored and tied in the way we have described, to a formed self-conception (even if formed just then), if it is self-subsuming and reflexive, leading to later (revokable) commitment, then it is a doing, not a happening merely. If all that context and stage setting (compare Wittgenstein) does not make it an action, what alternative conception of action is being presupposed? The actual bestowal of weights on reasons is a doing and not merely a happening; another and alternative bestowal of weights on reasons could have occurred instead—this one wasn't causally determined, and others aren't causally excluded—with all of the accompanying context and stage setting appropriate to it, so that alternative bestowal too would have been a doing and not merely a happening. The person could have bestowed differently.

## Notes

1. On this last point see Herbert Simon, *Models of Man* (New York: Wiley, 1957), essays 7, 8; and William Starbuck, "Level of Aspiration," *Psychological Review* 70 (1963), pp. 51–60, "Level of Aspiration Theory and Economic Behavior," *Behavioral Science* 8 (1963), pp. 128–36.

A realistic and illuminating picture of the process surrounding decision is presented in Irving Janis and Leon Mann, *Decision Making* (New York: Free Press, 1977).

2. Mortimer Adler and his associates give the following description of the view they term "the freedom of self-determination." "The individual's . . . freedom of choice . . . rests with his power of self-determination which, through its causal indeterminacy, is able to give dominance to one motive or one set of influences rather than another. Far from motives or other influences determining which of several decisions is made, it is the other way around . . . the self determines which motive or set of influences shall be decisive (i.e., which shall find expression in the decision made)" (*The Idea of Freedom* [New York: Doubleday, 1961]), vol. II, p. 232; see also pp. 292–93).

3. The notion of contracausal human freedom (though not the term) originated with Philo. In his view, God, in creating the world, reserved for himself the power to upset laws by working miracles, and gave to man a portion of that same power—although man's 'miracles' are not worked with respect to laws that he himself created. (See Harry A. Wolfson, *Philo* [Cambridge, MA: Harvard University Press, 1947], vol. I, pp. 431, 436.) The Epicureans denied causality altogether, and Chrysippus held that causality, by its nature, stopped at the will of man. The Philonic view is the first to place absolute free will within a world of some causality which otherwise would apply and which is suspended. (See H. A. Wolfson, *Religious Philosophy* [Cambridge, MA: Harvard University Press, 1961], p. 196; and *The Philosophy of the Kalam* [Cambridge, MA: Harvard University Press, 1976], p. 733.) It became a matter of controversy within Christian theology whether humans naturally retained this gift of free will from God, or whether, after Adam's fall, God withdrew it as a matter of course and bestowed it only as a matter of divine grace. (See H. A. Wolfson, "St. Augustine and the Pelagian Controversy" in his *Religious Philosophy,* pp. 158–76.)

It is instructive to apply to these matters the notion of an inegalitarian theory, wherein there is marked out a natural state, deviations from which have to be explained by special forces or reasons. There are at least three views: (1) Philo's view: man has free will as a gift from God, a gift bestowed in creating man's nature; hence free will is man's natural state, and could not be altered by Adam's sin; (2) man's natural state was unfree, but in one act God gave all men free will as a donation of some of his powers; (3) in response to Adam's act, God altered man's natural state (if [1] had been true) or revoked his general gift; he now has to bestow free will upon each person individually. (This last is Augustine's view.) Notice that proponents of each of these views can agree that all people have free will, yet disagree about its explanatory status or explanation.

4. Should we say the decision that bestows the comparative weights on reasons makes them, by some process of "backwards causality," always to have had those weights? One might speak either of temporally prior weights or of prior causal connections themselves being caused "backwards." Under the last, doing act A does not cause $R_A$ to occur or to have a certain weight; rather, doing A causes it to be true that $R_A$ caused A—while if B had been done, it would have caused it to be true that $R_B$ caused B. On this view, free actions are those that cause their causes' causing them. Thus is blocked the intuitive argument that if the causes of our actions go back to a time before we were born then we do not control the action: though we don't control the occurrence of earlier events, we do control which ones cause (which of the alternative) current actions. Even if

such a "backwards causality" theory (of either form) can be elaborated, I prefer to avoid such tangles here.

For a discussion of issues relevant to backwards causality, see Paul Horwich, "On Some Alleged Paradoxes of Time Travel," *Journal of Philosophy* 72 (1975), pp. 432–44; also John Wheeler, "The 'Past' and the 'Delayed-Choice' Double-Slit Experiment," in A. R. Marlow, ed., *Mathematical Foundations of Quantum Theory* (New York: Academic Press, 1978).

5. See Rolf Sartorious, "The Doctrine of Precedent and the Problem of Relevance," *Archives for Philosophy of Law and Social Philosophy* (1967); and Ronald Dworkin, "Hard Cases," in his *Taking Rights Seriously* (Cambridge, MA: Harvard University Press, 1977). Unlike Dworkin's model of the legal system (whether or not it is appropriate there), we do not claim people can make only one correct decision or that there is a uniquely correct set of weights.

6. Though it must sometimes be possible independently to check this if the claim is to have empirical content, it need not always be possible in order to put forth an explanation based on the claim. For further discussion of this point, see my "On Austrian Methodology," *Synthese* 36 (1977), note 21.

7. Even if this last assumption cannot be checked independently for this situation, there may be evidence from other situations of the stability of his preferences, namely, the repeated confirmation of the predictions made on the joint basis of the claim (about strongest preference) and the assumption.

8. See also the discussion of the strongest motive issue as applied to questions of free will in Rem B. Edwards, "Is Choice Determined by the 'Strongest Motive'?" *American Philosophical Quarterly* 4 (no. 1, 1967), pp. 72–78.

9. This subclass is treated as the whole by C. A. Campbell, *In Defense of Free Will* (London: Allen & Unwin, 1967), essays 2, 3.

10. See John von Neumann, *Mathematical Foundations of Quantum Mechanics* (Princeton, NJ: Princeton University Press, 1955).

11. For Simon's model see his *Models of Man*. I took this approach to the satisficing model in "The Normative Theory of Individual Choice" (unpublished doctoral dissertation, Princeton University, 1963), pp. 288–99.

12. See Sidney Winter, "Satisficing, Selection, and the Innovating Remnant," *Quarterly Journal of Economics* 85 (1971), pp. 237–61; and "Optimization and Evolution," in R. H. Day and T. Groves, eds., *Adaptive Economic Models* (New York: Academic Press, 1975), pp. 73–118.

13. See his "Deductive Nomological vs. Statistical Explanation," in H. Feigl and G. Maxwell, eds., *Minnesota Studies in the Philosophy of Science* (Minneapolis: University of Minnesota Press, 1962), vol. III, pp. 98–169; and *Aspects of Scientific Explanation* (New York: Free Press, 1965), pp. 376–412.

14. See Gilbert Harman, *Thought* (Princeton, NJ: Princeton University Press, 1973), pp. 135–40; and Peter Railton, "A Deductive-Nomological Model of Probabilistic Explanation," *Philosophy of Science* 45 (1978), pp. 206–26.

15. A proponent of this mode of understanding as the sole mode must be careful in stating his thesis. The thesis cannot be that we understand a notion only if we know how it would be decided by a Turing machine, for since the notion of 'effectively decidable by a Turing machine' is itself not; if the thesis were true we could not understand it. Various weakenings of the thesis also

fail—the set of Gödel numbers of Turing machines that are effective algorithms, which halt, is not even recursively enumerable—leaving it unclear how to state the thesis in a plausible form.

16. Compare W. V. Quine, *Ontological Relativity* (New York: Columbia University Press, 1969), pp. 14, 60.

17. "How can we know in that way, without reflective conceptual scrutiny? And will not all the knowledge be in the reflective scrutiny?" For a presentation of a view that avoids this philosophical picture but leaves much obscure (at least as judged by the mode of knowledge it claims is not the only one) see Aurobindo, *The Life Divine*, Book II, Pt. I, Ch. X, "Knowledge by Identity and Separative Knowledge."

18. A treatment of decision by someone within the phenomenological tradition is Paul Ricoeur's *Freedom and Nature* (Evanston, IL: Northwestern University Press, 1966); however, I have not found this work helpful.

19. See Israel Kirzner, *Competition and Entrepeneurship* (Chicago: University of Chicago Press, 1973), for a discussion of (the uses within economic theory of) the distinction between maximizing, in the manner of Lionel Robbins, a pregiven objective function among pregiven alternative actions, and entrepreneurial alertness. Since this essay was written, Kirzner has published a book of essays congenial to the position about weighting reasons presented here. See his *Perception, Opportunity, and Profit* (Chicago: University of Chicago Press, 1980), especially ch. 13.

20. Compare Wittgenstein's statement, *Philosophical Investigations*, paragraph 197.

21. *Philosophical Explanations* (Cambridge, MA: Belknap Press, 1981), ch. 1.

22. Does this have the consequence that that self could not have bestowed weights differently? Not if the bestowal itself receives only a limited weight in the actual self-synthesis, and if the alternative syntheses involving different bestowals would then have been the closest continuers of the same earlier self, the one the actual synthesized self most closely continued. By most closely continuing the same earlier self, the other (possible) syntheses around other bestowals would have been that self later, just as the actual synthesized self is. So the particular bestowal isn't essential to the self with the consequence that the self couldn't have done otherwise, yet as a weighted component of a self-synthesis, neither is it random and arbitrary in relation to that self.

23. Compare Gilbert Ryle's discussion of whether, on the volition theory, the having of a volition is a voluntary act which therefore needs its own separate volition, in *The Concept of Mind* (London: Hutchinson's University Library, 1949), p. 67.

# 8

# Two Kinds of Incompatibilism[1]

## ROBERT KANE

*I*

Can libertarians or incompatibilists—those who believe that freedom is incompatible with determinism—produce an intelligible account of free will or free agency? Most people believe they cannot. For they must assume that indeterminism or chance is somehow involved in free choice or action, and it is notoriously difficult to reconcile this requirement with the rationality and control demanded by free, responsible agency. Traditional attempts by libertarians to meet this requirement have led to a myriad of problems—confusions of freedom with indeterminism, infinite regresses, obscure or mysterious accounts of agency or causation, and so on. These problems in turn have led many respected thinkers to conclude that libertarian or incompatibilist accounts of freedom are "necessarily confused" or "essentially mysterious."

Even some of the staunchest defenders of incompatibilist views have lent support to this conclusion. Richard Taylor argues that while an incompatibilist view of freedom seems to be presupposed by our practical reasoning and moral consciousness, such a view is obscure to a discomforting degree, if not "positively mysterious."[2] No less a figure than Kant held that an incompatibilist account of freedom could not be made intelligible to theoretical reason, though it had to be assumed by practical reason—a discomforting situation if you cannot accept Kant's obscure notion of the noumenal self as the source of this freedom. More recently, works by Thomas Nagel and Galen Strawson[3] have argued powerfully for what many twentieth century philosophers have been saying, that incompatibilist accounts of freedom cannot in principle be made intelligible. "I conclude," Strawson says, that incompatibilists "can give no satisfactory positive answer to the question 'In what quality of an agent . . . or will does its being a free agent . . . or will consist?'—given that it is [the incompatibilist's] . . . strong notion of true-responsibility-entailing freedom that is in question." But surprisingly, neither Strawson nor Nagel is willing to lightly dismiss incompatibilist intuitions about freedom. Much like Kant, but without Kant's noumenal reality to rely upon, Strawson concludes that while we cannot "really [be] free . . . agents" in the incompatibilist sense, we nevertheless "cannot help believing we are." And Nagel thinks that while incompatibilist freedom does not make sense from an "objective standpoint," we are powerfully attracted to it from the "subjective standpoint" of our experience of freedom.

These charges of unintelligibility and incoherence of incompatibilist theories are serious. They influence the assessment of all arguments for the incompatibility of freedom and determinism, the most important of which in recent philosophy is the "Consequence Argument" defended by Carl Ginet, Peter van Inwagen, James Lamb, David Wiggins, and others.[4] Many find this argument persuasive, but its success, like that of other arguments for incompatibilism, rests upon accepting certain interpretations of terms like "power" and "could have done otherwise" which are part of the definition of the agent's freedom.[5] If incompatibilist theories of free agency turn out to be incoherent, so that adequate interpretations of these critical notions must be compatibilist interpretations, then the Consequence Argument and other such arguments for incompatibilism will fail. To defend incompatibilism, therefore, it is not enough merely to put forward such arguments and to criticize existing compatibilist analyses of freedom, as essential as these tasks may be. One must also give a "positive account" of incompatibilist freedom, showing that it can be intelligibly described.

The present essay is about this problem of the intelligibility of incompatibilist freedom. I do not think Kant, Nagel, and Strawson are right in thinking that incompatibilist theories cannot be made intelligible to theoretical reason, nor are those many others right who think that incompatibilist accounts of freedom must be essentially mysterious or terminally obscure. I doubt if I can say enough in one short paper to convince anyone of these claims who is not already persuaded. But I hope to persuade some readers that new ways of thinking about the problem are necessary and, more to the point, that new ways of thinking about the problem are possible. As Nagel says, "nothing approaching the truth has yet been said on this subject." Parts V and VI of this paper present one new way of thinking about the problem. Parts II through IV prepare for this way by distinguishing and discussing two kinds of incompatibilist theories.

*II*

The first step in rethinking the problem of intelligibility is to recognize that there are *two fundamentally different kinds of incompatibilist theories,* only one of which, I believe, has the potential for resolving the problem of intelligibility in a satisfactory way. The distinction between these two kinds of incompatibilism is not very well known; in fact it is almost entirely unknown. But if it is as important as I think it is, then it deserves to be widely discussed.

Theories of the first kind may be called "AC theories"—for "Agent Cause theories." They are well-known, though they come in many varieties. In fact, most traditional and current incompatibilist theories of freedom have been AC theories of one form or another. Theories of the second kind are more rare and less well known. They are the "TI theories"—for "Teleological Intelligibility theories," an expression I have borrowed from Gary Watson (note 5, p. 165). "Teleological Intelligibility" is a mouthful, but it is perfectly descriptive of the kind of theory I have in mind. Few philosophers have taken TI theories seriously as alternatives to Agent Cause theories, though a few, like Watson and David Wiggins, have at least recognized the possibility of doing so. And no developed TI theory has been available until recent times to compare with AC theories (though there have been hints in the history of philosophy to suggest what TI theories might look like).[6]

As a consequence, it is fair to say that most students of the free will issue identify libertarian or incompatibilist theories of agency with Agent Cause theories—an identification that is also encouraged by many text-book discussions. And they tend to think that incompatibilist accounts of free agency stand or fall with the intelligibility of AC theories. I think this is a mistake of some consequence. For if AC theories cannot by themselves solve the problems of intelligibility of libertarian freedom, it is too hasty to conclude that nothing will solve these problems. There are other options, and TI theories are worth considering.

The chief difference between AC theories and TI theories is that the former rely on a notion of *nonevent,* or *nonoccurrent,* causation by an agent. This is the distinguishing feature of "Agent Cause" theories of all kinds. TI theories rely on no such notion. To be more precise, we can make use of the following general account of an Agent Cause theory borrowed from C. D. Broad.[7] Broad defines agent causation, which he calls "non-occurrent causation," as the agency of a self with respect to its free choices or actions satisfying the following conditions. (a) The self or agent is the sole cause of its free choices or actions; (b) its causation can be exercised in two directions, to choose (or do) and to do otherwise; and (c) its causation of a free choice or action is the causation of an occurrence or event by a *thing* or *substance* which cannot be explained as the causation of an occurrence or event *by other occurrence or events*. The terms "occurrence" and "event" are used interchangeably here to mean either *states* (like something's being red or round) or *changes* (like something's moving or expanding). This is the broad interpretation of "event" used by Davidson and other contemporary thinkers, and it is Broad's sense of "occurrence." Condition (c) is the distinguishing feature of AC theories. Conditions (a) and (b), suitably interpreted, could be accepted by all incompatibilists.

All AC theories satisfy Broad's three conditions, but the thing or substance which causes nonoccurrently is differently described in different theories. Recent AC theorists, like Taylor and Roderick Chisholm,[8] follow Thomas Reid in identifying the nonoccurrent cause as the agent, or the human being, a substance in space and time having both mental and physical attributes. Kant identifies it with the noumenal self which is beyond spatial and temporal categories, and others identify it with a "transempirical ego" (Eccles) or a nonmaterial Cartesian ego (Mansel), likewise outside space and time. Still others have spoken (not altogether coherently, according to Locke and Hobbes) of that which causes nonoccurrently as something within the agent, like the agent's Will or Reason, considered almost as an agent within the agent.[9]

But whatever it is, the Agent Cause in all these theories satisfies Broad's three conditions, and in particular condition (c): its causation of its free choices or actions cannot be explained as the causation of events or occurrence by other events or occurrences. This third condition is problematic for a well known reason: while causation by things or substances is common, it can usually be interpreted as the causation of events by other events. "The stone broke the window" is elliptical for "The stone's striking the window caused the window to break," and "The cat caused the lamp to fall" is elliptical for "The cat's leaping onto the lamp caused it to fall." No such interpretations in terms of event or occurrent causation are possible for the causation by agents of their free choices or actions on an AC theory. We cannot say the agent caused its free choices *by* doing something else; nor can we fully explain why the agent chose rather than doing otherwise, or vice versa, by saying that the agent was in certain states, or had undergone certain changes, even if the states or changes were states or processes of mind. For this would be to completely explain the outcome in terms of other events or occurrences.

## III

Why do AC theorists insist upon such a strong requirement for genuine free agency? The answer takes us to the root of incompatibilist intuitions generally, which are expressed in the following quote from Aristotle's *Physics*:

> The stick moves the stone and is moved by the hand, which is again moved by the man; in the man, however, we have reached a mover that is not so in virtue of being moved by something else. (VIII, 256a6–8)

Compare Chisholm's statement: "Each of us, when we act, is a prime mover unmoved. In doing what we do, we cause certain events to happen, and nothing—and no one—causes us to cause those events to happen" ([3] ("Human Freedom," p. 32 [see note 8]). To many persons, this is a literally incredible notion. Yet, I think it embodies a central—perhaps *the* central—incompatibilist intuition. Of course, free agents are not prime movers in the sense of the First Cause of the cosmos. We are finite movers within the cosmos and cannot escape being influenced by the conditions of our existence—by heredity, environment and conditioning. The incompatibilist's question is whether there is anything left over by these conditions of our existence such that our free actions can be said to be (i\*) *our products* (i.e., caused by us) and such that (ii\*) their occurring rather than not occurring here and now, or vice versa, *has as its ultimate or final explanation the fact that they are caused by us*. Though the conditions of my existence narrow my choices to, say, doing A or doing B, there should be something left over that is wholly and ultimately "up to me here and now," that is, whether I do A *rather than* B or B *rather than* A. One should be able to explain the doing of A rather than B or vice versa as caused by me (condition (i\*)). And this explanation should be "ultimate" or "final" in the sense that no other explanation of the outcome beyond this one should be possible (condition (ii\*)).

These conditions are far from perspicuous and we will have more to say about them as we proceed. But even in their present crude form, they explain much of what motivates Agent Cause theories, and incompatibilist theories in general. Incompatibilists are very much concerned with the notion of being "ultimately responsible" for one's choices or actions. The "buck stops here (and now)" expresses their intuition. Since it is a necessary (though not sufficient) condition for being responsible for something that you cause it, or have some (direct or indirect) causal influence upon it, to be "ultimately responsible" is to be an ultimate cause, or causal influence—one whose operation or influence is not caused or explained by anything else. If our present choices or actions were completely explained or caused by our past character, motives and circumstances (if nothing were left over in the sense just described), then in order to find out whether we were ultimately responsible for our present choices or actions we would have to find out whether we were ultimately responsible in any respect for our *past* character, motives, and circumstances. The question of *ultimate* responsibility would then not be satisfactorily answered until we arrived at *some* choices or actions in the past that satisfied conditions (i*) and (ii*): they were caused by us, and their occurring rather than not occurring *then and there,* had as its ultimate or final explanation the fact that they were caused by us then and there.

AC theorists, like other incompatibilists, insist that, as a consequence of these requirements, choices or actions for which we are ultimately responsible cannot be completely explained or caused by past character, motives, and other circumstances. What distinguishes their (AC) view is that they deny this by denying that free actions can be completely explained *by events or occurrences or "circumstances" of any kind,* past or present, physical or psychological. The explanatory remainder is provided by the nonoccurrent causation of the agent. As Taylor says, "some . . . causal chains . . . have beginnings and they begin with the agents themselves." (p. 56) On the face of it, this move to nonoccurrent causation seems drastic and it does not seem to be the *only* way to get the desired result, i.e., ultimate responsibility. But it has appealed to many incompatibilists because less drastic moves have led to intractable puzzles and paradoxes.

To sum up, that which motivates Agent Cause theorists to make the requirements they do about free action is what motivates incompatibilists generally. They want to account for the idea that agents can be "ultimately responsible" for at least some of their actions in a way that is spelled out by conditions (i*) and (ii*). Let us state these conditions more fully and call them respectively the "Explanation" and "Ultimacy" conditions.

   (i)  (The Explanation Condition) A free action for which the agent is ultimately responsible is the product of the agent, i.e., is caused by the agent, in such a way that we can satisfactorily answer the question "Why did this act occur here and now rather than some other?" (whichever occurs) by saying that the agent caused it to occur rather than not, or vice versa, here and now.

   (ii) (The Ultimacy Condition) The free action for which the agent is ultimately responsible is such that its occurring rather than not here and now, or vice versa, *has as its ultimate or final explanation the fact that it is caused by the agent here and now.*

The explanation is "ultimate" or "final" in the sense that no other explanation of the outcome that goes beyond the explanation in (i) is possible. The full import of this requirement will be explained later. But the gist of it is that the agent not only causes the outcome, but is not caused by anything else to cause it. The agent is a "mover" (i), not "moved by something else" (ii).

Since free agents satisfying these conditions are finite agents whose options are limited by causal circumstances, such agents are not divine. But they could be said to be made in a divine image (*imagine Dei*), being the prime movers or first causes of at least some things in the universe, their own actions. It is not difficult to discern in this image of oneself as a free agent a certain dignity, which Kant and others saw. We have value as ends-in-ourselves because we are the *ultimate producers* through free choices of our own ends and actions guided by those ends. (*Choices* give rise to *intentions* whose contents express our purposes or *ends*.) Other creatures which seek ends are not the ultimate producers of their own ends.

## IV

These are nice thoughts, but does it make sense to say that one can be the ultimate producer of *anything* in the sense of conditions (i) and (ii)? AC theories begin to run into trouble when this question is seriously addressed.[10]

The main source of the trouble is that conditions (i) and (ii) imply that free choices or actions *cannot be determined.* In short, incompatibilism— with its requirement of indeterminism of free choices or actions—is a consequence of ultimate responsibility in the sense of (i) and (ii). More specifically, it is condition (ii), the Ultimacy Condition, which is the culprit. If a free action were determined by past circumstances, given the laws of nature, there would be an explanation for why the agent acted as he or she did that was other than, or went beyond, saying that the agent caused the doing or the doing otherwise here and now. This further explanation would be in terms of the relevant past circumstances and laws of nature, whose existence could not in turn be explained by saying that the agent caused them to be what they are by acting here and now.[11]

There is a lesson in this result that is all too often forgotten. Libertarians and incompatibilists do not want indeterminism for its own sake. If the truth be told, indeterminism is something of a nuisance for them. It gets in the way and creates all sorts of trouble. What they want is ultimate responsibility, and *ultimate responsibility requires indeterminism.* It has been said that all valuable things come with a price. In this case ultimate responsibility is the valuable thing, and indeterminism is the price. And indeterminism is a *high* price. For it threatens to subvert the entire incompatibilist project. The basic problem is this: given the requirement that free choicess or actions be undetermined, it becomes difficult to satisfy the other condition for ultimate responsibility, the Explanation Condition. In other words, the two conditions for ultimate responsibility are in conflict. The Ultimacy Condition implies indeterminism, but indeterminism makes it difficult to satisfy the Explanation Condition.

Why does indeterminism cause problems for the Explanation Condition? If the doing of A and the doing otherwise are undetermined, then either might occur *given all the same past circumstances and laws of nature.* (This is a simple consequence of the definition of a determined event: an event is determined just in case there are past circumstances (i.e., events or occurrences) and laws of nature, such that it is (logically) necessary that if the past circumstances and laws obtain, then the event occurs.) But this makes it difficult to answer the question required by the Explanation Condition: "Why did the agent here and now do A *rather than* do otherwise, or do otherwise *rather than* do A?" How can we explain either outcome, should it occur, in terms of exactly the same past? If we say, for example, that the agent did A rather than B here and now because the agent had such and such reasons or motives and engaged in such and such a deliberation before choosing to act, how would we have explained the doing of B rather than A given exactly the same reasons or motives and the same prior deliberation? If the deliberation rationalized the doing of A rather than B (or vice versa), would not the doing of B rather than A (or vice versa) as an outcome of the same deliberation be arbitrary or capricious relative to the agent's past—a kind of fluke or accident? To be sure, statistical explanations are compatible with the indeterminism of outcomes given the same past. But they will not answer the question required by the Explanation Condition because they will not explain why this particular outcome occurred here and now rather than not: it is not a satisfactory answer to the question "Why did the agent do A rather than do otherwise here and now (or vice versa)?" to say that, given the circumstances, he or she *might* have done either, or that there was a certain probability attaching to each of the possible outcomes. Thus, statistical explanations will not answer the question, and causal explanations of a deterministic sort are ruled out by the assumption of indeterminism.

One might respond that this line of argument does not really apply to explanation in terms of "reasons," (or "motives") because reasons cannot be assumed to be events or occurrences at all, and hence cannot be counted in the normal sense among the "past causal circumstances." (This is one line of defense of the familiar, though disputed, claim that reasons for action cannot be causes of action.) Reasons are either psychological attitudes (wants, beliefs, preferences, etc.) or the intentional contents of such attitudes. In either case, one might argue, reasons are not events or occurrences in any ordinary sense. Reasons in the first sense are psychological *attributes,* and reasons in the second sense are *propositional contents.* And even if reasons in the second sense could be regarded as states of affairs, they might be states of affairs that do not actually exist or will exist in the future, if they ever exist at all. They would not qualify, *qua* propositional contents, as actual past or present determining events or occurrences.

These points are well taken, but unfortunately, they will not solve the problem of the Explanation Condition. It may be true that reasons in these two common senses cannot strictly speaking be construed as causes in the sense of determining events or occurrences. But, in order to actually *motivate,* reasons as intentional contents must be the intentional contents of some psychological attitudes an agent actually *has.* And while wants, desires, beliefs and the like may be attitudes of mind and not themselves states or changes, an agent's *having* one or another of them at some time or other *is* a state of that agent, and hence an event or occurrence in the broad sense that includes states and changes. Thus, to explain the doing of A rather than B (or vice versa) in terms of the *having* of certain reasons or motives is to explain in terms of events or occurrences. For AC theorists, therefore, complete explanation of this sort would only push the question of ultimate explanation further backwards: what explains the agent's *having* these reasons or motives at this time?

Most AC theorists are well aware of this problem. Some, like Taylor, make a point of insisting that one cannot fully explain agent causation in terms of causes *or* reasons. (p. 55) The agent simply acts—does A or does otherwise—and that is the end of it. If one said that the agent did A rather than doing otherwise, or vice versa, because the agent had such and such character and motives, one would have to ask what caused the agent to have this character and these motives, thus pushing the question of ultimate responsibility backwards, but not resolving it. To stop the potential regress, AC theorists like Taylor disallow any explanations of agent causation in terms of reasons or causes. But, this leaves them without any answer to the critical question: "Why did the agent do A rather than B or B rather than A?"

Other AC theorists, like Chisholm, have a more complex attitude to this difficult issue. As Thalberg points out,[12] while Chisholm, like other AC theorists, insists that agent causation—which he calls "immanent causation"—cannot be completely explained in terms of reasons or motives of the agent, he also favorably invokes the well-known Leibnizian dictum that "reasons may incline without necessitating," thus giving reasons a role to play in the explanation.[13] Will appeal to the Leibnizian dictum resolve the problem? Certainly not by itself. If an agent's reasons incline her toward choosing A rather than B, it must still be possible on an incompatibilist view like Chisholm's for her to choose A or to choose

B, all circumstances remaining the same. Now if the agent chooses A, we can explain the choice by saying that the agent's reasons inclined to the choice of A rather than B. But what if B is chosen? How will this be explained, given exactly the same reasons that inclined to A? Is it true that the having of those reasons did not *determine* the choice of A? But it is not an adequate answer to the question "Why did the agent choose B here and now rather than A?" to say "The agent's reasons inclining her toward choosing A rather than B were not determining." Whatever else is needed to answer the question "Why did the agent choose B. . . ?" must be supplied by the Agent Cause. AC theorists must say that the agent just chose B even though her reasons inclined toward A, and one cannot adequately explain *that* by citing any further facts about her. Thus, the Leibnizian dictum by itself does not avert the need for a nonoccurrent causation which cannot be fully accounted for in terms of events or occurrences. And the appeal to nonoccurrent causation, either alone or with the Leibnizian dictum, does not provide a satisfactory answer to the "Why"-question associated with the Explanation Condition. It seems that AC theories to date do not have a satisfactory answer to this question. Can TI theories do better?

## V

TI theories do not appeal to nonevent or nonoccurrent causation. They try to explain incompatibilist free agency in terms of event causation alone. This would appear to make a difficult task even more difficult. I have often heard it said by knowledgeable philosophers that one does not stand a chance of making sense of freedom in an incompatibilist or libertarian sense without appealing to something other than event causation. Perhaps so. But the issue is worth another look because of the difficulties of AC theories, and for another related reason: many persons are ready to dismiss incompatibilist theories out of hand because nonoccurrent causation seems to have no place in the scientific picture of nature. How, if at all, does free will fit into the natural order? AC theories leave this a mystery and are often dismissed for doing so. There is something to be said for a theory that would bring the venerable free will issue into closer contact with modern scientific theories, and this suggests considering how far one can go with event causation alone. As Chisholm says, few would deny the existence of agent causation in the broadest sense—agents act and thereby bring things about. The matter of dispute is whether or not agent causation can be fully interpreted in terms of event causation.

But the denial of nonevent causation is only one feature of TI theories—a negative feature. The positive features of such theories are suggested by the following quote from Wiggins.

> Maybe all [incompatibilists] need to imagine or conceive is a world in which (a') there is some macroscopic indeterminacy founded in microscopic indeterminacy, and (b') an appreciable number of free actions or policies or deliberations of individual agents, although they are not even in principle hypothetically derivable from antecedent conditions, can be such as to persuade us to fit them into meaningful sequences. (p. 52)

Wiggins says very little beyond this about what such a theory would look like, but I think in this quote he sees deeply into the needs of the incompatibilist position. On a TI account, that position must do without nonoccurrent causes, but it needs (a') some macroscopic indeterminacy founded on microscopic indeterminacy, and (b') some account of the agent's willing and acting for reasons that will render choices or actions "teleologically intelligible," though not determined. The macroscopic indeterminacies, it would seem, must come about by some sort of amplification of microscopic indeterminacies in the brain. There are ways one could imagine this taking place, but no hard evidence that it does occur. What if it does not occur? What if the requisite indeterminacies are simply not there, or not there in an available way? Then I think libertarians cannot be comfortable. Their theory, I believe, is not entirely immune to empirical falsification. The Epicureans held that if there was to be room in nature for human freedom, the atoms must sometimes "swerve" from their determined pathways. If the atoms do not "swerve"—if the appropriate "causal gaps" are not there in nature—then there is no room for an incompatibilist free will in nature. One would need a Kantian noumenal order, or some similar strategem, to make sense of it, and this I think should make incompatibilists uncomfortable.

In any case, we shall return to the micro- and macroindeterminacies. Let us merely suppose at present and for the sake of argument that they are available in the brain. What, if anything, could we do with them if they were there? It has often been argued that quantum uncertainties in the brain, even if their macroscopic effects were not negligible, would be of no use to incompatibilists. If choices or decisions should result from them, those choices or decisions would be chance occurrences, neither predictable nor within the agent's control—more like epileptic seizures than free, responsible choices or actions. This is one issue TI theories must address.

To address it, I believe a successful TI theory must satisfy the following conditions which are put in the form of a definition.

(UR) An agent has *ultimate responsibility* for the choice of A and the choosing otherwise[14] (= it is "up to the agent here and now" in the sense of ultimate responsibility whether the agent chooses A or chooses otherwise), just in case the agent's choosing A here

and now rather than choosing otherwise, or vice versa (whichever occurs)

(1) (The Production Condition) is the intentional termination of an
effort of will that is the agent's effort of will, and

(2) (The Rationality Condition) the agent ($r_1$) has reasons for doing
so (whichever occurs), ($r_2$) does it *for* those reasons,[15] ($r_3$) does
not choose (for those reasons) compulsively, and ($r_4$) believes at
the time of choice that the reasons for which it is made are in
some sense the weightier reasons, more worth acting upon that
their alternatives, and

(3) (The Ultimacy Condition) given the facts of the situation, no
other explanation (other than the conjunction of (1) and (2)) for
the agent's choosing A or choosing otherwise (whichever occurs)
is possible, unless that explanation can in turn be explained by
the conjunction of (1) and (2) itself (i.e., the explanation provided by (1) and (2) is "ultimate" or "final"). In particular, any
explanation of the agent's making the effort of will in (1) and of
the agent's having the character and the reasons or motives for
choosing in (2) will not also explain the choice, even though (1)
and (2) will explain the choice.

Condition (3) of this definition corresponds to the Ultimacy Condition
(ii) defined earlier. Conditions (1) and (2) correspond to the Explanation Condition (i) defined earlier. I have broken the Explanation Condition into two parts to bring out the two aspects of that which needs
explaining in an ultimately free choice, as indicated in previous sections,
first, that the agent *produces* or *causes* the outcome, and second that the
agent's doing so is *rational*. Between them, these two conditions express
the idea of "teleological intelligibility," i.e., that the choice, whichever
way it goes, will be explicable in terms of the agent's purposes, efforts
and reasons. By saying in condition (1) that the termination of the effort
is "intentional," I mean to say that it is done by the agent both *knowingly*
and *purposefully*.[16] More will be said about this later, and also about
other features of the three conditions ("acting for reasons," etc.).

The task for TI theories is to account for all three conditions at once,
and the problem they face in doing so is similar to the one we identified in
Part IV. Because it implies indeterminism, the Ultimacy Condition (3) is in
apparent conflict with the Explanation Conditions, (1) and (2). If the
choice were determined by prior circumstances and laws of nature, the
Ultimacy Condition (3) would fail for the reasons given in Part IV. But if
ultimacy implies indeterminism, then indeterminism, once admitted,
seems to undermine the two Explanation Conditions. Indeterminism
seems to undermine the idea that the agent is in control of the outcome
whichever way it goes (condition (1)): call this the problem of *dual produc-*

*tion.* And indeterminism also seems to undermine the idea that the choice will be rational whichever way it goes (condition (2)): call this the problem of *dual rationality.* We have already seen that AC theories have difficulty accounting for dual rationality. It is worth adding that they also have trouble with dual production. Condition (1) of the above definition also presents a problem for AC theories because it says that the agent chooses as the termination of some sort of effort of will. AC theorists cannot avail themselves of such language because to do so would be to explain the agent's causing in terms of what appears to be a further event or occurrence, namely, the agent's making an effort of will—an occurrence which presumably would require further explanation.

Thomas Reid got into trouble on this point, as William Rowe nicely points out in his APA Central Division Presidential Address "Two Concepts of Freedom." (Rowe [see note 9]) Reid tells us that an Agent Cause must not only have the power to bring about an act of will but also must have *exerted* that power to bring about the act of will. But, as Rowe points out, "each exertion of power [on Reid's view] is an[other] *event* which the agent can cause only by having the power to cause it and by *exerting* that power. . . . The result . . . is that in order to produce any act . . . the agent must cause an infinite number of exertions." (pp. 53–54) Reid subverts the intentions of his Agent Cause theory by introducing exertions of will in this way. A consistent AC theory, as Rowe suggests, would not do so. The AC theorist should affirm that the agent can cause at least some of its actions without doing so *by* doing something else, and in particular, without doing so by some further act of will. Rowe seems to be right about this, so far as the logic of Agent Cause theories is concerned. But this feature of AC theories also creates problems that have always troubled persons about such theories. They seem to leave questions unanswered, not only about *why* the agent produced one effect rather than another (rationality), but also about *how* the agent produced one effect rather than another (production).

Returning to TI theories, how do *they* avoid an infinite regress of willings, given that according to condition (1), the agent chooses or chooses otherwise as the termination of an effort of will? The answer *in part* is that the acts for which we are ultimately responsible according to UR are choices or decisions, while the willings are efforts of will that precede the choices and terminate in them. These efforts I take to be tryings or strivings, in O'Shaughnessy's sense of "striving will," but they are mental efforts directed at getting one's ends (purposes, intentions) sorted out, rather than efforts to move one's body. Think, for example, of a situation of moral conflict or struggle where one must choose to resist the temptation to steal money or choose to steal the money. Or, think of a situation of prudential struggle where one must choose to resist the temptation to overeat in the interests of long range goals. In agreement with Kant, I think these are paradigm cases of libertarian free decisions, though not the only cases. And in these cases there is an effort of will involved to choose in a certain way, with other motives pulling in another way, and the outcome uncertain in our own minds until we choose.

There are clearly problems in such situations of inner conflict or struggle about dual production and dual rationality, especially in the cases where we succumb to temptation (weakness of will), but these problems must await consideration for a moment. Our present concern is with the regress of willings or exertions. On the theory I am suggesting that would satisfy UR, the choice terminates and is preceded by the effort to resist temptation. But what precedes the effort? Not necessarily some other effort. The effort may have simply been preceded by the agent's prior character and motives which provided *both* the reasons for trying to overcome temptation and the reasons for wanting to succumb to it. But, then, one might argue that the effort is explained by the character and motives, and if the agent is to be ultimately responsible, the character and motives must be explained by *earlier* efforts or exertions on the part of the agent. In other words, we get the regress anyway, though with intervening steps. Now this is true up to a point. There might have been earlier efforts, and they might have been involved in explaining the agent's responsibility here and now by explaining the agent's present character and motives. But on the present proposal the existence of earlier efforts is not necessary to account for ultimate responsibility here and now. The reason lies in the manner in which the Ultimacy Condition (3) of UR is satisfied: the Ultimacy Condition demands that "any explanation of the agent's making the effort of will" and any explanation of the "agent's having the character and the reasons or motives for choosing . . . *will not also explain*" why the agent *chooses A* rather than choosing otherwise or vice versa. In other words, while the choice (or doing otherwise) can be explained by saying that the agent (with such and such a prior character) intentionally terminated the effort of will (condition (1)) for such and such prior reasons or motives (condition (2)), the choice cannot be explained by the prior character and motives alone or by the prior character and motives plus the effort, *even if the prior character and motives can explain the effort*. If this condition could be satisfied, then anything which explains the prior character and motives would explain the effort, but not the choice, and the regress would have been stopped.

But how can this be? How can the prior character and motives explain the effort without explaining the choice that terminates the effort? The answer is in two parts. The first part consists in saying *how* the prior character and motives explain the effort in the cases of moral and prudential choices described above. In these cases, prior character and motives provide (A) the reasons and dispositions that account for the agent's trying to resist moral or prudential temptation, but they also provide (B) the self interested reasons, inclinations, and character traits that account for why it is *difficult* for the agent to act morally or prudentially in the situation. In other words, the complex of past motives and character explains the *conflict* within the will from both sides; it explains why the agent makes the effort to resist temptation *and* why it is an *effort*. It is because the effort is thus a response to an inner conflict which is embedded in the prior character and motives that the prior character and motives can explain the conflict and explain why the effort is being made, without also explaining the *outcome* of the conflict and the effort. Prior motives and character provide reasons for going either way, but not *decisive* reasons in the sense that would explain which way the agent would inevitably go. If the reasons were decisive, there would be no conflict of the kind we are now envisaging.[17]

This takes us to the second part of the answer to the question of how prior character and motives can explain the effort without also explaining the choice which terminates the effort. We must now turn out attention to the effort which intervenes between motives and character, on the one hand, and choice, on the other. And with regard to this effort, we must do what AC theories generally refuse to do, i.e., take indeterminacy seriously as a positive feature of incompatibilist free agency rather than merely a negative feature. Let us suppose that the effort of will which terminates in the choice is *indeterminate,* thereby making the choice which terminates it *undetermined.* Consider a quantum analogue. Imagine an isolated particle moving toward a thin atomic barrier. Whether or not the particle will penetrate the barrier is undetermined. There is a probability that it will penetrate, but not certainty, because its position and momentum are not both determinate as it moves toward the barrier. Whether it penetrates or not is therefore *undetermined* because the process leading up to it is *indeterminate.* Now imagine that the choice (to overcome temptation) is like the penetration event. It is *undetermined* because the process preceding it, and potentially terminating in it (i.e., the effort of will to overcome temptation), is *indeterminate.* So far as the argument is concerned, this effort might be, or might be correlated with, a brain process, though that process would have to be macroindeterminate as a result of amplification of microindeterminacies in the brain (Wiggins' condition (a')). Our problem is to say what could be done with these indeterminacies, assuming they were there. And the suggestion is that we imagine the effort of will that leads to choice as itself indeterminate like the particle trajectory in the analogy. Then the agent's character and motives could explain the occurrence of the effort on the part of the agent without explaining the outcome of the effort, i.e., the choice itself, because the choice (the penetration event) would not be determined. Prior character and motives would explain the effort because they would explain why the agent is motivated to make the effort *and* why the agent is motivated to resist it—i.e., why it is an *effort*. But they would not fully explain the outcome of the effort, because the effort itself is indeterminate.

To shore up these claims, however, we still have to deal with the problems of dual rationality and dual production that were put aside several paragraphs earlier, especially for the cases of weakness of will where one fails to act morally or prudentially. Note that if the outcome of the indeterminate effort of will is that the agent does overcome temptation and does not act out of weakness of will, then the Production Condition (1) and the Rationality Condition (2) would seem to be satisfied. When the agent in such conflict situations overcomes temptation and acts morally or prudentially it seems that the agent intentionally (i.e., knowingly and purposefully) terminates the effort to overcome temptation by choosing to do so, has reasons to do so (the moral or prudential reasons as the case may be), chooses *for* those reasons (with the intent of acting morally or prudentially), and so on. But we must look at the situation more closely. There are, for example, four rationality requirements, $(r_1)$–$(r_4)$, of the Rationality Condition (2), and it is time to consider each of these at greater length. We will do this by first trying to show how the easier cases of choosing from duty or prudence (and hence overcoming temptation) satisfy the Rationality Condition. The harder cases of weakness of will (or succumbing to temptation) may then be taken up, after we have a better understanding of the rationality requirements. Finally, we can return for a closer look at the Production Condition (1) in the light of what has been said about rationality.

The first requirements $(r_1)$ of condition (2) is that the agent *has* reasons for acting as he or she did whichever way the choice goes; and this seems clearly satisfied in the cases where one chooses morally or prudentially to overcome temptation. The relevant reasons in the moral case are *beliefs* about what is one's duty in the present situation and the *desire* to act from duty. In the prudential case, they are beliefs about what is required to attain some long term goal and the desire to attain that goal. For future reference, we might call these the "motives of duty" and the "motives of prudence," respectively. The second requirement $(r_2)$ of the Rationality Condition is that the agent not only has reasons for the choice but acts *for* those reasons. In order to spell out this requirement I am going to refer to Robert Audi's account of "acting for reasons" which is the most elaborate general account of this notion I have seen.[18] Audi insists that to perform an act A for a reason R (e.g., to do one's duty or to act prudentially) the agent must first *want* to R and must *believe* that having the reason R influences his or her A-ing. (He is here obviously using "reason" to refer to the *contents* of the relevant beliefs and desires or wants, whereas we have been using it to refer to the beliefs, desires and wants themselves. But this ambiguity, noted earlier, need not deter us from adapting his conditions if we keep the distinction in mind.) This condition is certainly satisfiable in the above situations where the reason is to act from duty or prudence and the act is the choice to avoid stealing or overeating. The agent *wants* to act from duty (or prudence) and *believes* that having a want with this content influences the choice. Audi insists further that the A-ing must be explicable, at least in part, by the agent's having the reason along with some relevant background beliefs. One must be able to answer the question "Why did the agent do A?" in part by citing the reason; and this one clearly can do in the case where the agent acts from duty or prudence. Further, he insists that the A-ing must actually be nonaccidentally produced (i.e., causally influenced) by the having of the reason and the relevant background beliefs (though not necessarily determined by them).[19] This condition can also be satisfied in the above examples even though the intervening effort is indeterminate, since the motives of duty or prudence may causally influence the choice even if they do not determine it. If the agent had not had these motives in the situation, the effort (to overcome temptation) would not have been made. Thus, they influence the outcome without determining it. Audi has noted in correspondence that he expressly insists that the motivating reasons and beliefs be causally influencing without requiring that they be determined in order not to beg the question at issue between compatibilism and incompatibilism. Though he inclines toward compatibilism, he could see no reason why the connecting motives or beliefs *had* to be determining rather than merely causally influencing in order to say the agent acted *for* them. Finally, Audi insists that the agent must be disposed to attribute the A-ing in part to the reason R and the relevant background beliefs, something that is also satisfied in the above cases of acting from duty or prudence. When the agent does overcome temptation in such situations, he or she is disposed to attribute this in part to the wanting to act from duty or for a long range goal and to the backgrounds beliefs that would make this want relevant to the situation at hand.

Requirement ($r_3$) of the Rationality Condition is that choosing for these reasons not be compulsive, or done out of compulsion. Compulsion has been insightfully analyzed by Harry Frankfurt [note 17] in terms of higher order desires and we can make use of his type of analysis here. Typical cases of compulsion can be described by assuming that one has a first order desire for something, say, a drug, and also a second order desire not to have the first order desire. In such cases, one acts compulsively when one cannot resist giving in to the first order desire; and one is free of compulsion when one can resist giving in to the first order desire. Now compulsion in this sense might well be involved in some moral or prudential choice situations; it is not implausible to suppose that people are sometimes compulsively moral or prudential. They cannot resist giving in to their desires to act from duty or prudence. But to say that moral and prudential choices are always compulsive in this sense would be tendentious and question begging. Where agents cannot resist the desire to act prudentially and morally, they lack freedom of will. Compatibilists and incompatibilists can agree on that. Incompatibilists can nevertheless insist (and most compatibilists I think would readily agree) that at least some, and probably many, of our everyday moral and prudential choices are not compulsive in this sense; and these would be the candidates for genuinely free choices. Moreover, if these candidates can be described as we have described moral and prudential choices in this section—namely, as choices in which the preceding effort of will to overcome temptation is indeterminate—they would *not* be compulsive in the sense just defined because acting against duty or prudence—acting immorally or imprudently—would always be *causally possible* in such cases. This is due to the indeterminacy of the effort and the resulting causal possibility that it may succeed *or* fail. In such cases, therefore, the desire to act from duty or prudence is always resistible. All the theory has to maintain is that such situations can occur. For they are the ones in which the agent is ultimately responsible. The theory does not have to deny that some moral or prudential choices might be compulsive in Frankfurt's sense.

The final rationality requirement $(r_4)$ of (2) is that the agent "believes at the time of choice that the reasons for which it is made are in some sense the weightier reasons, more worth acting upon at the time than their alternatives." The key idea here is that the agent not believe that choosing for these reasons rather than some others here and now is an arbitrary or flukish thing to do, inexplicable in terms of his or her total set of reasons. The ultimately responsible agent cannot believe that he or she chose randomly or arbitrarily, that the choice did not reflect his or her considered judgment about the relative merits here and now of the reasons for acting. This is an important condition for assessing responsibility as well as rationality, and it conforms, I think, to the experience—the phenomenology, shall we say—of free choosers.[20] They cannot believe their free choices just happened to occur in a manner that is inexplicable by their reasons. Now if we apply this condition to the cases at hand of moral and prudential choice, it seems clear that the condition is satisfied when we choose from duty or prudence to overcome temptation. For we clearly think in such cases that we have chosen for reasons that are weightier and more worth choosing for. Where the condition seems to be as *violated* is in the opposite cases where we succumb to temptation. But let us not judge too hastily. It is to these cases of succumbing to temptation that we now turn.

The opposite cases of succumbing to temptation are more problematic for *all* requirements of the Rationality Condition and for the Production Condition as well. Given the agent's commitment to moral or prudential reasons, how can it be rational to intentionally act against them? This question is, of course, a variant of the old problem of how weakness of will (or *akrasia*) is possible without being either irrational or compulsive. To address it in this context, the first step is to recognize that agents who succumb to temptation do not do so without reasons. Their reasons are reasons of self interest in the moral case, or desires for present or imminent satisfactions in the prudential case. This means that in situations of moral or prudential struggle, we are dealing with two conflicting sets of reasons—in the moral case, moral reasons or motives of duty, on the one hand, and reasons of self interest, on the other, in the prudential case, desires for long range goods or motives of prudence, on the one hand, and desires for present goods, on the other. When agents overcome temptation they are acting for the former reasons, when they succumb to temptation, they are acting for the latter reasons. In either case, it is important to note that the agents *had* the reasons of both conflicting kinds before they acted; it is just a question of which ones they will act upon.

If the two sets of reasons were regarded by the agent as being on a par—so that each motivated from its point of view (e.g., the moral point of view vs. the self interested point of view) and neither set outweighed or overrode the other—we might think of the choice as being rational from one or the other equally valid point of view, whichever way it went. The problem is that this supposition does not adequately describe the situation: the two sets of reasons or points of view are decidedly *not* on a par in the mind of the agent. Moral (or prudential) reasons are thought by the agent to be overriding; this is what creates a problem about moral or prudential weakness. But I think it is at this critical juncture that we need to take a closer look at the situation. If an agent is capable of inner moral or prudential struggle at all, then it must be assumed that the agent *consciously believes* and would *avow* that moral (or prudential) reasons ought to prevail; in *that* sense they outweigh or override in the mind of the agent. But if the agent's conviction about this was unshakeable and never was threatened by countervailing reasons (some of them perhaps unconscious) *there would be no inner conflict or struggle.* Many of our everyday choices in fact involve no such conflict or struggle; the desires on one side are so strong that they meet little or no resistance. But the lesson that TI theorists should derive from this is one that Kant was aware of: these latter kinds of choices, not involving conflict or struggle, are not the paradigms of choices for which we have ultimate responsibility in the incompatibilist sense. In other words, they should concede that Kant was right in a general way to recognize that the paradigm cases of undetermined free choices are those involving inner struggle and effort of will which must be exercised *against countervailing inclinations* (though I think they should also be wary of Kant's own interpretation of such cases, including his assimilation of all of them to action in accordance with the moral law).[21]

In cases where there is genuine conflict or struggle, desires on one side meet resistance from desires on the other. Whatever it is that persons engaged in moral or prudential struggle may avow or consciously believe about the priority of moral or prudential reasons, when there is conflict and uncertainty about the outcome their full psychological profiles (conscious and unconscious motives) will show that there is some doubt about this priority. The doubt may be hidden by self deception, but it will be there, I suggest, or there would be no struggle. And so long as the doubt is there, it is not *certain* that moral reasons outweigh self interested reasons or vice versa, "in the mind of the agent," considered as the total psychological profile. Whatever the agent consciously believes or avows, the issue is actually in doubt, undecided, so that, in effect, when the person does decide in such situations, and the indeterminate effort becomes determinate choice, the agent will *make* one set of reasons or the other prevail then and there *by deciding*. If the choice is weak-willed she may feel remorse thereafter, but that will be because she will believe that at the time of choice she made self-interested reasons prevail and acted *for* them.

Thus, concerning requirement ($r_1$) of the Rationality Condition, if the agent succumbs to temptation, the agent will *have* reasons for doing so—self-interested reasons in the moral case, desires for present or imminent satisfactions in the prudential case. Concerning ($r_2$), the agent will have acted *for* those reasons. The Audi conditions will be satisfied: the agent performs A (succumbs) for reason R (of self interest or for imminent satisfaction), the agent wants R and believes that having R influences her A-ing. The A-ing is explained in part by her having R. (One answers "Why did she do it?" in part by citing R.) The A-ing is causally influenced by the self interested reason or desire for imminent satisfaction, though not necessarily determined by it. Had she not had it, she would not have acted as she did. Yet, having it did not necessitate her acting as she did. Finally, she is disposed to attribute the succumbing to the self interested reason or desire; and this is what she will do, for example, if she should express remorse.

Concerning requirement ($r_3$), choosing out of self interest or for imminent satisfactions need not be compulsive. Some such choices *might* be compulsive in Frankfurt's sense, just as some choices for duty or prudence might be compulsive. Agents may sometimes compulsively act upon selfish or imprudent desires. But there is no good reason why we have to say that all selfish or imprudent choices are of this kind. And they will *not* be of this kind when they are preceded by indeterminate efforts of will in the manner of our account. For then it will have been causally possible for the agents to have acted otherwise—to have acted morally or prudently—given exactly the same prior character and motives.

We come finally to requirement (r₄), which, as indicated earlier, *seems* to be violated in weak-willed choice: the agent must believe "at the time of choice that the reasons for which it is made are in some sense the weightier reasons, more worth acting upon at the time than their alternatives." Despite the appearance, however, I suggest that if we attend to all that has just been said about weak-willed choice, we can see how this condition can also be satisfied. It is true that the agent believes and would consciously avow that the moral or prudential reasons were "better" in some sense, better *from* the moral or prudential point of view. But taking the entire psychological profile (conscious and unconscious motives alike) and considering the conflict and struggle within the will of the agent which is taking place, it is not clear that moral or prudential reasons are regarded as the weightier ones in the mind of the agent *all things considered*. In other words, the moral or prudential point of view is not the only point of view that carries weight *in the mind of the agent* prior to choice. If it were, there would be no conflict or struggle. Moreover, the implications of our earlier descriptions of such choice situations is that, whichever way we choose (to overcome or to succumb), we will be *making* the reasons for which we choose at that moment the weightier ones for us, all things considered, by choosing. Thus, in the weak-willed case, the choice will be to make self interested reasons or present inclinations prevail over moral or prudential reasons then and there, which will be tantamount to accepting and acting on the conviction at that moment that they are, all things considered, the weightier reasons, more worth acting on by the agent *at that moment* than their alternatives. We need not deny that weak-willed agents continue to believe that "in some sense" moral or prudential reasons are the "better" ones and that they would be better persons if they had acted otherwise—better from the moral or prudential points of view. They continue to have divided loyalties. But by choosing selfishly or imprudently they have made clear that, "in another sense," selfish or imprudent motives were regarded as better by them at the time of choice, more worthy of being acted on all things considered then and there. This is why remorse, regret or shame may be appropriate later. They do not see the choice as a fluke or accident, beyond their control at the time they made it. It is also why as Davidson notes, though we cannot explain, and much less justify, the weak-willed's behavior *in moral or prudential terms*, if we look at the entire psychological profile, we can *explain* it, as Davidson says, and even explain how it could be rational.

Having discussed the four requirements of the Rationality Condition (2) for weak-willed choice, let us now return to the Production Condition (1). One might question whether the requirement of the Production Condition, that the choice be an *intentional* termination of an effort of will, is satisfied by weak-willed choice. There is certainly no prior *intention* to make it on the part of the agent. But as students of intentional action know, intentionally doing some A does not always require a prior intention to-do-A. Cases of deliberation and trying are especially tricky. Suppose an agent is deliberating about whether to do A or B. The deliberation is intentional in the sense that the agent intends to do something or other, intends to-do-A-or-B. But before the deliberation terminates, it is not true that the agent intends to-do-A or intends to-do-B. We can put this in terms of Michael Bratman's plausible idea that intentions not only presuppose wants and beliefs, but are also *plans* of action.[22] The agent deliberating about whether to choose A or B does indeed plan to-choose-either-A-or-B. But it does not follow that prior to choice the agent plans to-choose-A or plans to-choose-B. The agent will choose one or the other, and the choice will be intentional, even though there was no prior intention to make just *that* choice, but only the general intention to resolve the matter in one way or the other. We carry out the general intention to resolve indecision *by* choosing one way or the other.

To be sure, our paradigm cases of choices involving moral and prudential struggle add a new twist to ordinary cases of practical deliberation, since in the moral and prudential cases agents are trying to make one outcome (say, A) prevail over the other, even while finding themselves drawn in the opposing direction. Yet the above point about the intentionality of choices is still relevant. Normally, when we are trying to do something (hit a target), but fail, the failure (missing the target) is unintentional. But this is just where the paradigm cases of choices involving inner conflict and stuggle are unique. Normally, the resistance to our tryings comes from outside our will (we miss the target because our arms quiver involuntarily or the wind moves the target). But in the paradigm cases of choice under conflict, the resistance to trying is coming *from our own will*. This is what makes these cases so important for understanding free will. If we fail to resist temptation it is because, though we wanted to resist, in another equally important sense we also wanted to succumb. Phenomenologically, we all recognize that these temptation cases are not like trying to hit a target and missing. In the temptation cases the resistance is coming from our own wills, and so the outcome is willed, whichever way it goes. To be sure, the weak-willed outcome is not planned. There was no prior intention to do it. But we have seen that where choices are involved, their being intentional does not require a prior intention to make the specific choice that is made. Once a choice is made, of course, there *is* a specific intention, or plan in Bratman's sense, to do A (or B, as the case may be). The making of the choice is the formation of just such an intention. But this is *after* the choice is made. Before the choice is made, there is no specific intention to make just that choice.

There is one important difference, however, in the manner in which the Production Condition is satisfied by principled (i.e., moral or prudential) behavior, on the one hand, and by weak-willed behavior, on the other—a difference that has probably not gone unnoticed. While in both cases the agent "intentionally terminates an effort of will" one way or the other, in the case of principled behavior it is proper to say that the choice is brought about *by* the effort (since the effort was an effort to resist temptation), while in weak-willed behavior it is not proper to say that the choice is brought about by the effort. Rather in the weak-willed case, the choice is brought about *by the character and (self interested or inclining) motives* which the effort *failed to resist*. But note that in both cases, since the effort *and* the character and resistant motives are both the agent's the outcome will be willed by the agent whichever way it goes.

To summarize, I have argued that in cases of moral and prudential struggle the Production and Rationality Conditions (1) and (2) of UR can be satisfied for weak-willed choice as well as for principled choice (from duty or prudence). In the weak-willed case, the agent's choice also terminates an effort of will to overcome temptation. The termination in this case is of course a *failure* to overcome temptation *from* the moral and prudential points of view, but the agent recognizes it as *his* or *her* failure, because the choice to succumb was intentionally (knowingly and purposefully) made by him or her *for* self interested reasons or to satisfy present inclinations. But we have also seen that the Ultimacy Condition (3) can be satisfied in either case of principled or weak-willed behavior because the effort of will that terminates in choice one way or the other is indeterminate. One could not predict the outcome even if one knew all one could know about the prior facts. Nor could one explain the critical difference—the choosing of A rather than choosing otherwise, or vice versa—in terms of past circumstances and laws of nature. The "ultimate" or "final" explanation for the choosing rather than doing otherwise, or vice versa, is the explanation embodied in (1) and (2): the agent intentionally terminated an effort of will, had reasons for doing so, did it for those reasons, etc. No further nonrational explanation for this "rather than" claim is possible given the facts of the case (including the fact *that the effort was indeterminate*). Deterministic explanations are ruled out. A statistical explanation is possible, but since it would assign only a probability to each outcome it would not explain why the agent here and now chose A rather than doing otherwise, or vice versa. We must invoke the explanation in terms of (1) and (2) to do that. Moreover, any explanation for the effort which terminated in the choice (in terms, for example, of past character and motives), or for the agent's having the reasons or motives he or she did have, would not also explain the choice itself.

Yet, there is one more thing to add. For one might still object that while the explanation by (1) and (2) may be ultimate or final in the sense that no other explanation is possible given the facts of the situation, it is not "ultimate" or "final" in the sense that it is an ultimately and finally satisfying rational explanation. For we might ask of the explanation in terms of (1) and (2) itself, "Why did the agent intentionally terminate the effort of will at the time in *this* way rather than that, and for *these* reasons rather than those, given that the alternative choice might also have been rational?" (Call this question "Q.") In answer to this objection, we must add one further twist to the theory, which for present purposes will be the final one. I want to suggest that even this ultimate question Q has an answer, so that one does not have to remain silent in the face of it. The answer, which is already implicit in our earlier discussion, is: "Because the agent came to believe at the time that these were all things considered the weightier reasons." (Call this explanation "E.") With respect to E we can, of course, ask in turn "Why did the agent come to believe at the time that that these were all things considered the weightier reasons?" But the answer to this question is: "Because the agent brought this about by intentionally terminating the effort of will in this way and for these reasons." In other words, the explanation E which explains (1) and (2) is in turn explained by (1) and (2). The agent brought himself or herself to believe by deciding, but since he or she did this, the deciding was rational given what was believed at the time of decision.

Of course, it will be objected that this is a shameless strategem which works because the "coming to believe they are the better reasons" and "intentionally terminating the effort of will for these reasons" are the same act "under different descriptions," so that the explanations are circular and vacuous. To which I respond "Circular, yes; vacuous, no." For it is significant and informative to say that acts of this kind *can* be described in these two different ways—one expressing a cognitive event, "coming to believe," the other a volitional event, "intentionally terminating"— mutually explanatorily supportive of each other. Indeed, I am suggesting that this is one of the crucial defining characteristics of any genuine act of free will. It is far from a trivial or empty fact about such acts. (It is noteworthy that philosophers and cognitive scientists have recently been giving more attention to the possibility that some of our beliefs and comings to believe may be influenced by our wills.[23]) As for the circularity of the explanations, I concede it, but think it is exactly what Ultimacy requires. Such an act is "ultimate" or "final" because it is in a way "self-explaining." One can answer the question of why it occurred under one description by citing it under another description, and vice versa. Only if acts are self explaining in this way, I believe, can regresses be avoided and Ultimacy secured. Nor am I the first to see or say something like this. A great tradition of French libertarians, from Jules Lequier, Charles Renouvier (who influenced William James), Emile Boutroux, Yves Simon, down to Jean-Paul Sartre and Paul Ricoeur has at least consistently hinted at the idea by insisting that in libertarian choice we must be choosing the reasons that in turn explain our action.

It should now be clear why the Ultimacy Condition was defined in UR by saying that no other explanation of the choice is possible, *unless* that explanation is in turn explained by (1) and (2) themselves. For of the two mutually supportive explanations—"coming to believe they are the weightier reasons" and "intentionally terminating the effort of will for these reasons"—the second is just a condensed statement of (1) and (2). The Production and Rationality Conditions provide an ultimate explanation of the choice because (as UR says) "no other explanation (other than the conjunction of (1) and (2)) for the agent's choosing A or choosing otherwise (whichever occurs) is possible, unless that explanation can in turn be explained by the conjunction of (1) and (2) itself."

But still, you will say that *something* remains unexplained. Yes. But remember that everything that *can* be explained, *given the facts of the situation,* is explained. Moreover, the outcome is *rational* whichever way it goes in the light of the agent's psychological history and is *produced* by the agent's will whichever way it goes, either by an effort of will or by the force of character and motives which the effort of will failed to resist. To insist that the explanation is inadequate given all these facts is, I suspect, to tacitly assume that reason explanations cannot adequately explain unless they are deterministic. For what is missing seems to be that the reasons and the effort do not determine the outcome. But, given the nature of this debate, such an assumption is question begging in the extreme. Charles Peirce insisted that it was the essence of *genuine* contingency that it entailed the absence of completely sufficient reasons. Libertarians have to live with that limitation. But they can try to explain whatever can be explained given the limitation.

## VI

The above is not a complete TI theory, but it does suggest the contours of such a theory and some of its essential features. Even if it were complete, I would not dare to say that it was the last word on incompatibilist theories of freedom, or even on TI theories. I have been involved in free will discussions for too long to become overly optimistic. But at least it provides us with a better idea of what an alternative to an Agent Cause theory might look like, something to sink our teeth into when discussing the problem of intelligibility of libertarian free will, and thus taking us a few further steps into the labyrinthe. Nor do I imagine that sceptics will be satisfied. Further objections beyond those already discussed will abound. So, without supposing that all the objections can be answered, let me conclude by addressing a few of the more significant ones.

*Objection 1:* "By making the choice outcome depend upon an indeterminate effort of will (and hence to some extent on chance), are you not *limiting* the *power* or *control* the agent has over those choices for which the agent is ultimately responsible? And does that not undermine the intent of an incompatibilist theory by denying that the agent's control over free choices is absolute or complete?"[24]

Yes, I am limiting the agent's power or control. But it is misleading to say the outcome depends "on chance," if this is going to suggest to the unwary that there are *two* separable events or processes involved, the "effort" and the "chance." Preceding the choice, we do not have the effort occurring and *then* chance, or chance occurring and *then* an effort. We merely have the effort, and it turns out that this effort is indeterminate. So we cannot say of an agent that she made just *this* much effort, and *then* she got lucky (or unlucky), because chance took over. Such claims will not make sense, because, first, there is no such thing as "this exact amount of effort" and, second, the chance is not separable from the effort, it is the indeterminacy *of* the effort.

With that said, however, it is true that the agent's power of control over the outcome is thereby limited. The agent cannot be sure of the outcome of the undetermined free choice up to the last minute, nor does the agent have absolute or complete control over it. I would not only say this, I would insist upon it. We have already seen that absolute or complete control is not available to finite agents, if it means that choices are not limited by heredity, environment, and conditioning. What else could absolute or complete control over choice mean? Given the present objection, one could guess that it might mean the choice was determined by a determinate effort of the agent, which was in turn determined by character and motives, so that, given the character, motives and effort, the result was inevitable. But if *that* is what is meant, then, as we have already suggested, *absolute* control is incompatible with *ultimate* control, because the former implies determinism and the latter indeterminism. This is an important point. Absolute control, in the sense just defined, and ultimate control are incompatible. One cannot have both. The choice between the two ought therefore to be given more attention by those concerned with the free will issue. I am not sure what the right choice is between the two, but it is clear what *incompatibilists* or *libertarians* must choose; they must go with ultimate control.

Nor do I deny that this limitation on the control involved in free agency is a source of uneasiness. But it is something that needs to be brought out into the open by incompatibilists and not swept under the rug. For I do not think an incompatibilist theory of free agency can be made intelligible without some such concession. Incompatibilists have often thought they could avoid the problem by getting *both* absolute and ultimate control over free actions. Though ultimacy requires that actions be undetermined by events or occurrences, they have thought that they could bring absolute or complete control back into the picture by inventing a special kind of agency or causation, like Agent Causation, to make up the difference and "determine" what events or occurrences did not determine. It turns out, however, that the manner in which this special cause is to fill the Explanation Gap remains a mystery for reasons we have discussed. And we should recall Schrödinger's statement: "at *that* price [mystery], one can have anything," even the reconciliation of absoluteness and ultimacy. But in the real world, I do not think they can be reconciled. If we are ultimately responsible agents, then our finiteness and limitations are even more profound than we expected. Among their implications is the uncertainty and risk involved in exercising one's free will—an uncertainty and risk that William James rightly described and eulogized in "The Dilemma of Determinism" as the price of living in an open universe.[25]

*Objection 2:* "You claim to be avoiding mystery and going all the way with event causation. But are you not substituting one mystery for another—the mystery of indeterminate efforts of will, described by quantum analogies, in place of nonoccurrent causes, noumenal selves, and the like. And is that a gain?"

If you believe that the "mysteries" of quantum theory are of the same order as those of nonoccurrent causes and noumenal selves, then this will seem a telling objection. I do not. To begin with, nonoccurrent causes do not explain what most needs explaining by an incompatibilist theory of free agency, namely, dual production and dual rationality, while quantum theory explains a great deal about the world around us, more even that it was originally introduced to explain. To be sure, there are many fascinating and unsolved problems about the interpretation of quantum phenomena and even more about any alleged effects they might have in the brain. But these problems represent a challenge. It would be a result of some significance if the problems dealt with by philosophers of quantum mechanics were found to be more intimately related to the venerable problem of free will than had previously been suspected. I think the relation is more intimate than is usually suspected. In fact, I would suggest that the best model of the transition from indeterminate efforts of will to choices as described in this paper—that is, the best model for the exercise of free will—is the collapse of the wave packet in quantum theory. This incredibly puzzling phenomenon involves a like transition from indeterminateness to determinateness and is tied up with deeper ontological issues about determinism and indeterminism. It is worth exploring the possibility that this phenomenon is related to free will, not just physically, but *conceptually*.

*Objection 3:* "Are indeterminate efforts of will really *events* or *occurrences* at all? If they are not, are you really 'going it alone' with event causation? If they are, you owe us more explanation of the kinds of events they are."

They are happenings, just as the movement of the particle toward the atomic barrier is a happening. They might even be conceived as processes in the brain that are, or involve, amplifications for microprocesses ("clocks over clouds" as Popper put it). In that case, the indeterminacy would come from the microparts, but it would have macroeffects by way of amplification, and the effort of will would be (or would be correlated with, or would have as its physical basis) the *comprehensive* brain process that includes microparts and macroeffects. We would then simply have to get used to some unusual ways of talking about human thought and behavior, just as physicists have had to do in their domain. And we should expect the same resistance to talk of indeterminate efforts of will in the debate about free will that was given to indeterminate particle trajectories in quantum theory by such scientists as Einstein, Planck, and De Broglie, who would not accept the fact that indeterminacy was an ultimate feature of the cosmic order. Indeterminate particle trajectories and indeterminate efforts of will may both cause intellectual discomfort and we may yearn to get back to the familiar ground of classical trajectories and determinate outcomes. Or, alternatively, we may be looking at a whole new way of viewing the physical world, on the one hand, and the life histories of human beings, on the other, a way that does not involve exact or determinate trajectories or life histories. In any case, the theory does not appeal to nonoccurrent causes in the traditional sense. And if you say, "What you are doing is replacing nonoccurrent causes with *fuzzy* events," I would say, "Well, that is one way of putting it, though not my favored way."

I said in Part V that these indeterminate efforts of will should be thought of as tryings or strivings in O'Shaughnessy's sense of "striving will," except that they are efforts to get our purposes or goals straightened out. They are what we ordinarily describe as efforts to overcome temptation. Phenomenologically, I have nothing special to add to their description beyond the general descriptions of efforts of will given by O'Shaughnessy, Ricoeur, McCann, and others who have discussed notions of trying or striving.[26] What I would add is that if there are brain events corresponding to these efforts (either correlated with or identical to the efforts, or the physical bases on which the mental efforts supervene), those brain events are physically indeterminate macroeffects of amplified microindeterminacies in the brain of the kind required by Wiggins condition (a'). Moreover, I contend that there is nothing in the phenomenology of such efforts to suggest that their physical bases *have* to be determinate, and could not be indeterminate. Indeed, the indeterminacy in the physical bases could be reflected in our phenomenology as the *uncertainty* we feel about the outcome of such efforts and the *tension* we feel in situations in which the will is in conflict with itself. Is the indeterminacy there in the brain? I do not know. As I said earlier, there is an empirical aspect of the free will issue that philosophical reflection cannot co-opt. But unless there is some indeterminacy in appropriate parts of the physical world—some "causal gaps" in nature as the Epicureans opined—I do not see how *any* incompatibilist theory can succeed.

*Objection 4:* "Can events in general, and choices in particular, be *caused* if they are not determined by their causes? If not, does the Production Condition (1) of UR make sense?"

In her Inaugural Lecture, "Causality and Determination," Elizabeth Anscombe has argued—convincingly in my view as well as in the view of many others—that such causation is conceivable.[27] One can be said to cause or "produce" an outcome even if that outcome is not inevitable given one's effort. Suppose the karate master swings his arm down on a thick board, and suppose (contrary to fact) that there were nonnegligible indeterminacies in the motion of his arm that made the outcome (breaking the board or not breaking it) undetermined. If the board breaks, the indeterminacy of the outcome does not lead us to deny that the motion of the arm *caused* the board to break (or failed to do so, as the case may be). The difference between this example and the case of free will, is that where the effort fails, and one succumbs to temptation, the outcome is also intended by the agent. In other words, the *resistance* of the board in the karate master example, corresponds, in the free will example, to the resistance *of the agent's own will.* Thus, for free will, but not in the karate master case, the outcome will be willed, whichever way it goes.

*Objection 5:* "What about cases where there is no moral, prudential, or practical conflict or struggle in the mind of the agent—cases, for example, where the agent does the right or prudent thing without being tempted to do otherwise, or cases where the agent has no reason to do otherwise that has any motivational force? The agent cannot be *ultimately* responsible for such actions in the sense of UR because the Rationality Condition is not satisfied? But cannot the agent be *morally responsible* for them? And if so, does this theory adequate capture the notion of moral responsibility?"[28]

In an important recent paper, Peter van Inwagen has argued that free choices or actions which satisfy the requirements of incompatibilists would occur in everyday life less frequently than incompatibilists usually acknowledge.[29] His argument is that most everyday choices and actions in which the agent does the right or prudent or reasonable thing without being tempted to do otherwise, or without having any good reasons to do otherwise, would not count as free in the sense intended by incompatibilists. We need not reproduce his argument here to see the point of it in the light of what has been said in this paper. Consider, for example, that such choices would not satisfy the Rationality Condition of UR for both of the possible outcomes. But van Inwagen goes on to argue that this result does not mean that we cannot be *morally* responsible for these everyday choices or actions where we are not tempted to, or have no good reasons for, doing otherwise. We can be morally responsible for these everyday choices or actions which issue unopposed from our present character and motives, *insofar* as we were responsible for forming our character and motives in the past by making free choices that *did* satisfy incompatibilist requirements.

I think van Inwagen is correct about both these claims. Let me put what I think is right about them in the terms of this paper. Incompatibilist free choices arise at those critical junctures of human life when we are engaged in moral, prudential, and practical struggle, where there is inner conflict and the outcome is not obvious. It is at these points, as Kant saw, that we are truly "making ourselves" in such a way that we are ultimately responsible for the outcome. They are "hard choices," to use Isaac Levi's expression, and it is through them that we design a future that is reasonable given our past, but is not determined by our past. But even though these hard choices are a subset of the totality of our everyday choices (van Inwagen's first point), it does not mean that we are not morally responsible for other choices and actions (van Inwagen's second point). For, other everyday choices and actions issue from our motives and character, and we can be ultimately responsible for our present motives and character by virtue of past choices which helped to form them and for which we were ultimately responsible. Thus, moral responsibility presupposes ultimate responsibility, but we can be morally responsible for many everyday choices and actions generally that do not themselves satisfy the conditions for ultimate responsibility, UR. And we are morally responsible for ultimate choices in a two-fold way, by virtue of our already formed character and motives which influence them, and by virtue of the present efforts of will which bring them about.

*Objection 6:* "Is a TI theory like yours necessarily opposed to an AC theory? Could not AC theorists like Taylor and Chisholm simply accept much of your account of 'teleological intelligibility' and incorporate it into their Agent Cause theories? Your indeterminate efforts, for example, might be interestingly conceived as examples of Chisholm's 'endeavorings'."

The first thing to note here is that, strictly speaking, TI and AC theories are incompatible because the former reject and the latter require nonoccurrent or nonevent causation. Nonetheless, it would be possible for an AC theorist like Taylor or Chisholm to simply *add* Agent, or nonoccurrent, Causation to a TI theory like mine, making it an AC theory. This would be a particularly interesting exercise, I think, with regard to Chisholm's "endeavorings" (or, for that matter, Reid's "exertions of will"). But any such reconciliation or confrontation between AC theories and this, or any, TI theory will have to come to grips with the following kinds of questions. What would the addition of Agent Causation add to the explanatory power of the theory? Would it add anything essential to the explanation of how and why the agent did A rather than B, or B rather than A, which is not already accounted for, say, by conditions (1) and (2) of UR? If those conditions are satisfied, we can say that the agent terminated an effort of will at a certain time by choosing A (or B), and that the agent had reasons for doing so and chose for those reasons; in addition we can say that the agent may have terminated the effort otherwise, would have had reasons, if he or she had terminated it otherwise, would have done so for those reasons, etc. What would we be adding to this by saying that the agent brought about the choice of A (or B) *nonoccurrently?* Perhaps we would be underlining the fact that it was the agent who *did* the terminating, or that it was the *agent* who did it. But, by asserting UR, the TI theorist is already saying that the agent did it. The conditions of UR are meant to spell out what it *means* to say "the agent did it." It is not agent causation that TI theorists are suspicious of, but Agent (i.e., nonoccurrent) Causation. Perhaps the introduction of nonoccurrent causation would make up for some of the uncertainty and limitation produced by indeterminate efforts, as discussed in objection 1? Whereas indeterminate efforts of will would leave the outcome uncertain, the nonoccurrent cause would make the outcome determinately one choice or the other. But how does nonoccurrent causation do this? Why are its outcomes certain rather than uncertain? Why is its control absolute rather than limited? What more will we have learned about why the agent determinately chose A rather than B or B rather than A, if we are told that the agent chose A (or B) nonoccurrently? Any attempted reconciliation between AC and TI theories must come to grips with such questions. We can express the issue with the following friendly but firm challenge to AC theorists. If you wish to incorporate this or a similar account of teleological intelligibility into your view and simply add an appeal to Agent or nonoccurrent Causation to it, what are you thereby adding beyond an endorsement of the fact that the agency is such that, after you have accounted for its teleological intelligibility, *there is nothing else to explain?*

*Objection 7:* "Suppose there are two agents A and B, both of whose free choices are 'teleologically intelligible' in the sense that they can be explained in accordance with the conditions (1) and (2) of UR: they brought about their choices, had reasons for them, etc. Then 'it is incredible to suppose that the additional information that determinism holds in A's world but not in B's confers some special value or dignity to B's life. For it implies no special *powers* for B. In whatever way A is supposed to be powerless, B is as well, if that [indeterminism vs. determinism] is the only difference between them'."

This objection, which I quote from Gary Watson (note 5, p. 165) (and which has been stated in somewhat different terms by Bruce Waller [note 24]) goes to the heart of what many people may feel is inadequate about TI theories in general. What can indeterminism add to teleological intelligibility to confer dignity? It does not seem to add any powers to the agent. In fact, it seems to *limit* the agent's power, as we have already seen. Of course, as Watson concedes, if teleological intelligibility (described by Wiggins as the ability to fit behavior "into meaningful sequences") *implied* indeterminism, then we would have a reason for introducing indeterminism. But Watson suggests that there is no good reason to think that teleological intelligibility implies indeterminism. On this point, I think he is clearly right. So, what then does indeterminism add?

My general answer to this question should now be evident. It is not teleological intelligibility itself that requires indeterminism. Compatibilists can get teleological intelligibility. What requires indeterminism is the *ultimacy* of choice. Teleological intelligibility is then brought in to reconcile ultimacy with the idea that choices and actions can be the causal results of character, motives, and efforts even when the choices are not determined. To put it another way, conditions (1) and (2) of UR, the Explanation Conditions—which represent the "teleological intelligibility" of free choices—do not imply indeterminism. What implies indeterminism is condition (3) of UR, the Ultimacy Condition. The role of conditions (1) and (2) is to make ultimate choices "teleologically intelligible," by showing how they can be explained as rational products of the agents though they are not determined.

What special *power* then does indeterminism confer on free agents? Agents in the undetermined world have the *power to make choices for which they have ultimate responsibility.* They have the power to be the *ultimate* producers of their own ends in a sense that satisfies the Ultimacy Condition of UR as well as the teleological intelligibility conditions (1) and (2). That is to say, they have *the power to make choices which can only and finally be explained in terms of their own wills* (i.e., character, motives, and efforts of will). No one can have this power in a determined world. If we must give this power a name, let us call it "free will."

## Notes

1. I am indebted to the following persons who helped sharpen my thoughts on the topics of this paper through correspondence, conversation, or

recent writing, some unpublished: Robert Audi, Mark Bernstein, David Blumenfeld, Richard Double, George Graham, William Hasker, Fred Kronz, Noah Lemos, William Rowe, Thomas Talbott, Bruce Waller, Gary Watson, and Peter van Inwagen. I would especially like to thank Bernstein, Graham, Rowe, Waller, and van Inwagen for commentary on earlier drafts, as well as two anonymous referees of *Philosophy and Phenomenological Research* whose questions and suggestions helped improve some of the paper's important formulations. The usual disclaimer is more than usually necessary in this case: these acknowledgements do not imply agreement on the part of the above people with what I have to say—an unlikely prospect since they hold differing views about free will. The view expressed here is mine alone, as are its shortcomings.

2. *Metaphysics* (Englewood Cliffs, NJ: Prentice-Hall, 1974), p. 57.

3. See their essays in this volume.

4. Ginet "Might We Have No Choice?" in K. Lehrer, ed., *Freedom and Determinism* (New York: Random House, 1966), pp. 87–104, and "A Defense of Incompatibilism," *Philosophical Studies* 44 (1983), pp. 391–400; van Inwagen, *An Essay on Free Will* (Oxford: Oxford University Press, 1983); Lamb, "On a Proof of Incompatibilism," *The Philosophical Review* 86 (1977), pp. 20–35; Wiggins, "Towards a Reasonable Libertarianism," in T. Honderich, ed., *Essays on Freedom and Action* (London: Routledge & Kegan Paul, 1973). For critical discussion of the argument, see the introduction by John Martin Fisher to *Moral Responsibility* (Ithaca, NY: Cornell University Press, 1986); and also Watson, ed. *Free Will* (New York: Oxford University Press, 1982), D. Lewis, "Are We Free To Break the Laws?" *Theoria* 47 (1981), pp. 112–21, M. Slote, "Selective Necessity and the Free Will Problem," *Journal of Philosophy* 79 (1982), pp. 5–24, and T. Flint, "Compatibilism and the Argument from Unavoidability," *Journal of Philosophy* 74 (1987), 423–40.

5. For recent contributions to this much discussed topic from opposing points of view, see Ginet, "The Conditional Analysis of Freedom," and K. Lehrer, "Preference, Conditionals and Freedom," both in van Inwagen, *Time and Cause* (Dordrecht: Reidel, 1980), and for overviews see Fischer, *Moral Responsibility*, and Watson, "Free Action and Free Will," *Mind* 94 (1987), pp. 145–72.

6. R. Kane, *Free Will and Values* (Albany: State University of New York Press, 1985), discusses such a theory and its historical precedents. Suggestions that point in the direction of TI theories without going all the way are made by Wiggins, "Reasonable Libertarianism"; J. Thorp, *Free Will: A Defense Against Neurophysiological Determinism* (London: Routledge & Kegan Paul, 1980); J. Trusted, *Free Will and Responsibility* (Oxford: Oxford University Press, 1984); van Inwagen "A Definition of Chisholm's Notion of Immanent Causation," *Philosophia* 7 (1978), pp. 567–81; R. Nozick, *Philosophical Explanations* (Cambridge, MA: Harvard University Press, 1981) [see the excerpt reprinted in this volume]; and Rem Edwards, *Freedom, Responsibility and Obligation* (The Hague: Nijhoff, 1969). The suggestions of Thorp, Trusted, and van Inwagen are meant to be refinements of the Agent Cause view. But they seem to point beyond it toward a TI theory (as van Inwagen himself concedes of his own paper). Nozick's treatment of free will in his widely read *Philosophical Explanations* has been criticized by reviewers as less successful than other parts of the book, but it contains many valuable insights that point in the direction of TI theories. The traditional philoso-

pher who probably comes closest to a TI theory is William James (see Donald Viney, "William James on Free Will and Determinism," *The Journal of Mind and Behavior* 7 [1986], pp.555–65).

7. "Determinism, Indeterminism and Libertarianism," in S. Morgenbesser and J. Walsh, J., eds., *Free Will* (Englewood Cliffs, NJ: Prentice-Hall, 1962), pp. 115–32.

8. Chisholm, "Freedom and Action," in Lehrer, ed., *Freedom and Determinism;* "The Agent as Cause," in M. Brand and D. Walton, eds., *Action Theory* (Dordrecht: D. Reidel, 1976), pp. 199–211; "Human Freedom and the Self," in Watson, ed., *Free Will;* and *Person and Object* (London: Allen & Unwin, 1976); see also C. A. Campbell, *In Defense of Free Will* (London: Allen & Unwin, 1967).

9. Despite the prevalence of AC theories in discussions of free will, historical studies of them are few and far between. Some recent work of William Rowe on seventeenth and eighteenth conceptions of freedom have begun to remedy the situation. See his "Causality and Free Will in the Controversy Between Collins and Clarke," *Journal of the History of Philosophy* 25 (1987), pp. 57–67, and "Two Concepts of Freedom," *Proceedings of the American Philosophical Association* 61 (1987), pp. 43–64 (reprinted as Chapter 9 in this volume).

10. Criticisms of AC theories appear in C. D. Broad, T. Nagel, and I. Thalberg, "How Does Agent Causality Work?" In Brand and Walton, eds., *Action Theory;* L. Bonjour, "Determinism, Libertarianism and Agent Causation," *The Southern Journal of Philosophy* 14 (1976), pp. 145–56; and A. Goldman, "Chisholm's Theory of Action," *Philosophia* 7 (1978), pp. 583–96. The Thalberg essay is a good account of the differences between the AC theories of Taylor and Chisholm, as well as a challenging critique of both.

11. It is noteworthy that if genuine "backwards causation" were possible, all bets would be off. Ultimacy would not necessarily preclude determinism and incompatibilists would have to rethink their position. I think many incompatibilists have recognized this, as least tacitly (some explicitly, e.g., P. Forrest, "Backwards Causation in Defense of Free Will," *Mind* 94 [1985], pp. 210–17). Backwards causation, if it existed, would change the rules of the game regarding free action, and it is interesting that the Ultimacy Condition shows why. Similarly, the Ultimacy Condition allows for the possibility of so called "soft facts" about the past in the sense of facts whose existence in the past depends upon what agents do in the present. The kind of determinism that Ultimacy rules out, usually called "causal determinism," involves determination by "hard facts" about the past. Thus, throughout this paper, when I speak of "determinism" and "indeterminism" I mean "causal determinism" in this sense and its denial "causal indeterminism."

12. Thalberg, "How Does Agent Causality Work?" pp. 230–31.

13. Chisholm, "Freedom and Action," p. 25.

14. I apply this definition specifically to choices because I believe that choices or decisions (the traditional *libera arbitria voluntatis*) are the primary *loci* of free*will.* Free action on my account is derivative from free will. I do not argue for these points here, having done so elsewhere (Kane, *Free Will and Values,* ch. 2).

15. Acting "for a reason" involves more than merely "having a reason and

acting" as Robert Audi has shown in "Acting for Reasons," *The Philosophical Review* 95 (1986), pp. 511–46. I try to show later in this paper that the conditions Audi lays down in his paper for "acting for a reason" (pp. 537–38) are all satisfied by the examples I cite later in support of this account of ultimate responsibility.

16. There are common elements of most accounts of intentional action, despite differences. See, for example, J. Meiland, *The Nature of Intention* (London: Methuen, 1970); Audi "Intending," *The Journal of Philosophy* 70 (1973), pp. 387–403; M. Bratman "Intention and Means-End Reasoning," *The Philosophical Review* 90 (1981), pp. 252–65; and M. Brand, *Intending and Acting* (Cambridge, MA: MIT Press, 1986).

17. In other words, these are not cases of compulsion, which have been analyzed by Frankfurt in terms of higher order volitions ("Freedom of the Will and the Concept of a Person," *Journal of Philosophy* 68 [1971], pp. 5–20). We discuss why such choices need not be compulsive later on.

18. See note 15.

19. He says "non-accidentally produced" in order to eliminate much discussed cases of "wayward causation" in which a reason might influence the occurrence of the act for which it is a reason, but by an accidental series of causal events unknown to the agent, rather than in the "normal" way. We cannot get into this complicated topic here. Suffice it to say that in cases of choosing from duty or prudence, wayward causation might be involved (though it is hard to imagine exactly how), but *need* not be involved. When it is involved, the choices would not be free in the desired sense, that is, would not satisfy UR.

20. The condition also expresses some of what is true, I think, in Galen Strawson's claim that "believing one is a free agent is a necessary condition for being a free agent" (Strawson, Chapter 1 in this book).

21. It should be noted that Kant also recognized that the problem we are addressing here—the problem of acting contrary to the moral law—was a critical one for his account of human freedom. He wrestled with it unsuccessfully well into his latest written words (notably in *Religion Within the Bounds of Reason Alone*), as recent writers on Kant's doctrine of freedom such as G. Prauss and Henry Allison have reminded us. See Allison, "Morality and Freedom: Kant's Reciprocity Doctrine," *The Philosophical Review* 95 (1986), pp. 393–425.

22. See Bratman, "Intention."

23. See, for example, Bas van Fraassen, "Belief and the Will," *The Journal of Philosophy* 81 (1985), pp. 235–56.

24. This objection has been made by Bruce Waller, "Free Will Gone Out of Control," *Behaviorism* 16 (Fall, 1988), pp. 149–57; also by Clifford Williams and by Thomas Talbott, Mark Bernstein, and David Blumenfeld in correspondence and discussion. My response to it and the distinction between "absolute" and "ultimate" control upon which the response rests were clarified by discussions with Waller, Blumenfeld, Talbott, and Richard Double.

25. *The Will to Believe and Other Essays* (New York: Dover, 1956), pp. 145–83.

26. Paul Ricoeur, *Freedom and Nature*, E. Kohak, trans. (Evanston, IL: Northwestern University Press, 1966), parts I and II; and Hugh McCann, "Volition and Basic Action," *The Philosophical Review* 83 (1974), pp. 451–73.

27. *Metaphysics and the Philosophy of Mind: Collected Philosophical Papers,* vol. III (Minneapolis: University of Minnesota Press, 1981). See also van Inwagen, *An Essay,* chapter 1.

28. This objection and others relating to moral responsibility are also made in Waller, "Out of Control," and by Talbott.

29. "When Is the Will Free?" reprinted as Chapter 12 in this volume.

# 9

# Two Concepts of Freedom

## WILLIAM L. ROWE

In his life of Samuel Johnson, Boswell reports Johnson as saying: "All theory is against freedom of the will; all experience for it." The first part of this remark would be agreeable to many eighteenth century philosophers: those believing that certain theoretical principles concerning explanation or causality support the doctrine of necessity. But the second part, that experience is on the side of free will, would be somewhat puzzling to those eighteenth century philosophers who hold that free will is a power and that a power, as opposed to an activity, is not something we can directly experience or be conscious of.[1] In his journal, however, which presumably was written shortly after the actual conversation with Johnson, Boswell reports Johnson's remark differently. There he has Johnson saying: "All theory against freedom of will, all practice for it."[2] Here the second part makes better philosophical sense, for that our practice of moral praise and blame is on the side of free will was a standard theme among eighteenth century advocates of free will, and it is perfectly understandable, therefore, that Johnson would have cited practice as on the side of freedom. But what is the *concept* of freedom that lies behind this remark by Johnson? And more generally, what *conceptual issues* were at the center of the controversy over freedom and necessity that occupied the last half of the seventeenth and most of the eighteenth century, a controversy bringing forward as its champions, on one side or another, such formidable figures as Hobbes, Locke, Samuel Clarke, Leibniz, Hume, and Thomas Reid? I want to answer these questions, not simply in order to deepen our understanding of this historical episode in the controversy over freedom and necessity, as important as that may be, but because I believe a clear understanding of this episode in the controversy can help us in our current thinking about the problem of freedom and necessity.

My belief is that when all is said and done there are two fundamentally different conceptions of freedom that occupy center stage in the controversy that we may arbitrarily date as beginning with Thomas Hobbes and Bishop Bramhall (in the second half of the seventeenth century) and ending with Thomas Reid and Joseph Priestley (in the late eighteenth century). Vestiges of these two conceptions are very much alive in the twentieth century. I intend, however, to examine these two conceptions in their earlier setting, analyzing and evaluating them in the light of criticisms advanced against them, both then and now. The first of these conceptions, of which John Locke is a major advocate, I will call *Lockean freedom*. The other conception, of which Thomas Reid is the leading advocate, I will call *Reidian freedom*. The history of the controversy in the period we are considering is fundamentally a dispute over which of these two concepts of freedom is more adequate to our commonsense beliefs about freedom and our general metaphysical and scientific principles.

Before we begin with Locke's conception of freedom, it is best to note that all participants in the controversy embraced what has come to be known as the volitional theory of action. Since this theory is common to the controversy we are examining, it plays no significant role in the controversy itself. Nevertheless, some brief description of it will help us understand certain points that emerge in the controversy. According to this theory, actions are of two sorts: those that involve thoughts and those that involve motions of the body. What makes the occurrence of a certain thought or bodily motion an *action* is its being preceded by a certain act of will (a volition) which brings about the thought or motion. Volitions, then, are "action starters." On the other hand, they are also themselves referred to as "actions." Of course, if we do classify volitions as actions, we cannot say that *every* action must be preceded by a volition. For then no action could occur unless it were preceded by an absolutely infinite number of volitions. But we still can say that thoughts and bodily motions are actions only if *they* are preceded by volitions that cause them. It is not clear whether volitions that start actions are viewed as distinct from the actions started, or as a part of the actions. It is also unclear just what the agent wills when his volition starts (or is part of) a certain action. These uncertainties, however, will have little bearing on our examination of the two conceptions of freedom that dominated eighteenth century thought.

## *I. Lockean Freedom*

Locke distinguished between a free action and a voluntary action. For your action to be voluntary all that is required is that you will to do that action and perform it, presumably as a result of your willing to do it. Suppose you are sitting in your chair and someone invites you to go for a walk. You reject the idea, choosing instead to remain just where you are. Your so remaining, Locke would say, is a voluntary act. But was it a free act? This is a further question for Locke, and it depends on whether you could have done otherwise had you so willed. If I had injected you with a powerful drug, so that at the time—perhaps without your being aware of it—your legs were paralyzed, then your act of remaining in the chair was voluntary but not free, for you could not have got up and walked had you willed to do so. A free act, says Locke, is not just a voluntary act.[3] An act is free if it is voluntary *and* it is true that had you willed to do otherwise you would have been able to do otherwise. For Locke, then, we can say that you are free with respect to a certain action provided it is in your power to do it if you will to do it *and* in your power to refrain from doing it if you should will to refrain. Locke tells us that a man who is chained in prison does not stay in prison freely—even if that is what he wants to do—because it is not in his power to leave if he should will to leave. But if the prison doors are thrown open, and his chains are removed, he is free to leave and free to stay—for he can do either, depending on his will.

So far, of course, little or nothing has been said about the question of whether the will is free. And this was what Locke preferred, thinking on the whole that the question of freedom is the question of whether you are free *to do* what you will; much confusion, he thought, results from asking whether you are free *to will* what you will. But the chief merit of Locke's conception of freedom, or so it seemed to many, is that it fits nicely with the belief that our acts of will are causally necessitated by prior events and circumstances. Anthony Collins, Locke's friend and follower, took up this topic in his book, *A Philosophical Inquiry Concerning Human Liberty*, published in London in 1717. Collins argued that all our actions are subject to causal necessity; he argued, that is, that our actions are so determined by the causes preceding them that, given the causes and circumstances, no other actions were possible. What are the causes of our actions? Well, the immediate cause of the action is you decision or act of will to perform that action. What is the cause of your making that decision? According to Locke and Collins, the cause of that act of will is your desires, judgments, and the circumstances that prevailed just prior to that decision. Given your desires and judgments at the time, and given the circumstances that prevailed, it was impossible for you not to will as you did. And given the desires, judgments, circumstances, and the act of will, it was impossible for you not to act as you did. Now this impossibility of willing and acting otherwise does not conflict with Lockean freedom. For Lockean freedom does not require that *given the causes,* we somehow could have acted differently. All it requires is that *if* we had decided or willed differently *then* we could have acted differently. Indeed, Locke is careful to note that the absolute determination of the will or preference of the mind does not preclude freedom so far as the action flowing from the will or preference of the mind is concerned. He remarks:

> But though the preference of the Mind be always determined . . . ; yet the Person who has the power, in which alone consists liberty to act, or not to act, according to such preference, is nevertheless free; such determination abridges not that Power. He that has his Chains knocked off, and the Prison doors set open to him, is perfectly at liberty, because he may either go or stay as he best likes; though his preference be determined to stay by the darkness of the Night, or illness of the Weather, or want of other Lodging. He ceases not to be free; though that which at that time appears to him the greater Good absolutely determines his preference, and *makes* him stay in his Prison.[4]

Let us call those who believe both that we have Lockean freedom and that our actions and acts of will are subject to causal necessity, 'necessitarians.' It is likely that Locke was a necessitarian; Hobbes and Collins most certainly were. Those who, like Clarke and Reid, hold that necessity and freedom are really inconsistent with one another do not disagree with the necessitarians concerning the consistency of *Lockean freedom* with the causal necessity of our actions and acts of will. What they reject is the whole notion of Lockean freedom. Before we state their conception of freedom, however, we had best consider what their objections are to the Lockean idea of freedom.[5]

Lockean freedom, as we saw, exists solely at the level of *action:* you are free with respect to some action provided that you have the power to do the act if you will to do it, and have the power not to do it if you will not to do it. But what about the *will?* What if you don't have the power to will the action, or don't have the power not to will it? To see the difficulty here, let's return to our example where you are sitting down, someone asks you get up and walk over to the window to see what is happening outside, but you are quite satisfied where you are and choose to remain sitting. We earlier supposed that I had injected you with a powerful drug so that you can't move your legs. Here Locke would say that you don't sit freely, since it was not in your power to do otherwise if you had willed otherwise—say, to get up and walk to the window. But let's now suppose that instead of paralyzing your legs I had hooked up a machine to your brain so that I can and do cause you to will to sit, thus depriving you of the *capacity* to will to do otherwise. It's still true that you have the power to get up and walk *if* you should will to do so—I haven't taken away your physical capacity to walk, as I did when I paralyzed your legs. Here the problem is that you can't *will* to do anything other than sit. In this case, it seems clear that you sit of necessity, not freely. You can't do otherwise than sit, not because you lack the power to get up and walk if you should manage to choose to do that, but because you lack the power to *choose* to get up and walk. On Locke's account of freedom, however, it remains true that you sit freely and not of necessity. And this being so, we must conclude that Locke's account of freedom is simply inadequate. It is not sufficient that you have the power to do otherwise *if* you so will; it must also be true that you have the power to will to do otherwise. Freedom that is worth the name, therefore, must include power *to will*, not simply power *to do if we will.*

There is a second objection to Lockean freedom, an objection based on the fact that Lockean freedom is consistent with the causal necessity of our actions and decisions. According to the necessitarians, you are totally determined to will and act as you do by your motives and circumstances. Indeed, Leibniz quotes with favor Bayle's comparison of the influence of motives on an agent to the influence of weights on a balance. Referring to Bayle, Leibniz remarks: "According to him, one can explain what passes in our resolutions by the hypothesis that the will of man is like a balance which is at rest when the weights of its two pans are equal, and which always inclines either to one side or the other according to which of the pans is the more heavily laden."[6] Bayle's idea is that just as the heavier weight determines the movement of the balance, so does the stronger motive determine the movement of your will. If your motive to get up and walk to the window is stronger than whatever motive you have to remain sitting, then it determines you to will to get up and walk to the window. Given the respective strength of these motives, it is no more possible for you to will to remain sitting than it is possible for a balance to stay even when a heavier weight is placed in one of its pans than in the other. Motives, on this view, are determining causes of the decisions of our will in precisely the way in which weights are the determining causes of the movements of the balance. But if all this is so, claim the opponents of the necessitarians, then no one acts freely, no one has power over his will. For it was generally agreed that our motives are determined by factors largely beyond our control, and if these motives determine our acts of will as weights determine the movement of a balance, then we can no more control our will than the balance can control its movements. Just as a balance has no freedom of movement, so the person would have no freedom of will. Freedom would be an illusion if our will is subjected to causal necessity by motives and circumstances. Since Lockean freedom is consistent with such causal necessity, Lockean freedom is really not freedom at all.[7]

We've looked at two major objections to Lockean freedom. According to Locke, freedom to do a certain thing is (roughly) the power to do that thing if we will to do it. Our first objection is that we might have the power to do something if we willed to do it and yet lack the power to will to do it. Surely, freedom must include the power to will, and not just the power to do *if* we will. Our second objection is against the necessitarian view that our acts of will are causally necessitated by prior events and circumstances. If that is so then we *now* have no more control over what we will to do than a balance has over how it moves once the weights are placed in its pans. Causal necessitation of our acts of will denies to us any real power over the determinations of our will. And without such power we do not act freely. To be told, as Locke would tell us, that we could have done something else if we had so willed, is of course interesting, and perhaps not unimportant. But if we are totally determined to will as we do and cannot will otherwise, then it is absurd to say we act freely simply because had we willed otherwise—which we could not do—we could have acted otherwise.

I believe these objections to Lockean freedom are in the end totally convincing. Indeed, it puzzles me that the notion of Lockean freedom continues to survive in the face of such utterly devastating objections. But before passing on to the second concept of freedom, *Reidian freedom,* we should note an attempt or two to defend or amend Lockean freedom so that it will appear less implausible.

At the level of action we are free, for Locke, provided we could have done otherwise if we had chosen or willed to do otherwise. Basically, our objections to Lockean freedom point out the need to supplement freedom at the level of action with freedom at the level of the will. The problem for the necessitarian is how to do this without abandoning the causal necessitation of the will by our motives and circumstances. Now one might be tempted to suggest that at the level of the will we are free provided we could have willed to do otherwise *if* we had been in different circumstances or had different motives—a thesis that in no way conflicts with the act of will being causally necessitated by our actual motives and circumstances. Such a suggestion of what it means to have free will fully merits, I believe, the contempt and ridicule that Kant meant when he spoke of a "wretched subterfuge" and William James meant when he spoke of "a quagmire of evasion."[8] If Lockean freedom is to be saved, we need a better account of free will than this suggestion provides.

In his discussion of Locke's account of freedom, Leibniz generally endorses Locke's view but points out its failure to provide any account of free will. He suggests two accounts of free will, one in contrast to the bondage of the passions, an account drawn from the Stoics; a second in contrast to necessity, an account that is Leibniz's own.[9] Although neither account removes the causal necessitation of the will, the first account does appear to soften the blow. Leibniz remarks: "the Stoics said that only the wise man is free; and one's mind is indeed not free when it is possessed by a great passion, for then one cannot will as one should, i.e., with proper deliberation. It is in that way that God alone is perfectly free, and that created minds are free only in proportion as they are above passion; . . ."[10] Here we have a nice amendment to Lockean freedom. For an action to be free it must not only be willed and such that we could have done otherwise if we had willed otherwise, but also the act of will must have been free in the sense of resulting at least partially from the proper exercise of reason. If the passions totally determine the act of will and the consequent action, we need not say that the person acts freely. However, if the judgments of reason and our circumstances totally determine our will so that given those judgments and circumstances no other act of will was possible, we can still say that we act freely, provided we could have done otherwise had we chosen or willed to do otherwise, for as rational beings we are willing as we should. This amendment, I believe, softens the necessitarian view; but it fails to solve the basic problem. For to will as we should is one thing, and to will freely is another. The problem with Lockean freedom is not that it fails to rule out necessitation of the will *by the passions;* the problem is that it fails to rule out the necessitation of the will *period.* It is time to turn to our second concept of freedom.

## II. *Reidian Freedom*

The clearest statement of our second concept of freedom is by the Scottish philosopher, Thomas Reid. Here is what Reid says.

> By the *liberty* of a moral agent, I understand, a power over the determinations of his own will.
> If, in any action, he had power to will what he did, or not to will it, in that action he is free. But if, in every voluntary action, the determination of his will be the necessary consequence of something involuntary in the state of his mind, or of something in his external circumstances, he is not free; he has not what I call the liberty of a moral agent, but is subject to necessity.[11]

It is helpful, I believe, to divide Reid's view of freedom into two themes: a negative thesis and a positive thesis. The negative thesis is this: if some action of ours is free then our decision or act of will to do that action cannot have been causally necessitated by any prior events, whether they be internal or external. If I have a machine hooked up to your brain in such a manner that my flip of a switch causally necessitates your decision to get up and walk across the room, it follows that you are not free in your action of getting up and walking across the room. In this case your decision to do that action is causally necessitated by some prior *external* event, the flipping of the switch. On the other hand, if your decision to do the act was causally necessitated by your motives and circumstances, then the causally necessitating event is *internal*, and the action again is not free. You are free in some action only if your decision to do that act is not causally necessitated by any involuntary event, whether internal or external. This is the negative thesis.

All too often, it is assumed that this second concept of freedom, which I have called *Reidian freedom*, consists in nothing more than this negative thesis. And the major objection of the necessitarians to Reidian freedom is based on this assumption. According to Reid, our free acts of will are not caused by any prior events, whether external or internal. And the difficulty with this, so the objection goes, is that it conflicts with the view that every event has a cause, a view that most eighteenth century philosophers, including Reid, accepted. What this objection reveals, however, is that the necessitarians hold to only one sort of causation, causation by prior events. Thus once it was denied that our free acts of will are caused by any prior events, the necessitarians concluded that the advocates of Reidian freedom were committed to the view that our free acts of will are totally uncaused events. But Reid, following Samuel Clarke, Edmund Law, and others, believed in another sort of causation, causation by persons or agent.. And what they affirmed in their positive thesis is that free acts of will are caused by the agent whose acts they are. Reid, then, no less than the necessitarians affirmed that all events, including our free acts of will, are caused. As he remarks: "I grant, then, that an effect uncaused is a contradiction, and that an event uncaused is an absurdity. The question that remains is whether a volition, undetermined by motives, is an event uncaused. This I deny. The cause of the volition is the man that willed it."[12]

What we've just seen is that the advocates of Reidian freedom agree with the necessitarians in holding that every event has a cause. What they deny is that every event has an event-cause. In the case of our free acts of will the cause is not some prior event but the agent whose acts they are. To understand Reidian freedom, therefore, we need to look at the foundation on which it rests, the idea of agent causation.

Reid believed that the original notion of 'cause' is that of an agent who brings about changes in the world by *acting*. To be such a cause, Reid held that a thing or substance must satisfy three conditions: first, it must have the power to bring about the change in the world; second, it must exert its power to bring about that change. It will help us understand and appreciate his view if we contrast two examples. Suppose a piece of zinc is dropped into some acid, and the acid dissolves the zinc. In this example, we might say that the acid has the power to bring about a certain change in the zinc. We might also be willing to say that in this instance the acid *exerted* its power to bring about this change, it *exerted* its power to dissolve the zinc. But can we reasonably say that the acid had the power not to bring about this change? Clearly we cannot. The acid has no power to refrain from dissolving the zinc. When the conditions are right, the acid must dissolve the zinc. So Reid's third condition is not satisfied. The acid, therefore, is not an agent-cause of the zinc's dissolving. Turning to our second example, suppose I invite you to write down the word "cause." Let's suppose that you have the power to do so and that you exert that power with the result that a change in the world occurs, and the world "cause" is written on a piece of paper. Here, when we look at Reid's third condition, we believe that it does obtain. We believe that you had the power to refrain from initiating your action of writing down the word "cause." The acid had no power to refrain from dissolving the zinc, but you had the power not to bring about your action of writing down the word "cause." If these things are so, then in this instance you are a true agent-cause of a certain change in the world, for you had the power to bring about that change, you exerted that power by acting, and finally, you had the power not to bring about that change.

There is one very important point to note concerning Reid's idea of agent causation. We sometimes speak of causing someone to cause something else. But if we fully understand Reid's notion of agent causation we can see, I think, that no event or agent can cause someone to agent-cause some change. And this, again, is because of Reid's third condition of agent causation, the condition that requires that you have the power to refrain from bringing about the change. Suppose an event occurs that causes you to cause something to happen—some boiling water spills on your hand, say, causing you to drop the pot of boiling water. Now if the spilling of the boiling water on your hand really does cause you to bring about your dropping the pot, if it causally necessitates you to cause your dropping of the pot, then given the spilling of the boiling water on your hand it wasn't in your power not to bring about your dropping the pot. But you are the agent-cause of some change only if it was in your power at the time not to cause that change. This being so, it is quite impossible that anything should ever cause you to agent-cause some change. Since having the power not to cause a change is required for you to be the agent-cause of some change, and since being caused to cause some change implies that you cannot refrain from causing that change, it follows that no one can be caused to agent-cause a change. If you are the agent-cause of some change, it follows that you were not caused to agent-cause that change.

Having taken a brief look at Reid's notion of agent causation, we can return to what I have been calling Reidian freedom. According to Reidian freedom, any action we perform as a result of our act of will to do that action is a free action, provided that we were the agent-cause of the act of will to perform that action. And since to agent-cause an act of will includes the power not to cause it, we can say that every act of will resulting in a *free* action is an act of will we had power to produce and power not to produce. As Reid says: "If, in any action, he had power to will what he did, or not to will it, in that action he is free."

Suppose someone wills to perform a certain action, say revealing a secret of great importance that he has been entrusted with. Since his act of will must have a cause, either it is caused by the agent himself—in which case he is the agent-cause of that act of will and his action is free—or something else causes his act of will and his action, although voluntary, is not free. In some cases, it will not be difficult to decide the matter. Suppose our person has been offered a small bribe and, as a result, reveals the important secret. Here, we would judge that the person does act freely, believing that the desire for the bribe is not sufficient of itself to cause the agent to will as he did. On the other hand, if our agent is placed on the rack and made to suffer intensely over a period of time and finally, after much pain, divulges the secret, we would all judge that the intense pain was such as to cause directly the volition to reveal the important secret. The volition was not agent-caused and the action of revealing the secret was not *free*. But these are the easy cases. Clearly, between these two extremes there is a continuum of cases in which we would find the judgment between agent-cause and other cause extraordinarily difficult to make with any assurance. To help us here, we need to note another important element in Reid's theory of human freedom.

Reid believes that freedom is a *power,* a power over the determinations of our will. Now power is something that can come in degrees—you may have more or less of it. Presumably, under torture on the rack, your power over your will may be reduced to zero and your freedom thereby destroyed. On the other hand, your desire for a small bribe is unlikely to diminish significantly your power not to will to reveal the secret. Between these two extremes the mounting strength of your desires and passions will make it increasingly difficult for you to refrain from willing to reveal the secret. But so long as their strength is not irresistible, if you do will to reveal it, you will be at least a *partial agent-cause* of your act of will, and, therefore, will act with a certain degree of freedom and a corresponding degree of responsibility. Of course, people may differ considerably in terms of the power they possess over their wills. So a desire of a given strength may overwhelm one person while only slightly diminishing another person's power over his will. Therefore, in order to determine whether a person acted freely and with what degree of freedom, we need to judge two things: we need to judge the degree of power over the will that the person possesses *apart* from the influence of his desires and passions; and we need to judge the strength of his desires and passions. Clearly these are matters about which at best only reasonable or probable judgments can be made.

Leibniz once remarked concerning a version of the free will doctrine: "What is asserted is impossible, but if it came to pass it would be harmful."[13] This remark nicely captures most of the objections to the view of Reid and other free will advocates. For these objections divide into those that argue that the view is impossible because it is internally inconsistent or inconsistent with some well-established principle of causality or explanation, and those that argue that the possession of free will would be harmful because the agent's actions would then be capricious, uninfluenced by motives, rewards or punishment. I want here to look at two different objections that fall into the first category. The first of these, and by far the most popular, is, I believe, a spurious objection. Since it is spurious, I will bury it in a footnote.[14] The second, however, is a very serious objection, revealing, I believe, a real difficulty in Reid's agent-cause account of freedom.

The second objection (the serious one), like the first, arrives at the absurd conclusion that any action requires an infinite series of antecedent events, each produced by the agent who produces the action. This absurd conclusion, I believe, does follow from Reid's view of agent-causation in conjunction with the principle that every event has a cause. I propose here to explain how this absurdity is embedded in Reid's theory and what can be done to remove it.

On Reid's theory, when an agent wills some action, the act of will is itself an event and, as such, requires a cause. If the act of will is free, its cause is not some event, it is the agent whose act of will it is. Being the casue of the act of will, the agent must satisfy Reid's three conditions of agent-causation. Thus the agent must have had the power to bring about the act of will as well as the power to refrain from bringing about the act of will, and she must have *exerted* her power to bring about the act of will. It is the last of these conditions that generates an infinite regress of events that an agent must cause if she is to cause her act of will. For what it tells us is that to produce the act of will the agent must *exert* her power to bring about the act of will. Now an exertion of power is itself an event. As such, it too must have a cause. On Reid's view the cause must again be the agent herself. But to have caused this exertion the agent must have had the power to bring it about and must have *exerted* that power. Each exertion of power is itself an event which the agent can cause only by having the power to cause it and by *exerting* that power. As Reid reminds us, "In order to the production of any effect, there must be in the cause, not only power, but the exertion of that power: for power that is not exerted produces no effect."[15] The result of this principle, however, is that in order to produce any act of will whatever, the agent must cause an infinite number of exertions. Reid's theory of agent-causation, when conjoined with the principle that every event has a cause, leads to the absurdity of an infinite regress of agent-produced exertions for every act of will the agent produces.

It is remarkable that Reid appears never to have seen this difficulty in his theory. Occasionally he joins the causal principle and his view of agent-causation into a single remark, with the result that the difficulty fairly leaps up from the page. For example, in discussing Leibniz's view that every action has a sufficient reason, Reid remarks: "If the meaning of the question be, was there a cause of the action? Undoubtedly there was: of every event there must be a cause, that had power sufficient to produce it, and that exerted that power for the purpose."[16] If exertions of power are events—and what else could they be?—the infinite regress of exertions produced by the agent who performs any action is abundantly apparent in this remark. Perhaps Reid didn't see the problem because he always had in mind the basic distinction between the *effects* agents produce by their actions and the *actions* of the agents by which they produce those effects. With this distinction in mind, it is natural to suppose that *everything* an agent causes (the effects) she causes not simply by virtue of having a certain power but by acting, by exerting that power. Put this way, Reid's notion that an agent can cause something only by acting, by *exerting* her power, is intuitively attractive—so attractive, perhaps, that one may be blind to the difficulty that appears when actions themselves are held to be among the things that an agent causes.

One solution to the difficulty requires that we view some acts of the agent as caused by the agent, but not caused by some *exertion* of the agent's power to produce them. Perhaps we should think of the act of will as in some way a special sort of action, a *basic act*. A basic act of an agent is one that she causes but not by any exertion of power or any other act. Short of some such view, it seems that we must either accept the absurdity of the infinite regress, view some act of the agent as itself uncaused (thus abandoning the causal principle), or take the view that an act of will is not itself an event and, therefore, does not fall under the causal principle. This last move, however, would leave the act of will as a surd in Reid's theory and plainly conflicts with his stated position that acts of will are effects. "I consider the determination of the will as an effect."[17]

The solution I've proposed requires a significant change in Reid's view of agent-causation. Not every act of the agent can be produced by the agent only by the agent's *exerting* her power to produce it. Acts of will that are produced by the agent whose acts they are, we shall say, are such that the agent causes them but not by any other act or any exertion of the power she has to produce the acts of will. We thus can halt the regress of acts of exertions that is implied by the conjunction of the causal principle and Reid's analysis of what it is to be a cause "in the strict and proper sense." The price, of course, is a significant modification of Reid's account of agent-causation.

Can we afford this price? Many philosophers would agree with Jonathan Edwards in holding that it is simply impossible that the agent should *cause* his act of will without an *exertion* of his power to produce that act of will, an exertion that is *distinct* from the act of will that is produced.[18]

The answer to Edwards is that although some actions (moving one's arm, e.g.) can be caused by the agent only by the agent exerting his power to produce his action of moving his arm, other actions such as acts of will are produced directly by the agent and not by means of exertions that are distinct from the acts of will produced. To deny the possibility of the latter is simply to claim that ultimately only events can be causes of events—thus if there is no exertion of power by the agent (and no other event causes the volition), no act of will can be produced. But the whole idea of agent-causation is that agents are causes of events, that in addition to event-causes there are causes of a wholly different kind—agents. If we take the view that persons really are active, rather than passive, in the production of their acts, then the modification I've suggested is precisely what one might expect the theory of agency embraced by Reid ultimately to imply. For, on the one hand, it is Reid's view that events and circumstances and other agents do not cause the person to agent-cause his acts of will. If other agents or prior events cause the person to do something, then the person lacks power to refrain and, therefore, is not the agent-cause of those doings: he is in fact passive with respect to his actions. And, on the other hand, if the person is the agent-cause of some act of his then on pain of infinite regress there must be some exertion or act he brings about without engaging in some other exertion or act in order to bring it about. In short, once we fully grasp the idea of agent-causation we can see, I believe, that it implies that when an agent causes his action there is some event (an act of will, perhaps) that the agent causes without bringing about any other event as a means to producing it.[19]

### III. Reidian Freedom and Responsibility

We started with Johnson's remark that although all theory is against free will, all experience or practice is for it. Among the several arguments Reid advanced in favor of free will, his argument from our *practice* of holding persons morally responsible for their actions and decisions is undoubtedly the strongest. I believe that Reid's argument from the fact of moral responsibility to the existence of Reidian freedom merits careful examination. But I have no time here to do that. Instead, I want to sharpen our grasp of Reidian freedom by considering just what it implies with respect to the vexing question of whether the agent could have done or willed otherwise. For there are, I believe, good reasons to doubt the traditional claim that an agent is morally responsible for doing A only if she could have avoided doing A. And there appear to be good reasons to doubt the claim that an agent is morally responsible for doing A only if she could have refrained from willing to do A. Now if this should be so, then if Reidian freedom implies either of these claims, it will *not* be true that an agent is morally responsible only if she possesses Reidian freedom—Reid's strongest argument for Reidian freedom will stand refuted.

According to Locke, the agent freely does A only if she could have refrained from doing A had she so willed. Reid says that freedom must include power over the determinations of our will. Perhaps then, Reidian freedom is simply Lockean freedom with the addition of the power to will to do A and the power to will to refrain from doing A.[20] If so, I'm afraid that moral responsibility does not entail Reidian freedom. For moral responsibility does not entail Lockean freedom. One of Locke's examples is of a man who wills to stay in a room, not knowing that he is locked in. We may hold such a person responsible even though he would not have been able to avoid staying in the room had he willed not to stay in the room. For the agent who willingly does what he does, believing it to be in his power to do otherwise, must be distinguished from the person who stays in the room unwillingly because he is unable to leave. And if such a person is morally accountable for what he does, moral responsibility does not entail Reidian freedom *if* Reidian freedom is correctly understood as Lockean freedom with the addition of power over the will. But a careful look at Reid's account of a free action shows that it is a mistake so to understand Reidian freedom. What he says is this: "If, in any action, he had power to will what he did, or not to will it, in that action he is free." There is nothing in Reid's account to suggest that the agent must have had the power to do otherwise had he so willed. What Reid says is that if a person wills to perform some action and does so, then he performs that action freely provided he had the power not to will to do that action.

An interesting challenge to the idea that we are morally responsible for our action only if we could have refrained from willing it has been advanced by Frankfurt and Nozick.[21] To see the challenge, consider the following example. Suppose a mad scientist has gained access to your volitional capacity and not only can tell what act of will you are about to bring about but, worse yet, can send electrical currents into your brain that will cause a particular act of will to occur even though it is not the act of will that you would have brought about if left to your own devices. We will suppose that you are deliberating on a matter of great concern: killing Jones. Our mad scientist happens to be interested in Jones's going on to his reward, but he wants Jones to die by your hand. His complicated machinery tells him that you are about to conclude your deliberations by willing *not* to kill Jones. Quickly, he pushes the buttons sending certain currents into your brain with the result that the volition to kill Jones occurs in you and results, let us say, in your actually killing Jones. Clearly you are not here morally accountable for your act of will and subsequent action of killing Jones. Were matters left to you, you would have willed not to kill Jones and would not have killed him. Although on Reid's account of this case it would be true that you willed to kill Jones, it is also true that you were not the agent-cause of your act of will and are therefore not morally accountable for your willing and your action.

Our second case is similar to, but also crucially different from, the first case. The mad scientist is intent on seeing to it that Jones is killed by your hand. But rather than activate the machine to cause your act of will to kill Jones, he would prefer that you bring about that act of will and the subsequent action of killing Jones. This time, however, your deliberations result in your act of will to kill Jones. The mad scientist could and would have caused that act of will in you had you been going to will not to kill Jones. But no such action on his part was necessary. There is a process in place (the machine, etc.) that assures that you shall will to kill Jones. But the process is activated *only if* you are not going to initiate your act of will to kill Jones. Given the machine, it was not in your power to avoid willing to kill Jones. But this fact *played no role* in what actually led to your willing to kill Jones and the actual killing that resulted. In this case, we do wish to hold you morally responsible for your act of will and the resulting action. And this is so even though it was not in your power to prevent your willing to kill Jones and not in your power to refrain from killing Jones.

Frankfurt argues that the fact that there are circumstances that make it impossible for an agent to avoid performing a certain action diminishes or extinguishes moral accountability for the action only if those circumstances in some way *bring it about* that the agent performs the action in question. This is true in our first case, where the mad scientist pushes the buttons that send the current causing your volition to kill Jones. Here the circumstances that prevent you from *not* willing to kill Jones *bring about* your volition to kill Jones. But in the second case, the circumstances that make it impossible for you not to will to kill Jones *play no role* in bringing it about that you willed to kill Jones. As Frankfurt remarks: "For those circumstances, by hypothesis, actually had nothing to do with his having done what he did. He would have done precisely the same thing, . . . , even if they had not prevailed."[22] It is because these circumstances play no role in what the agent willed and did that the agent bears moral responsibility for his volition and act even though it was not in his power to refrain from doing what he did. I believe Frankfurt is right about this matter. What remains to be seen, however, is whether Reid's basic intuition of a necessary connection between moral accountability and power over the will is unable to accommodate the case in which the agent is morally accountable but cannot prevent willing to kill Jones.

The second mad scientist example shows that an agent may be morally accountable for an act of will to do A even though it is not in the agent's power not to will that action. This certainly *appears* to conflict with Reid's theory. But we need to recall here that what is *crucial* for Reid's view of moral accountability is that the person be the *agent-cause* of her volition to do A. His view is that the agent is morally accountable for her voluntary action only if she is the agent-cause of her volition to do A. Now we already have seen that she may be the agent-cause of her volition to do A and not have it in her power not to will that action. This is what we learned, in part, from our second mad scientist case. But here, I believe, we need to distinguish between

1. It was in the agent's power not to will doing A.

and

2. It was in the agent's power *not* to cause her volition to do A.

In our second mad scientist case, (1) is false. But (2) is not false. The agent does have the power not to cause her volition to do A. The mad scientist has so arranged matters that the machine automatically causes the volition to do A in our agent if, but only if, the agent is about not to will to do A. This being so, (1) is clearly false. The agent cannot prevent her willing to do A; for if she does not cause her willing to do A the machine will cause her act of will to do A. But it still may be up to the agent whether *she* shall be the cause of her volition to do A. This power, Reid would argue, depends on a number of factors: the will of God, the continued existence of the agent, the absence of prior internal events and circumstances determining the occurrence of the volition to do A, etc. It also depends on the mad scientist's decision to activate the machine *only if* the agent is about not to will to do A. The scientist can cause our agent to will to do A. He does this by causing that act of will in the agent.[23] But if he does so then the agent does not agent-cause her volition to do A. The real agent-cause is the scientist. So if the agent has the power to cause her volition to do A she also has the power *not to cause* that volition. If she does not cause the volition and the machine activates, she, nevertheless, wills to do A—but *she* is not the cause of that act of will. I propose, therefore, the following as representing Reid's basic intuition concerning the connection between moral accountability and power:

> (P) A person is morally accountable for his action A only if he causes the volition to do A and it was in his power not to cause his volition to do A.[24]

(I believe this principle expresses Reid's view of our moral accountability for volitions as well. Simply replace "action A" with "volition to do A.")

Principle P accords with our intuitions concerning both of the mad scientist's cases. In the first case, when the machinery causes the volition to kill Jones, we do not wish to hold the agent morally accountable for the volition and its causal products. After all, if left to himself he would have willed to refrain from killing Jones. In the second case, where the machinery is not activated, we do hold the agent responsible for the volition and the action of killing Jones. And this is just what principle P will support. For the agent caused his volition to kill Jones and had it in his power not to cause that volition. I suggest, therefore, that the Frankfurt–Nozick examples do not refute the thesis that moral responsibility for a voluntary action implies Reidian freedom with respect to that action.[25]

## Conclusion

Some philosophical questions eventually yield to fairly definitive answers, answers which succeeding generations of philosophers accept, thereby contributing to our sense of progress in the discipline. Other philosophical questions seem to defy progress in the sense of definitive answers that are commonly accepted. Progress regarding them consists largely in deeper understanding and clarity concerning the questions and their possible answers. These are the deep philosophical questions. My conviction is that the question of human freedom is of the latter sort. I know that by setting forth the two concepts of freedom that were at the center of the eighteenth century controversy over freedom and necessity, and by criticizing the one, Lockean freedom, and recommending the other, Reidian freedom, I have not contributed to philosophical progress in the first sense. I haven't given any definitive answer. And in these compatibilist days, I certainly haven't given any answer that would be commonly accepted in my own department, let alone the discipline. My hope is that I have made some of these issues clearer and more understandable and have thereby contributed to philosophical progress in the second sense, helping us to grasp more clearly the philosophical question of human freedom and its relation both to causality and to moral responsibility.

## Notes

1. Thus Thomas Reid remarks: "Power is not an object of any of our external senses, nor even an object of consciousness" (*Essays on the Active Powers of Man*, IV, ch. I, p. 512; references are to the 1983 printing by Georg Olms Verlag of *The Works of Thomas Reid DD*, 8th ed., edited by Sir William Hamilton [James Thin, 1895]).

2. I am grateful to the distinguished Johnson scholar, Donald Green, for pointing this out to me.

3. Don Locke in "Three Concepts of Free Action" *Proceedings of the Aristotelian Society* (suppl., 1975), p. 96. fails to see that John Locke distinguishes between a voluntary and a free act. Thus he wrongly interprets Locke as holding "that to act freely is to act as you want to: the man who wants to get out of a locked room does not remain there freely but, Locke insists, a man who wants to stay there, to speak to a friend, does stay freely, even if the door is locked."

4. *An Essay Concerning Human Understanding*, Peter H. Nidditch, ed. (Oxford: Clarendon Press, 1975), bk. II, section 33.

5. There is an objection by J. L. Austin that also should be considered, since it attacks a point that is assumed by the other objections. Locke and Collins, as we just saw, took the view that given the causes of your action A, you could not have done anything other than A. Yet this does not preclude it being true that you could have done something else if you had willed to do something else. For with a difference in the causes, we might expect a difference in our powers. Now this nice harmony of causal necessity and freedom of action presupposes that the "if" in statements of the form 'S could have done X if S had chosen or willed to do X' is an "if" of causal condition. And Austin had an apparently devastating argument to show that the "if" in 'S could have done X if S had chosen or willed to do X' is not the "if" of causal condition. (See "Ifs and Cans," *Proceedings of the British Academy* 42 (1956), pp. 107–32.) The argument is this: if we consider an "if" of causal condition, as in the statement "This zinc will dissolve if placed in that acid," we can note two points. First, it will follow that if this zinc does not dissolve then it has not been placed in that acid. Second, it will not follow simpliciter that this zinc will dissolve. Just the opposite holds, however, of statements of the form 'S could have done X if S had chosen or willed to do X.' First, it will not follow that if S could not have done X, then S has not chosen or willed to do X. And second, it will follow simpliciter that S could have done X. From these premises Austin concludes that the "if" in 'S could have done X if S had chosen or willed to do X' is not the "if" of causal condition. But all that really follows from these premises is that the "if" in 'S could have done X if S had chosen or willed to do X' does not present a condition of the *main clause*, 'S could have done X.' It may still be, for all Austin has shown, an "if" of causal condition of something else. What else? Clearly, as Kurt Baier has argued, it would have to be of S's doing X ("Could and Would," *Analysis* 13

[suppl., 1963], pp. 20–29). The "if" in 'S could have done X if S had chosen or willed to do X' is an "if" of causal condition of the doing of X by S. What statements of this form tell us is that a set of conditions necessary for S's doing X obtained at the time in question, and had S chosen or willed to do X there would then have been a set of conditions sufficient for S's doing X. On this account, 'S could have done X if S had chosen or willed to do X' implies the genuinely conditional statement form, 'S would have done X if S had chosen or willed to do X.' So Austin's argument fails to establish that Locke and Collins were wrong to suppose that the "if" in 'S could have done X if S had chosen or willed to do X' is an "if" of condition.

6. *Theodicy*, Austin Farrer, ed., and E. M. Huggard, trans. (LaSalle, IL: Open Court, 1985), para. 324.

7. These two objections, and others, are expressed by Reid, Clarke, and Edmund Law. Perhaps their most forceful presentation is contained in Clarke's stinging attack on Collin's work. See *Remarks upon a Book, entitled, A Philosophical Enquiry Concerning Human Liberty* (1717), in Samuel Clarke, *The Works* (1738), vol. 4. The 1738 edition has been reprinted by Garland Publishing, 1978.

8. See Kant's *Critique of Practical Reason*, Lewis W. Beck, trans. (Indianapolis: Bobbs-Merrill Co., 1956), p. 99. Also see W. James's "The Dilemma of Determinism," in *The Writings of William James*, John J. McDermott, ed. (Chicago: The University of Chicago Press, 1977), p. 590.

9. In his second account of free will, Leibniz insists that the act of will must be free in the sense of not being necessitated by the motives and circumstances that give rise to it. His often repeated dictum on this matter is that motives "incline without necessitating." This remark has the appearance of giving the free will advocate just what he wants, the power to have willed otherwise even though the motives and circumstances be unchanged. But Leibniz meant no such thing. The motive that inclines most determines the will and the action, just as the weight that is heaviest determines the movement of the balance. Motives and circumstances necessitate the act of will in the sense that it is logically or causally impossible that those motives and circumstances should obtain and the act of will not obtain. Leibniz's claim that they don't necessitate the act of will means only that the act of will *itself* is not thereby rendered an absolute or logical necessity. Since Spinoza, Hobbes, and Collins held that the act of will is itself absolutely necessary, Leibniz's point is well taken. But, as we noted, it does nothing to remove the causal necessity of the act of will.

10. *New Essays on Human Understanding*, P. Remnant and J. Bennett, trans. and ed. (Cambridge: Cambridge University Press, 1982), bk. II, ch. xxi, sect 8.

11. *Active Powers*, IV, ch. I, p. 599.

12. Letter to Dr. James Gregory, 1793, in Hamilton, *Works*, p. 87.

13. "Observations on the book concerning 'The Origin of Evil,'" in *Theodicy*, p. 406.

14. The spurious objection is that the doctrine of the freedom of the will implies that each act of will that is free is itself the result of a prior act of will, ad infinitum. According to the free will position, an action is free provided it is willed and the agent freely determined or brought about that act of will. But, so

the spurious objection goes, to determine freely an act of will is to will freely that act of will. So an act of will is freely determined only if it is freely chosen. But an agent freely chooses an act of will only if his choice of that act of will is itself freely determined by the agent, in which case the choice of the act of will is itself the result of a prior free choice by the agent. And so we are off to the races, each determination of the will by the agent being preceded by an infinite series of determinations of the will by the agent. This objection fails, however, because it supposes that what it is for the agent to determine his will (that is, bring it about that he wills X, rather than something else) is for the agent to *Will* that his will be determined in a certain manner. (See, for example, Jonathan Edwards, *Freedom of the Will*, Paul Ramsey, ed. [New Haven, CT: Yale University Press, 1957], p. 172). But it is very doubtful that any free will advocate held this view. Many free will advocates attributed to the agent a power of self-determination, a self-moving principle. But by this they meant only that when the volitional act is produced by the self-moving principle, it is produced by the agent himself and not by any other thing or agent. (See "Unpublished Letters of Thomas Reid to Lord Kames, 1762–1782," collected by Ian Simpson Ross, *Texan Studies in Literature and Language* 7 [1965], p. 51.) They did not mean that in causing his volition the agent first chose or willed to produce that volition. To attribute such a view to them is to misunderstand what they claimed. According to the free will advocates, the soul or mind determines the will but does not do so by choosing or willing that the mind will X, rather than some other act. This objection, therefore, fails.

   15. *Active Powers*, IV, ch. II, p. 603.
   16. Ibid., ch. IX, p. 625.
   17. Ibid., ch. I, p. 602.
   18. See Edwards, *Freedom of the Will*, pp. 175–76.
   19. The solution I present in the text requires a major modification of Reid's theory of agent causation: dropping the requirement that the agent must *exercise* his power to bring about an act of will if the agent is to *cause* that act of will. There is, however, a way of solving the problem of the infinite regress that leaves Reid's theory intact. The whole problem vanishes if we take the view that the *exercise* of the agent's power (in order to produce his volition) is not itself an *event*. Not being an event, we require no cause of it, thus preventing the regress from starting. Is there any basis for such a view? Perhaps so. First, we must note that on Reid's view an event is a *change* in a substance. (Actually, Reid also includes the coming into existence of a substance as an event.) The occurrence of a volition in the agent is an event. The agent causes that event by exercising his power to cause it. What then of the agent's *exercise of power?* Here we may turn to Aristotle and his view of a *self-mover*. A self-mover is distinguished from a moved-mover. The latter (for example, a stick moving a stone) has a capacity to bring about movement in something else (the stone), but the exercise of that capacity is itself a movement. The *exercise* of the moved-mover's capacity to bring about motion in another is, therefore, an event. But the agent who causes the stick to move must be an unmoved mover—the exercise of its capacity to cause movement in another is *not itself a movement*. Not being a movement, it is not a change in a substance and is, therefore, not an event. Thus Aristotle holds that a

*self-mover* has a part that is moved (undergoes a change) and a part that moves but is not itself in motion (does not undergo a change). The part that moves but is not itself in motion must, of course, *exercise* its capacity to produce motion in the part that is moved. But this *exercise* of the unmoved part's capacity to produce motion is not itself a change in the part that is not itself in motion (not itself a change in the part that is an unmoved mover; see Aristotle's *Physics*, bk. viii, sections 4 and 5). Following Aristotle, we might take Reid to hold that the exercise of the agent's power to produce the volition to do A is *not itself* a change in the agent, it is not a change the agent undergoes. Now the causal principle, as Reid interprets it, holds that every event (every change in a substance) has a cause. The exertion of power to produce a *basic* change (e.g., an act of will), however, is not itself a change the substance undergoes. Therefore, it is not an event, and, therefore, does not require a cause. It would be an interesting and important addition to historical scholarship to see if Reid's theory can bear this interpretation.

20. For such an account of Reid, see Timothy Duggan's essay, "Active Power and the Liberty of Moral Agents," in Stephen F. Barker and Tom L. Beauchamp, eds. *Thomas Reid: Critical Interpretations* (Philadelphia: Philosophical Monographs, 1976), p. 106.

21. See Harry G. Frankfurt's "Alternate Possibilities and Moral Responsibility," *Journal of Philosophy* 66 (1969), pp. 829–39.

22. Frankfurt, "Responsibility," p. 837.

23. I take Reid to hold (rightly) that causing a volition to do A in an agent is to cause *the agent's willing to do A.* Thus, when an agent wills to do A we can raise the question of whether the cause of his so willing is the agent himself or something else.

24. Of course, we hold persons accountable for actions that they do not will. If I will to open my car door and do so, with the result that I knock you off your bicycle, I may be accountable for what I did through culpable ignorance— knocking you off your bicycle—even though I did not will to do it. But we may take Reid's account of freedom as what is entailed by those *voluntary* actions for which we are morally responsible.

25. Could not a supersophisticated scientist so arrange his machine that if the agent were about not to cause his volition to do A the machine would activate, causing him to *cause* his volition to do A? If so, and if our agent does cause his volition, with the result that the machine is not activated, isn't our agent responsible even though it is not in his power *not to cause* his volition? The Reidian reply to this is that it is *conceptually impossible* to cause an *agent* to cause (in Reid's sense) his volition. For an agent has active power to cause only if he has power not to cause. This last is a conceptual truth for Reid. "Power to produce any effect, implies power not to produce it" (*Active Powers,* IV, ch. I, p. 523).

# 10

# Agent Causation

TIMOTHY O'CONNOR

## I. Introduction

A natural way of characterizing our typical experience of making decisions and acting upon them—one that would, I think, gain widespread assent—goes something like this: When I decide, say, to go for a walk on a cool autumn evening, I am conscious of various factors at work (some consciously articulated, some not) motivating me either to do so or to do something else instead. And there are some courses of action which, while it is *conceivable* that I might choose to follow them, are such that they do not represent 'genuine' possibilities for me at that time, given my current mood, particular desires and beliefs, and, in some cases, long-standing intentions of a general sort. But within the framework of possibilities (and perhaps even relative likelihoods) that these present conative and cognitive factors set, it seems for all the world to be *up to me* to decide which particular action I will undertake. The decision I make is no mere vector sum of internal and external forces acting upon me during the process of deliberation (if, indeed, I deliberate at all). Rather, *I* bring it about—directly, you might say—in response to the various considerations: I am the source of my own activity, not merely in a relative sense as the most proximate and salient locus of an unbroken chain of causal transactions leading up to this event, but fundamentally, in a way not prefigured by what has gone before. Or, again, so it seems.

But a thesis that enjoys unusual consensus among contemporary philosophers is that this pretheoretic conception is not at all like the way things really are with respect to ordinary human activity. Indeed, most would claim that any attempt to theoretically articulate this common-sense picture of agency will inevitably be incoherent or, at best, irremediably mysterious. However, arguments on behalf of this thesis are not nearly as strong as the confidence with which it is generally held. This observation, together with an examination of the nature of such arguments, leads me to suspect that many philosophers are deeply in the grip of a certain broad picture of the physical world, one which has come to seem overwhelmingly obvious to them, despite the fact that it rests, so far as I can see, on certain empirical assumptions that are as yet unsubstantiated. I will address this intoxicating picture below, though I fear that my rhetorical skills are not up to the task of breaking the grip it has on some.

In what follows, I will contend that the commonsense view of ourselves as fundamental causal agents—for which some have used the term "unmoved movers" but which I think might more accurately be expressed as "not wholly moved movers"—is theoretically understandable, internally consistent, and consistent with what we have thus far come to know about the nature and workings of the natural world. In the section that follows, I try to show how the concept of 'agent' causation can be understood as a distinct species (from 'event' causation) of the primitive idea, which I'll term "causal production," underlying realist or non-Humean conceptions of event causation. In Section III, I respond to a number of contemporary objections to the theory of agent causation. Sections IV and V are devoted to showing that the theory is compatible with ordinary reasons explanations of action, which then places me in a position to respond, in the final section, to the contention that we could never know, in principle, whether the agency theory actually describes a significant portion of human activity.

Let me be clear from the outset about two tasks that I do not propose to undertake here. First, I will in no way attempt to argue or adduce evidence for the claim that the theory described actually applies to human action. (I will, however, briefly suggest what sort of considerations could count as evidence in favor of its applicability.) Nor will I attempt to address the epistemological question of whether it is reasonable to suppose, in the absence of strong, directly confirming evidence, that the agency theory gives a correct schematic account of (a significant portion of) human activity, though I am inclined to answer this in the affirmative. What follows is strictly an essay in "descriptive metaphysics," charting the internal relationship among concepts in what I believe to be part of the commonsense picture of the world.

## II. *Event Causation and Agent Causation*

I begin with a strong, highly controversial assumption about the general concept of causality. This assumption is that the core element of the concept is a *primitive* notion of the 'production' or 'bringing about' of an effect. This entails the negative thesis that a satisfactory reductive analysis of causality along Humean lines (in any of its versions) cannot be given. It should be readily apparent that if, contrary to this anti-Humean assumption, a satisfactory reductive analysis of causality *can* be given, the agency theorists's project of defending a variant species of causality immediately collapses into incoherence. For such reductive analyses are either committed to a general connection between certain *types* of causes and effects or equate causation with a form of counterfactual dependence. Neither approach is consistent with the agency theorist's claim that a causal relation can obtain between an agent and some event internal to himself, since his understanding of this is such as not to imply that the sort of event effected on that occasion will or would always (or generally) be produced given relevantly similar internal and external circumstances.

Acceptance of this assumption naturally (though not inevitably) points one in the direction of some sort of 'necessitarian' account of event causation. It is debatable, of course, whether the necessity in question is to be identified with broadly logical (or metaphysical) necessity or is rather to be thought of as a special, contingent form. Though the accounts I rely on in sketching a broadly necessitarian view take the former route, all that I want to assume here is that there is some form or other of objective necessity attaching to event-causal relations, as it is quite compatible with my purposes that this be held to be a primitive, contingent variety.[1] (Let me forestall confusion by emphasizing at the outset that, in drawing upon the necessitarian view of *event* causation in order to explicate the notion of agent causation, I am not suggesting that there is anything analogous to a necessary connection between prior circumstances and agent-caused events. Indeed, I will argue below that this is impossible. Rather, as will become clear shortly, the sole aspect of the necessitarian view that I carry over to agent causation is the necessary connection between an object's instantiating a certain set of properties and its possession of a causal power or powers. The two sorts of causation differ sharply, however, in terms of the manner in which causal powers are exercised: of necessity, when the object is placed in the appropriate circumstances, for event causation; under the voluntary, unnecessitated control of the agent, for agent causation.)

A recent elucidation of a necessitarian approach to causality is found in Harré and Madden (1975).[2] The central notion in their theory is that of the "powerful particular." When placed in the appropriate circumstances, an object manifests its inherent causal powers in observable effects. The particular powers had by a given object have their basis in its underlying nature—its chemical, physical, or genetic constitution and structure. Events figure in the causal relation in virtue of "stimulat[ing] a suitable generative mechanism to action, or [clearing away] impediments to the activity of a powerful particular already in a state of readiness to act." (p. 5) An example of the first sort of causal event is the detonation of a stick of dynamite. The other sort—the removal of an impediment to action—is exemplified by the removal of the air from an underwater cylinder, thereby enabling the body of water to exercise its power to crush the object. Certain effects are 'characteristic' of objects in the appropriate circumstances in a strong sense—"given the specification of the causal powers of the things and substances of the world, the denial of statements describing these effects of those powers, when the environment allows them to be exercised, would be inconsistent with the nature of those things" (p. 5). "While natures are preserved, the world must go on in its usual way," although "[n]ecessity might, and probably, does, hold in some cases only between the productive circumstances and a certain distribution of possible outcomes or productions" (p. 153).

Now it is natural to link the causal powers an object possesses at a given time directly to its properties. Shoemaker (1984)[3] provides a helpful explication of this idea. First we are told that the possession of a causal power by an object is to be thought of as its being the case that "its presence in circumstances of a particular sort will [of necessity] have certain effects" (p. 211). Properties figure into the picture in the following way:

> Just as powers can be thought of as functions from circumstances to causal effects, so the properties on which powers depend can be thought of as functions from properties to powers (or, better, as functions from sets of properties to sets of powers). One might even say that properties are second-order powers; they are powers to produce first-order powers (powers to produce certain sorts of events) if combined with certain other properties. (P. 212)

This implies that the relationship between an object's properties and its causal powers is a logically necessary one: "what makes a property the property it is, what determines its identity, is its potential for contributing to the causal powers of the things that have it" (p. 212).

If one wishes to hold, by contrast, that causal necessity is logically contingent, then one may say that properties are contingently associated with such functions from properties to powers, rather than being identified with (or logically connected to) them. And another possible wrinkle on the broad position, as Shoemaker notes, is to allow that

> the [causal] laws . . . may be statistical, the powers to which the properties contribute, may, accordingly, be statistical tendencies or propensities, and the causation may be nonnecessitating. (P. 232)

With this thumbnail sketch of a standard necessitarian account of event causation before us, I now turn to the central task of showing how the notion of agent causation may be seen as a distinct species or embodiment of the basic, primitive notion of causal production. The core idea is quite simple: First of all, according to my preferred understanding of the agency theory, wherever the agent-causal relation obtains, the agent bears a *property* or set of properties that is volition-enabling (i.e., in virtue of this property, the agent has a type of causal power which, in accordance with traditions, we may term "active power"). In this way, then, claims of the form "agent A caused event e" also satisfy a weak version of Davidson's Humean dictum that "causal statements are implicitly general": such assertions may be thought to imply that a similarly situated agent (i.e., such that the relevant internal and external properties are instantiated) will always *have it directly within his power to* cause an event of the e-type.

Thus, the agency theory (as I interpret it) affirms the completely general claim (i.e., one applicable to both of the basic sorts of causation) that objects have causal powers in virtue of their properties, so that objects sharing the same properties share the same causal capacities, but it denies that all such causal powers may be thought of as (or as being intimately associated with) simple "functions from circumstances to effects" (as Shoemaker puts it). For it maintains that some properties contribute to the causal powers of the objects that bear them in a very different way from the *event*-causal paradigm, in which *an object's possession of property P in circumstance C* necessitates or makes probable a certain effect. On this alternative picture, a property of the right sort can (in conjunction with appropriate circumstances) *make possible* the direct, purposive bringing about of an effect *by the agent* who bears it.

Such a property thus plays a different functional role in the associated causal process. It gives rise to a fundamentally different type of causal power—one that in suitable circumstances is exercised at will by the agent, rather than of necessity, as with objects that are not partly self-determining agents.

To repeat, then, the fundamental tenet of the agency theory may be taken to be the claim that there are two basic *sorts* of (causal) properties, one of which applies uniquely to intelligent, purposive agents.[4] The thesis that there are two fundamental sorts of causation is a consequence of the thesis concerning types of properties.

Now some may be willing to grant the basic internal coherence of this alternative paradigm, but will maintain that special assumptions would have to be made concerning the nature of the agent in whom such a property were instantiated, assumptions that are not plausible. The most common thought here is that it presuppose some form of substance dualism.

Let us consider, therefore, the compatibility of the agency theory with the view that the only substances to be found in the natural world are material substances. (I intend this to be noncommital on the question of whether certain material substances, such as living human brains, can have irreducibly mental [i.e., nonphysical] *properties*.) A human agent, in particular, is a wholly biological organism, whose macroproperties are either constituted by or dependent on the properties of certain elementary physical particles, organized into complex subsystems at a number of levels. Now some philosophers, it seems, are convinced that this basic picture inexorably leads to the following:

> Since all of the surface features of the world are entirely caused by and realized in systems of microelements, the behavior of microelements is sufficient to determine everything that happens. Such a 'bottom up' picture of the world allows for top-down causation (our minds, for example, can affect our bodies). But top-down causation only works because the top level is already caused by and realized in the bottom levels.[5]

But why does the author (John Searle) consider it an assured result that this bottom up picture is applicable to everything that happens in nature? Certain passages in the text from which this quotation is taken seem to suggest that it simply *follows* from the view that nature consists of material substances built up out of elementary particles, while others may be read as claiming that there are strongly confirming *empirical* grounds.

Surely the former reason is without merit. How can we deduce a priori that the organization of matter into certain highly complex systems will never result in novel *emergent* properties—either properties that themselves exert (in certain circumstances) an irreducibly "downward" form of causal influence, or ones that enable the objects that bear them to do so "at will"? Thomas Reid saw this point clearly. Although he was a substance dualist who thought that no purely material substances are capable of thought, he considered the implications for material agency if he were mistaken in this assumption:

> [But if matter] require only a certain configuration to make it think rationally, it will be impossible to show any good reason why the same

configuration may not make it act rationally and freely. . . . Those . . . who reason justly from this system of materialism, will easily perceive, that the doctrine of necessity[6] is so far from being a direct inference, that it can receive no support from it.[7]

Unfortunately, I haven't the space here to explore at any length the concept of an emergent property on which I'm relying. Suffice it to say that an emergent property is a macroproperty that is generated by the properties of an object's microstructure, but whose role in the causal processes involving that object are not reducible to those of the micro-properties.[8] I'm inclined to think that any tendency to suppose that the emergence of macrodeterminative properties in material substances is strictly inconceivable must be diagnosed as an instance of the withering effect on one's imagination that results from long-standing captivation by a certain picture of the world.

So whether there are any emergent properties of matter is an empiri-cal question to be decided ultimately on the basis of our success in identifying macrolevel properties of complex systems with relational complexes of microlevel properties. Now the agency theorist, as we have seen,[9] is committed (on the assumption of a substance monism) to the emergence of a very different *sort* of property altogether. Instead of pro-ducing certain effects in the appropriate circumstances itself, of necessity, such a property enables the *particular* that possesses it (within a certain range of circumstances) to freely and directly bring about (or not bring about) any of a range of effects. (The number of alternatives genuinely open to an agent will doubtless vary from case to case.) This further commitment leaves the theory's proponent open to a special sort of objection, not applicable to emergentist claims generally: given the unique nature of the *sort* of property the theory postulates, it is unclear whether it is really conceivable that such a property could *emerge* from other natural properties. It will be claimed that only a very different sort of *substance* from material substances, such as is posited by Cartesian dualism, could possess such a property. (It is noteworthy that many philosophers who discuss the agency theory seems to simply *assume* that its adherents are dualists.[10] But given that there is nothing inconsistent about the emergence of an "ordinary" causal property, having the poten-tial for exercising an irreducible causal influence on the environments in which it is instantiated, it is hard to see just why there could not be a sort of emergent property whose novelty consists in its capacity to enable its possessor directly to effect changes at will (within a narrowly limited range, and in appropriate circumstances). And if such a possibility claim is difficult to evaluate on a purely abstract level, it is perhaps more plausible when considered in relation to entities such as ourselves, con-scious, intelligent agents, capable of representing diverse, sophisticated

plans of action for possible implementation and having appetitive attitudes that are efficacious in bringing about a desired alternative.

The likely reply to this, of course, is that the incoherency of such a
view cannot be demonstrated only because we have been given so very
"thin" a model to go on. Here, too, I believe, it must be admitted that
there is some truth to this charge. Taking the agency theory seriously
within a basically materialist framework brings forth a whole host of
theoretical problems and issues such as the following:[11] When does a
physical system qualify as an "agent"? What structural transformations
in the human nervous system would result in long-standing (or perma-
nent) loss of the agent-causal capacity generally? Precisely to what extent is an ordinary human's behavior directly regulated by the agent
himself, and to what extent is it controlled by microdeterministic processes? (Put more generally, how do event- and agent-causal processes
interact?) These, however, are obviously empirical matters, requiring
extensive advancements within neurobiological science (and advancements favorable, of course, to the agency theorist's commitment to a
significant measure of indeterminacy in human behavior). The answers
to such questions will not be shown by philosophical work in action
theory.

## III. Some Contemporary Objections to the Agency Theory

However, we have yet to examine a few other challenges to the tenabil-
ity of the agency theory that have been raised in the literature, challenges that clearly are within the province of the philosophical theorist.

Donald Davidson has famously contended that the agency theorist
faces an inescapable dilemma, once the question is posed, How well
does the idea of agent causality account for the relation between an
agent and his action?[12] The dilemma that Davidson sees may be expressed thus: either the causing by an agent of a primitive action[13] is a
further event, distinct from the primitive action, or it is not.

Suppose first that the agent-causing is a further event. If so, then it is
either an action or it is not. If it is an action, then the action we began
with was not, contrary to the assumption, primitive. If it is not an action,
then we have the absurdity of a causing that is not a doing. Therefore, it
seems that we should not say that an agent's causing a primitive action
is an event distinct from the action.

Suppose, then, that we grasp the second horn of the original dilemma
and maintain that the agent's causing his action does not consist of some
further event distinct from his primitive action. Davidson replies:

> [T]hen what more have we said when we say the agent caused the
> action than when we say he was the agent of the action? The concept

of *cause* seems to play no role. . . . What distinguishes agent causation
from ordinary causation is that no expansion into a tale of two events is
possible, and no law lurks. By the same token, nothing is explained.
There seems no good reason, therefore, for using such expressions as
'cause', 'bring about', 'make the case' to illuminate the relation between an agent and his act. (P. 52–53)

Now there are several highly dubious assumptions being made in
this passage, but the first response to be made to the putative dilemma is
to deny Davidson's assumption that the agency theory maintains that
there is an irreducible causal relation between the agent and his (free)
*action*. For from this perspective, what is most intimately my activity is
the causal *initiation* of my behavior, the causal production of determinate (immediately executive) intentions or volitions. Thus, Bishop
writes that on the agency theory,

> [T]he action *is* the existent relation, and may not be collapsed into one
> of its terms. The object of the agent-causal relation, then, is not the
> action itself but certain events or sequences of events which, in virtue
> of their standing in this relation, count as *intrinsic* to the agent's inten-
> tional action.[14]

In the case of an observable bodily movement such as waving my
hand, my action consists of the causal relation I bear to the coming-to-
be of the state of determinate intention to wave my hand, plus the
sequence of events that flow from that decision.[15] How shall we think of
the primitive mental action at the core of this larger action? Does it
simply consist, as Bishop suggests, of an existent (agent-causal) relation
alone? I think that this suggestion is ill conceived, for the reason that the
*production* of the internal event is not to be identified with the instantiated relation alone, somehow isolatable from its relata, but rather it is
the complex event or state of affairs, *S's production of e*.

Now this, of course, is somewhat at odds with the conventional
analysis of actions as consisting of the events or sequences of events
*produced by* an appropriate causal factor. There is good reason to think
the conventional analysis is mistaken, however. Consider first the orthodox account of the production of action, viz., the causal theory. On this
account, actions are causally produced (at least in part) by desires and
beliefs. Such theorists generally claim that there is a sense in which an
action may be thought of as produced by its agent on the causal
theory—*I* am the source of my decision to wave my hand in virtue of the
fact that my desire to raise my hand (together with certain beliefs) is
causally efficacious in bringing that decision about. Thinking of the
matter in this way, the event that is my decision, then, is (at least partially) constitutive of an action of mine not solely in virtue of its intrinsic
features, but also in virtue of the fact that it is causally related to me in a

certain way. But this is problematic. Is not the production of internal mental events and/or bodily movements an essential part of my activity? If so, then we cannot avoid the conclusion that my primitive action (on the causal account) is to be identified with *DB's causing e,* where 'DB' is the causally efficacious desire-belief complex.[16]

It will be objected by many that it is simply a mistake to think of the relevant beliefs and desires as components of the action. But whatever unnaturalness this claim appears to possess is to be attributed to the failure of the causal theory to reflect the commonsense view of the etiology of ordinary behavior. If we *are* inclined to adopt this picture of the springs of action, then since I am active only in virtue of the productivity of properties that constitute my mental state, my being in that state is inseparable from my core activity—that of producing, e.g., a bodily movement.

I will hazard the suggestion that the fact that most action theorists do not individuate actions in this way is in part a result (in some cases indirect) of the influence of Hume's views on causation. Hume and his followers conceive a sequence of events over time as composed of discrete and essentially unconnected elements, "time slices." We may, as a wholly contingent matter of fact, discern various patterns of regularity in the sequences we observe over time, but there are no existent causal relations in nature between events. But if we repudiate this reductionist picture of causality, and allow that causes truly *produce* their effects, then, as I've just argued, the causal theorist ought to allow that actions are partly constituted by the causal relations that (he maintains) exist between an agent's reasons and resulting behavior.

To return, though, to the task of responding to the dilemma that Davidson attempts to construct, we thus begin by noting that on the agency theory, rather than there being a causal relation between agent and action, the relational complex *constitutes* the action. Suppose, however, that Davidson were to reformulate his dilemma in terms of the relation between the agent and the event constituents of a primitive (or core) action.[17] The first horn of the dilemma (which assumes that the agent's causing some event is distinct from his action) will then clearly be idle. But what of the second horn? If we say that the agent's causal activity is identical to his action, is it true, as Davidson asserts, that the concept of cause plays no role in what we assert? That nothing is explained, since we are not connecting the event-constituents of the action to a law?

As far as I can see, Davidson offers absolutely no reason to think we should say this. And, prima facie, such an assertion does seem at least partly explanatory: for if one points to that which causally produced an event, how could one have nonetheless failed to so much as contribute to an explanation of its occurrence? To be sure, such an explanation is far from *complete*. We have yet to indicate, for example, with what reasons the agent acted as he did. And we have said nothing in specific terms of the sort of nature possessed by the agent, in virtue of which he was capable of bringing about such effects. But one has surely been given *something* by way of explanation. It seems that Davidson's understanding of the matter here has been clouded by the deleterious effects of Hume, to the effect that explanation of events can only come about through subsumption under a law. But this dogma is essentially tied to the Humean framework, and I take it that there are good reasons for rejecting this.[18] We may safely conclude, therefore, that Davidson's supposed dilemma poses no serious threat to the agency theory.

Another well-known attack on the coherence of the agency theory is made by C. D. Broad (1952).[19] Broad writes:

> I see no *prima facie* objection to there being events that are not completely determined. But, in so far as an event *is* determined, an essential factor in its total cause must be other *events*. How can an event possibly be determined to happen at a certain date if its total cause contained no factor to which the notion of date has any application? And how can the notion of date have any application to anything that is not an event? (P. 215)

It is far from clear to me just what the difficulty is that Broad takes himself to be pointing out here. It is true that persisting objects such as human agents are not, in the ordinary sense, 'datable' entities, although we may specify the temporal interval through which they exist. But we may, of course, quite unproblematically speak of certain facts being true of an agent at one time that do not hold of him at another. And such is the claim of the agency theorist. Consider, for example, my deliberation a while ago concerning whether to continue working on this paper for another hour or to stop and do something else. After a brief moment of consideration, I formed the intention (at time $t$, say) to continue working. According to the agency theory, we may suppose that at $t$ I possessed the power to choose to continue working or to choose to stop, where this is understood as the capacity to cause either of these mental occurrences. And, in fact, that capacity was exercised at $t$ in a particular way (in choosing to continue working), allowing us to say truthfully that Tim at time $t$ causally determined his own choice to continue working. But we needn't, in order to make sense of this, analyze it as the claim (of dubious intelligibility) that a 'datable entity', Tim-at-$t$, was the occurrent cause of the decision to continue working.

But, you might say, given the fact that your producing your decision occurs at a specific time (and how could it be otherwise?), doesn't it seem appropriate to identify the particular *mental state* you were in at that time as what was ultimately responsible for that decision (though perhaps in a causally indeterministic fashion, if you like)? What is it about the nature of the causal process as you envision it that prevents us from properly saying this?

My answer is that the alternative wrongly implies that it is whatever is *distinctive* about the state that the agent was in at the time of his action—distinguishing it from his state just prior to that moment, say—that triggers the action. But while there are various *necessary* conditions on an agent's producing a decision to X, these conditions may obtain over a protracted period of time, and so cannot be thought to be themselves causally efficacious (with respect to the decision).

Perhaps underlying Broad's remarks, though, is the thought (made explicit in Ginet, *On Action*) that the proposition that I caused the decision at *t* cannot explain why I decided *when* I did, nor can it explain *why* I decided as I did. Now this is certainly true, and, we may add, it is further true that analogous questions are answered when we give an event-causal explanation of an event (setting aside complications raised by indeterministic event-causal processes). For causal properties are (ordinarily) such as to immediately give rise to their characteristic effects in the right circumstances, and the effects to which they give rise are *characteristic*, i.e., it is impossible (either physically or metaphysically) that any *other* effect should come about in just those circumstances.

But, as I have been at pains to emphasize, agent-causes operate in a different fashion, and corresponding to this is a difference in the way they are involved in the *explanation* of the effects they produce.[20] An agent-cause does not produce a certain effect by virtue of its very nature, as does an event-cause, but does so at will in the light of considerations accessible to the agent at that time. And so a full explanation of why an agent-caused event occurred will include, among other things, an account of the reasons upon which the agent acted. (The nature of such reasons-explanations, and their degree of explanatory power vis-à-vis fully event-causal explanations, will be considered in the following two sections.)

Yet another instance of an objection that attempts to insist that the agency theory meet standard requirements within an event-causal paradigm, which, upon reflection, are seen to be simply inappropriate in the context of agent-causality, is noted by the agency theorist Chisholm:

> Our account presupposes that there are certain events which men, or agents, cause to happen. Suppose, then, that on a certain occasion a man does cause a certain event e to happen. What, now, of that event—the event which is his thus causing e to happen? We have assumed that there is no sufficient condition for his causing e to happen. Shall we say it was not caused by anything? If we say this, then we cannot hold *him* responsible for his causing e to happen.[21]

I believe that the proper line of response here begins with the observation that the very idea of there being sufficient causal conditions for an agent-causal event is unintelligible. One agency theorist who has endorsed the opposing view is Richard Taylor:

> [T]here is nothing in the concept of agency [where this involves an irreducible causal relation between agent and act], as such, to entail that any events must be causally undetermined, and in that sense "free," in order for some of them to be the acts of agents. Indeed, it might well be that everything that ever happens, happens under conditions which are such that nothing else could happen, and hence that in the case of every act that any agent ever performs there are conditions that are causally sufficient for his doing just what he does. This is the claim of determinism, but it does not by itself require us to deny that there are agents who sometimes initiate their own acts. What is entailed by this concept of agency, according to which men are the initiators of their own acts, is that for anything to count as an act there must be an essential reference to an agent as the cause of that act, whether he is, in the usual sense, caused to perform it or not.[22]

We may say that I am free and responsible for some behavior of mine, then, just in case I originate or cause it and am not determined to do so. This would be allowed by Reid and other agency theorists who followed him. Taylor departs from the standard view of agency theorists only in suggesting that the first of these conditons may obtain in the absence of the second. He suggests as a simple, likely case of this sort my grasping my seat tightly while on a ski lift (where my timidity and fright are causally sufficient in the circumstances for my doing so). He notes that it would be odd to say that this is not something I *did* (compare my concurrent perspiration), and concludes from such examples that it is perfectly intelligible that I should be determined to (agent) cause my own actions. (In Reid's terminology, one may be unfree in the exercise of one's active power.)

Now it is one thing to argue in this way: it is perfectly intelligible that one should be determined on occasion to act as one does; on this theory, one is always the agent cause of one's acts; hence, this theory is constrained to allow for the possibility that an agent is determined to cause his own action. But it is quite another directly to defend the idea of causally determined agent causation against the charge of incoherence. Just how are we to understand the notion of there being a sufficient causal condition for an exercise of active power?

Unfortunately, Taylor himself never tries to spell this out, and he is apparently unaware of the difficulty one faces in trying to do so coherently. Note that what we are to envisage is not that there are sufficient causal conditions for event e independently of my causing it, but rather conditions sufficient precisely for the event that is *my causing e* (and only *thereby* for *e*). (This event is constituted by the holding of a causal relation between myself and the subevent *e*). It is *this* sort of event for which, Taylor claims, there may be sufficient causal conditions.

For the purpose of evaluating this claim, it will be useful to consider first the case of event causation. The cause of *A's causation of B* is none other than the cause of A itself.[23] What, then, of *S's causation of e*? There appears to be no way of getting a grip on the notion of an event of *this* sort's having a sufficient, efficient cause. Because of its peculiar causal structure, there is no event at its front end, so to speak, but only an enduring agent. And there cannot be an immediate, efficient cause of a causal relation (i.e., independently of the causation of its front end relatum). In general, that which is causally produced in the first instance is always an event or state having a causally *simple* structure: an object O's exemplifying *intrinsic* properties $p_1, p_2, \ldots$ at time $t_0$. Causally complex events can also be caused, of course, but only in a derivative way: where they have the form *event X's causing event Y*, whatever causes event X is a cause *thereby* of *X's causing Y*. In the special case of an *agent's* causing an event internal to his action, however, there is no causally simple component event forming its initial segment, such that one might cause the complex event (*S's causing e*) in virtue of causing *it*. Therefore, it is problematic to suppose that there could *be* sufficient causal conditions for an agent-causal event.

If I am right in claiming that it is strictly impossible for there to be sufficient causal conditions for an agent-causal event, we may readily dispose of the objection introduced by Chisholm that if *my causing e* itself has no cause, then I cannot be responsible for it. For it would appear from the above that no answer *could* be given to the question of what was the cause of a given agent-causal event, and hence that the question is ill framed, resulting from a failure to understand the peculiar nature of such an event. In this type of complex event, there is no first subevent bearing a causal relation to a second. So it seems that the libertarian may acknowledge without embarassment that events of *this* type are uncaused.[24]

To support the point I am trying to make here, I want to emphasize the contrast between the scenarios envisaged by the agency theorist and those envisaged by the simple indeterminist. The simple indeterminist claims that a (causally) simple mental event of the proper sort (e.g., a volition), if causally undetermined, is intrinsically such as to be under the control of the agent who is its subject.[25] I have tried elsewhere to give reasons for supposing that the claim is in fact false.[26] Agent-control—the type of immediate control we take ourselves to have over our own actions—is clearly causal in nature.

But now consider an instance of *S's causing e*. This event is intrinsically a doing, owing to its internal causal structure (i.e., an agent's

bearing a direct causal relation to another event). Its very nature precludes the possibility of there being a sufficient causal condition for it (as
I argued earlier), being an event that is the agent's causing the event
internal to it (*e*). Now the event *e* is itself clearly under the control of the
agent, since *he* caused it (directly). But would it not, then, be perfectly
absurd to raise a doubt concerning whether the agent controlled *his
causing e?* Indeed, it seems to me that the question of whether the agent
has control over this event is ill framed—*it* is simply an instance of an
agent's *exercising* direct control over another event.

Chisholm, by contrast, would have the agency theorist maintain
that the agent himself causes his agent-causing. It seems that the following line of thought underlies Chisholm's commitment to this perplexing
suggestion:

(1) An agent S bears responsibility for an event x only if S has
causally contributed to the occurrence of x.
(2) Any instance of an agent's causing an event is itself an event.
(3) Agents are responsible for their agent-causings.
∴ (4) Agents cause the events which are their agent-causings.

And, of course, if the agent is responsible for an instance of agent-
causing by causing *it*, then we must say that he is responsible for this
further event of his causing his agent-causing. And thus in this way we
are led (with Chisholm) to fabricate an infinity of simultaneous events.
But while statement (1) seems quite evident when we focus on events
that either lack internal causal structure or are constituted by two or
more such simple events causally connected to one another, if one allows for the possibility of events that simply are the direct causal activity
of agents, then one ought not to suppose that (1) holds with unrestricted
generality.

## IV. Two Objections to Indeterministic Reasons Explanation

I have yet to address an issue that critically bears on the viability of the
agency theorist's general project of providing an adequate theoretical
framework for understanding how free agency operates. We explain
the actions of ourselves and others around us by citing or ascribing
reasons for which the action was performed. How do reasons figure
into the performance of actions as the agency theorist conceives them?
It is astonishing to me to see how often critics of the agency theory
make the mistaken assumption that the agency theory is either incompatible with reasons-based accounts of action or is advanced as an
independent alternative to such accounts. This leads naturally enough
to the conclusion that it is simply confused[27] or explanatorily superflu-
ous.[28] In this section and in the one that follows, I try to show how

agent causality plays a necessary role in reasons explanations, once we abandon the causal theory's model of reasons as influencing actions by causally producing them.

I begin by considering two recent objections of a highly general character against the possibility of a satisfactory account of noncausal reasons explanations. The first of these is Galen Strawson's claim that the indeterminist's conception of of an agent as acting in view of prior motives while not being determined by them ineluctably leads to a vicious regress. For, he claims, we can conceive of an agent sitting in detached judgment on the matter of whether to act in accordance with motive X or motive Y only if he has some *further* desires or principles of choice that decisively inclines him in one of these directions. But if this is the case, then the agent is self-determining in making his choice only if he is somehow responsible for the presence of those further factors, which requires his having chosen to be that way. . . .[29]

Strawson is not alone in holding that the libertarian is unwittingly committed to this (problematic) picture. The same suggestion was colorfully made by Leibniz:

> One will have it that the will alone is active and supreme, and one is wont to imagine it to be like a queen seated on her throne, whose minister of state is the understanding, while the passions are her courtiers or favourite ladies, who by their influence often prevail over the counsel of her ministers. One will have it that the understanding speaks only at this queen's order; that she can vacillate between the arguments of the ministers and the suggestions of the favourites, even rejecting both, making them keep silence or speak, and giving them audience as it seems good to her. But it is a personification or mythology somewhat ill-conceived.[30]

But while we may wholeheartedly agree with Leibniz's assessment of this conception as "somewhat ill-conceived," we should also reject the suggestion that the libertarian *must* be assuming (if the account is to avoid positing fortuitous, irrational choices) that the agent has further, second-order reasons that explain why he chose to act in accordance with one set of motives rather than another. Consider a scenario in which an agent is deliberating between two courses of action X and Y, each of which has considerations in its favor. (I will refer to these sets of considerations as {X} and {Y}, respectively.) Suppose further that the agency theory is correct and the agent herself brings about the decision to take option X. The question, "Why did the agent perform that action?", is meaningfully answered by citing {X}, even though these reasons did not produce the agent's decision, and she could have chosen differently in those very same circumstances. In citing {X}, we are explaining the motivating factors that were in view when the agent made a self-determining choice. It is not necessary to try to ascend to a level of second-order reasons (for acting on first-order reasons) in a desperate bid to render this conception of action intelligible.

Perhaps underlying Strawson's charge is the belief that an action would be irrational or at least arbitrary (in a pejorative sense of that term) if, at the time of acting, the agent did not believe that her reasons decisively favored the course of action chosen, that she had reasons for performing X *rather than* Y. The first thing to notice here is that even if we were to accept this, it does not clearly imply that the agent-causationist model must be mistaken. For we should then say, in any given case, that while the agent has it in her power to choose any of a range of alternatives, only one choice would be rational from the standpoint of her own reasons. Why would it still be "rationally-speaking random," as Strawson puts it (in a portion of the text not quoted here), if the agent makes the *preferable* choice? And, furthermore, don't we sometimes make irrational decisions? It is open to Strawson to accept my claim that choices of the most preferable option would be rational, but then suggest that the power the agency theory confers on free agents is worthless. For it is nothing but the power to make irrational decisions, and who wants *that?* I do not accept the suggestion that there is no value in an agent's *freely* choosing to be (for the most part) rational. But we can say something further. And that is that many situations of choice simply do not point to one course of action as "the thing to do" in the circumstances, as being preferable to all the rest.[31] Moral choices are commonly of this sort, but it is not limited to these. And if this claim is right, then there will be situations in which the agency theory confers a power on agents beyond that of determining whether they shall act rationally or irrationally.

In responding to Strawson's contention that the indeterministic aspect of the agency theory leads to a regress of reasons, I have begun to stray into the territory of the second, related objection to indeterministic reasons explanation that I want to consider, and so it is appropriate now to make this objection explicit. Suggested by various remarks in Kane (1989),[32] the objection I have in mind may be put thus: Any genuinely explanatory response to the question, "Why did S do X?", will ipso facto be an answer to the question, "Why did S do X rather than any of the available alternatives?", and a proper answer to the latter of these must incorporate *all* the relevant psychological features of the agent at the moment of choice. This requires some elaboration. The question, "Why did S do X rather than, say, Y or Z?", might be interpreted as simply a request for the reason that motivated S's making the choice S made (as opposed to reasons there may have been for any of the alternatives to X). When the question is construed in this way, however, we needn't cite all the considerations before S's mind at the time of the decision, but only those that provided a motive for doing X. But the sort of reading of this question that Kane has in mind is a much stronger one, which requests an account of why it was *necessary* that S do X in those circumstances rather than any of the alternatives. And citing whatever motive(s) there were for doing X at that time is clearly insufficient for this purpose. Rather, we need an account that implies that those motives were enough to tip the balance in favor of the actual outcome, as against its competitors.

Consider the following remarks in Kane ("Two Kinds of Incompatibilism"):

> How can we explain either outcome, should it occur, *in terms of exactly the same past?* If we say, for example, that the agent did [X] rather than [Y] here and now because the agent had such and such reasons or motives and engaged in such and such a deliberation before choosing to act, how would we have explained the doing of [Y] rather than [X] *given exactly the same reasons or motives and the same prior deliberation?* (P. 228, emphasis added)

In simply assuming that an explanation of the action will cite *all* the salient psychological features of the agent at the time of his decision, Kane is clearly presuming that there is only one type of adequate explanation of a choice, the type that explains why only that choice *could* have been made at that point in the agent's psychological history. But this is unsupported. The agency theorist may cheerfully concede that explanations of *that* sort are precluded by actions that are described by his theory—i.e., explanations that cite factors that could put an observer in a position to predict outcomes with certainty. And though we may grant that explanations of that sort are highly desirable for scientific purposes (among others), no reason has been given why we cannot allow explanations that account for an occurrence by characterizing it as the freely initiated behavior of an agent motivated by such and such a reason.[33]

The element of causal initiation is critical, I think, to the viability of this alternative explanatory framework. Some philosophers have failed to see that the prior presence of consciously considered reasons and agent-causal initiation are each necessary components in the agency theorist's explanatory scheme, and so have drawn the conclusion that the role of reasons in explaining actions obviates appeal to agent causation. Thus, Goetz (1988), for example,[34] writes:

> [I]f the reasons for which an agent acts help explain her freedom and responsibility with respect to that action, and her causing of her action can only be explained by appeal to the reason for which she acts, it is clear that the agent's causing of her action cannot help explain how it is that the agent is free and responsible with respect to her action. *Any*

*explanatory power which the causation by the agent of her action might have would have to be derived from or parasitic upon the explanatory power of the reason she has for performing that action.* Thus, not only is it the case that agent-causation cannot help explain an agent's performance of a free action, but also it is not needed for this explanatory role, once the agent's reason for performing that action has been invoked to explain it. (P. 310, emphasis added)

The sentence I have highlighted in the preceding passage involves a mistaken claim. It is doubtful that we can form a conception of an agent's causing an event internal to his action without his having any sort of pro-attitude toward that action, and so to that extent the agent's causing the component event is dependent on the reason he has (or, his having *a* reason) for acting in that way. Nonetheless, the relative dependency of reasons and agent-causal initiation with respect to explanatory power is precisely the reverse of what Goetz suggests. For the agent's free exercise of his causal capacity provides a necessary link between reason and action, without which the reason could not in any significant way explain the action. It allows us to claim that the reason had an influence on the *production* of the decision, while not causing it. Were we to remove the element of causal production of decision altogether, and simply claim that the decision was uncaused, then noting the fact that the agent had a reason that motivated acting in that way would not suffice to explain it (as Davidson has famously argued). For in that case, any number of actions may have been equally likely to occur, *and* the agent would not have exercised any sort of *control* over which of these was actually performed (either via the efficacy of his reasons or in the direct fashion suggested by the agency theory). And it seems sufficiently obvious that where there are no controlling agents or factors of even a relatively weak, indeterministic sort, there can be no explanation of the occurrence.

It will be observed that the crucial claim I am making here is that any genuine explanation of an occurrence must involve an account of how that occurrence was *produced*. It has often been thought that, given this requirement, the only way in which reasons can play a role in the explanation of an action is by functioning as the central features of a set of conditions that determine the action. One alternative to this is to suppose that reasons cause actions without determining them. I do not deny that this is a viable indeterministic account of reasons explanation rival to the one I am offering here. But while it provides for the possibility of reasons explanation, I think it must be rejected ultimately on the grounds that it fails to show how it can be up to an agent to determine which among a range of possible courses of action he will actually undertake.[35] If I am right in supposing this, then the only account of reasons explanation that is consonant, in the final analysis, with a picture of free and responsible agency is the one suggested by the agency theory.

## V. An Account of Reasons Explanation

So far, however, I have only spoken impressionistically of the sort of reasons explanation appropriate to the agency theory. I now attempt to give a more careful account by laying out conditions sufficient for the truth of each of two general sorts of ordinary reasons explanation. (What I say about these cases is readily adaptable to other sorts, such as explanation by a prior intention.)

The first sort that I want to consider involves explaining action by reference to a prior desire that $\Phi$, where this is construed broadly (and beyond everyday usage) as including any kind of "pro-attitude" or positive inclination towards the state of affairs $\Phi$. The following general conditions seem to me to suffice for the truth of an explanation of an action in terms of an antecedent desire:

> S V-ed, then, in order to satisfy her antecedent desire that $\Phi$ if:
> (i) prior to this V-ing, S had a desire that $\Phi$, and believed that by V-ing, she would satisfy (or contribute to satisfying) that desire, and
> (ii) S's V-ing was initiated (in part) by her own self-determining causal activity,[36] and
> (iii) concurrent with this V-ing, S continued to desire that $\Phi$ and intended of this V-ing that it satisfy (or contribute to satisfying) that desire.

Condition (iii) is necessary[37] because were I to cease to have the original desire and act for a completely different reason, it clearly would not have a genuinely explanatory role to play. It also handles cases in which I continue to have the desire but it is not the reason for which I act (and hence I don't intend of my action that it satisfy that desire).

This third condition is an adaptation of the central component of Ginet's account[38] of reasons explanation, although there is an important difference in how it functions in our overall accounts. I am in agreement with Ginet that the part of the explanation that involves a connection between the prior desire and the present intention need not be causal in nature (apart from the causal connections involved in continuing to have the desire), but may, rather, be wholly *internal* (similarity of content) and *referential*. If it is my purpose or intention in V-ing that I carry out a prior desire that $\Phi$, then the prior desire may figure in the explanation of this action even if it does not constitute part of a set of conditions that causally produce the action. *Contra* Ginet, however, this will be the case only if the noncausal connection between desire and intention is coupled with some other, appropriate sort of factor that produces or initiates the action, viz., the agent herself (hence, the necessity of condition (ii)).

In discussing Ginet's simple indeterminist, noncausal account of reasons explanations (which lacks anything analogous to my condition (ii)), Lawrence Davis writes:

> "[S]he opened the window in order to let in fresh air" only if she opened the window *because she believed* she would or might let in fresh air thereby. And this "because" must be causal—nomic—else I do not see a plausible distinction between [this sentence] and (1') She opened the window knowing she would let fresh air in thereby. . . . If I am right that something causal is needed, . . . [then] Ginet has not shown that undetermined acts can be explained in terms of their antecedents.[39]

I think that Davis is right in supposing that "something causal is needed" to make possible an explanatory link between antecedent reason and action, but that causal element needn't be a *nomic* connection between reason and action. The agency theory provides a coherent framework in which reasons can influence the production of an action without themselves forming part of a causally sufficient condition for the action.

I might note that there may be further factors that enter into the explanation of my V-ing. Suppose my prior desire was relatively indeterminate with respect to *when* it should be realized. There will often be certain considerations or other factors at the time of acting that elicited my action (by suggesting that this was a particularly opportune time to satisfy the desire), and these will certainly figure in a full explanation of my action. But, by the same token, it's not obvious that there *needs* to be such environmental stimuli. Perhaps I am only concerned that I act within a certain time frame, and any particular moment is as good as any other. In such a case, there may not be an explanation of why I acted just *then* (rather than at some other time).

The set of sufficient conditions for an explanation of action by prior reasons just given are consistent with the agent not having a clear preference for the action performed over any available alternative. However, we often do act on such preferences; in such cases, we can explain (in terms of antecedent reasons) not only why the agent V-ed, but also why she V-ed *rather* than doing something else instead. Can we give nondeterministic sufficient conditions for the truth of such explanations, similar to those sketched above? I think that we clearly can. Consider the following:

S V-ed then rather than doing something else because she preferred V-ing to any alternative if:
(i) prior to this V-ing, S had a desire that $\Phi$, and believed that by

V-ing, she would satisfy (or contribute to satisfying) that desire, and

(ii) S preferred V-ing as a means to satisfying the desire that $\Phi$, and
also preferred satisfying $\Phi$ over the satisfaction of any other
desire, and

(iii) S's V-ing was initiated (in part) by her own self-determining
causal activity, and

(iv) concurrent with this V-ing, (a) S continued to desire that $\Phi$ and
intended of this V-ing that it satisfy (or contribute to satisfying)
that desire, and (b) S continued to prefer V-ing to any alternative action she believed to be open to her.

It is quite consistent with the *antecedent* circumstances expressed in
these conditions that S have *failed* to V at that time. She might, for
example, have come to prefer on reflection some alternative (or have
ceased to desire that $\Phi$ altogether), or she might have decided to continue seeking out further relevant considerations, or, finally, she might
have simply succumbed to some temptations despite her continuing to
believe that V-ing represented the best course of action open to her
(thereby exhibiting the phenomenon of "weakness of will").[40]

It might be claimed, however, that the fact that our set of conditions
does not rule out these possibilities goes to show that they are not truly
*sufficient* for the truth of explanations of why an agent performed a
particular action rather than any alternatives she had considered. Statements (i)–(iv) must be supplemented with conditions that rule out the
possibility of these alternative scenarios. Only then, it will be claimed,
will we have adequately explained why S performed the action she did,
rather than some other action.

But while similar charges have often been made by critics of libertarianism, as best I can see, there are no good reasons to accept them. We
may suppose that it is a wholly contingent matter of fact that none of the
alternative scenarios I envisaged occurred, that the prior circumstances
did not necessitate their nonoccurrence. How does this show our set of
conditions to be inadequate? If what we are seeking to explain is why a
particular action was *in fact* undertaken rather than some other, as opposed to why the action *had* to occur, why is it not enough that we refer
to those antecedent reasons the agent had for preferring the chosen
action over the alternatives, reasons the agent continued to have at the
time of the action and that she intended to satisfy in performing it?
Providing such an explanation clearly makes it teleologically intelligible
that the agent chose to perform that action rather than any of the others,
though it does not imply that no other action could have occurred in just
those circumstances. Therefore, I cannot see why one should think that
it fails genuinely to explain the action in any meaningful sense—unless,

again, the critic is failing to note the difference between agent-causal and entirely noncausal reasons explanations, a difference that is embodied in my third condition above.

## VI.  *Is Agent Causation Distinguishable from Mere Randomness?*

The final objection to the agency theory that I consider here is epistemological in nature: it seems that it is impossible, in principle, for us ever to know whether any events *are* produced in the manner that the agency theory postulates, because such an event would be indistinguishable from one which was essentially random, not connected by even probabilistic laws to events preceding it.[41] (Alternatively put, the objection claims that we could never know whether the unique sort of property or properties that give rise to active power is instantiated.)

However, if my earlier contention that simple indeterminism is incompatible with genuine reasons explanations of action is correct, then I believe that the present objection must be judged mistaken. The simple indeterminist supposes that (in many cases) an agent's decision is not the outcome of any determinative causal influence—neither the agent's prior reasons, as on the causal theory, nor simply the agent qua agent (as on the agency theory). I claimed, though, that reasons explanations require a mechanism of control that 'hooks up', so to speak, the agent's reasons and consequent decision (and action). On the causal theory, this is supplied by an event-causal relation between the decision and matching reason(s). On the agency theory, an agent's capacity directly to produce a decision in the light of consciously held reasons fills the bill. We cannot *simply* appeal, as, for example, Ginet ("Reasons Explanation of Action") does, to *internal* (and referential) relations between concurrent intention and prior motives, on the one hand, and that same concurrent intention and the decision (or action), on the other. Without the mediation of a (necessarily causal) 'mechanism of control', prior motives cannot *explain* a decision, even though (as it happens) they may *coincide* with it.

Returning now to the objection under consideration, let us suppose that our knowledge of natural processes were to progress to such a point as to provide unmistakable evidence of significant indeterminism in the nature of ordinary human action. Would we have no reason, in such an eventuality, to prefer the agent-causal hypothesis to that of simple indeterminism? Surely not. Surely it would be preferable to adopt a theory of action in virtue of which our reasons-based explanations could remain largely intact. And it seems that, in such a scenario, only the agency theory would allow this. Furthermore, given a detailed knowledge of neurophysiological processes, we could go beyond the bare postulation of the appropriate property (i.e., one on which the power to cause directly any of a certain range of alternative events supervenes). We could explain in some detail, for instance, the systemic conditions under which such a property is instantiated, as well as the subtleties of its interplay with other causal processes involved in the production of behavior.

Thus, the employment of the concept of active power is not irremediably at odds with the attempt to give a scientific account of natural processes, including human behavior (as is sometimes alleged). The use of this concept in explaining human behavior is consonant with scientific methodology, broadly construed, and could in principle be mapped onto other explanatory theories concerning biological subsystems of the human organism. It does run counter to the general program of microreductive explanation, which has been highly successful in other contexts. But this, it surely must be recognized, is simply a research *strategy*. Given its explanatory potential, it obviously should be pushed as far as it can go in the understanding of human behavior. (And there is a further reason that agent-causal mechanisms should be appealed to in theoretical accounts only after the alternatives have been exhausted: we simply cannot know in advance the details of how event- and agent-causal processes interact, nor the precise sorts of circumstances in which agent-causal processes do not figure at all in the production of behavior.) But if limits of the right sort persist, I see no reason that explanatory theories invoking the concept of agent causality should not be adopted.[42] The alternative—to regard much of our behavior as without explanation (save for the fact that it falls within certain parameters)—is simply not credible.

This reply to the charge that we could never have reasons for preferring the agent-causal form of explanation to that of causal randomness may be bolstered by a simple appeal to how things seem to us when we act. It is not, after all, simply to provide a theoretical underpinning for our belief in moral responsibility that the agency theory is invoked. First and foremost (as I suggested at the outset), the agency theory is appealing because it captures the way we experience our own activity. It does not seem to me (at least ordinarily) that I am caused to act by the reasons which favor doing so; it seems to be the case, rather, that *I* produce my decision *in view of* those reasons, and could have, in an unconditional sense, decided differently. This depiction of the phenomenology of action finds endorsement not only, as might be expected, in agency theorists such as Reid, Campbell, and Taylor, but also in determinists such as Bradley,[43] Nagel,[44] and Searle,[45] and in Ginet's "actish phenomenal quality".[46] If these largely similar accounts of the experience of action are, as I believe, essentially on target, then it is natural for the agency theorist to maintain that they involve the *perception* of the agent-causal relation. Just as the non-Humean is apt to maintain that we not only perceive, e.g., the movement of the axe along with the separation of the wood, but the axe *splitting* the wood (Madden and Harré, *Causal Powers*, pp. 49–51), so I have the apparent perception of my actively and freely deciding to take Seneca Street to my destination and not Buffalo instead.[47] Such experiences could, of course, be wholly illusory, but do we not properly assume, in the absence of strong countervailing reasons, that things are pretty much the way they appear to us? I will not delve into this further epistemological issue here, my concern being that of descriptive metaphysics, but I will note that skepticism about the veridicality of such experiences has numerous isomorphs that, if accepted, appear to lead to a greatly diminished assessment of our knowledge of the world, an assessment that most philosophers resist.

## Notes

Many people have given me helpful suggestions and criticisms of material presented in this paper, some of which was presented in a pair of lectures at the Free University in Amsterdam. I wish to acknowledge in particular the help of Randolph Clarke, Mark Crimmins, Norman Kretzmann, Al Plantinga, Dave Robb, Sydney Shoemaker, René van Woudenberg, and, especially, Carl Ginet.

1. As has recently been suggested, for example, by David M. Armstrong (*What Is a Law of Nature?* [Cambridge: Cambridge University Press, 1984]) and Michael Tooley (*Causation: A Realist Approach* [Oxford: Clarendon Press, 1987]).

2. *Causal Powers: A Theory of Natural Necessity* (Oxford: Basil Blackwell, 1975).

3. "Causality and Properties," in *Identity, Cause and Mind* (Cambridge: Cambridge University Press, 1984).

4. As Reid clearly saw, the notion of a particular actively (or agent-causally) bringing about an effect is intelligible only on the supposition that the particular be an agent capable of representing possible courses of action to himself and having certain desires and beliefs concerning those alternatives. (The reader is invited to try to form the conception of an object constituting a counterexample to this claim.) This simple observation is sufficient to dismiss the derisive query of Watson ("Free Action and Free Will," *Mind* 94 [1987], pp. 145–72) as to whether it is conceivable that spiders should turn out to be "agent-causes in Chisholm's sense" (p. 168).

5. Searle, in *Minds, Brains, and Science* (Cambridge, MA: Harvard University Press, 1984), p. 94.

6. Reid would not have recognized *in*deterministic natural processes as an alternative to causal necessity. Hence, his claim that there is no reason to suppose that intelligent material substances (if such there be) could not be capable of free action is a defense of the possibility of a material system's exercising agent-causality.

7. Reid, *Essays on the Active Powers of the Human Mind* (Cambridge, MA: MIT Press, 1969), p. 367.

8. For further details, see my "Emergent Properties" (*American Philosophical Quarterly,* 31 [April 1994], pp. 91–104; cf. Brian McLaughlin, "The Rise and Fall of British Emergentism," in A. Beckermann, H. Flohr, and J. Kim, eds., *Emergence or Reduction? Essays on the Prospects of Nonreductive Physicalism* (Berlin: Walter de Gruyter, 1992).

9. Because agent-causality is a distinct species of causation, only an emergent type of property could enable its occurrence.

10. Two examples among many are Honderich (*A Theory of Determinism,* Oxford: Oxford University Press, 1988) and Levison ("Chisholm and 'the Metaphysical Problem of Human Freedom'," *Philosophia* 8 [1978], pp. 537–41).

11. Actually, an adherent of a viable dualist version of the agency theory would have to answer much the same sort of questions as those suggested above.

12. "Agency," in *Essays on Actions and Events* (Oxford: Oxford University Press, 1980), p. 52.

13. That is, an action that one performs without doing anything else in order to perform it. Theories of action differ on the question of the class of actions that fall within one's repertoire of primitive or basic actions, but plausible candidates include decisions and simple bodily movements.

14. "Agent-causation," *Mind* 92 (1983), p. 71.

15. It would be a mistake, I think, to characterize a decision of the action-triggering type as simply the *occurrence* of an event that is, as I've been putting it, the coming-to-be of a state of intention to $\Phi$. While this construal is natural, of course, on causal theories of action, the agency theory conceives of the activity of decision formation as centrally involving the agent causation of such an event. Consequently, the formation of decision is most properly defined as a complex state of affairs consisting of the agent's bearing a causal relation to a causally simple mental event (which, I have suggested, we may take to be the coming-to-be of a state of intention to $\Phi$). Some agency theorists have spoken of "causing one's own decision"; I suggest that they are best interpreted as expressing the above idea in shorthand. In what follows, I will make use of this convenience also from time to time, and the reader should interpret such statements in the preceding manner.

16. Fred Dretske has argued for just this claim in *Explaining Behavior* (Cambridge, MA: MIT Press, 1988), ch. 2.

17. Bishop, "Agent-causation," pp. 72–73, suggests this reformulation of Davidson's argument. However, I have differed with Bishop's interpretation of Davidson's remarks in posing the second horn of the dilemma, and consequently my response to it takes on a different form from his.

18. Most fundamentally, I fail to see how merely indicating that an event falls under a pattern of regularity—no matter how "lawlike" the formal characteristics of that pattern may be—is, in and of itself, explanatory. It is only by indicating something concerning the causal mechanism(s) at work (as a broadly realist position understands this notion) that genuine explanation can be accomplished. Most Humeans, of course, do not see the matter this way.

19. "Determinism, Indeterminism, and Libertarianism," in *Ethics and the History of Philosophy* (London: RKP, 1952). Broad's argument has been endorsed by Ginet (*On Action* [Cambridge: Cambridge University Press, 1990], pp. 13–14), although Prof. Ginet has told me in conversation that he no longer feels certain that the apparent difficulty Broad raises is decisive. And a similar (though, to my mind, less clear) sort of objection to Reid's agency theory is raised by Baruch Brody in his introduction to a 1969 edition of Reid's *Essays on the Active Powers* (Cambridge: MIT Press).

20. As I noted above in responding to Davidson.

21. "Reflections on Human Agency," *Idealistic Studies* 1(1971), p. 40.

22. *Action and Purpose* (Englewood Cliffs, NJ: Prentice-Hall, 1966), pp. 114–15.

23. Assuming, that is, that what we are after is the "triggering" cause of the event, rather than what Fred Dretske calls a "structuring" cause—roughly, that which establishes a causal pathway between two objects or systems so that when the first is operated upon (by the triggering cause) in the right manner, it brings about a result in the latter.

24. Of course, there will be a large number of *necessary* causal conditions for the occurrence of any instance of an agent's directly causing some internal mental event at a particular time $t$. (And, hence, where any of these are absent, a sufficient condition for the *non*occurrence of such events.) Many of these will have to do with the internal state of the agent prior to $t$. To note only the most obvious such conditions, for an agent to cause, say, his decision to immediately engage in $\Phi$-ing, the option must be one that is accessible to his conscious awareness, he must believe it to be within his power, and, it would seem, he must have some positive inclination to $\Phi$. There will of course also be numerous conditions in terms of the structural constitution of the agent's neurophysiological system. It is evident from our acquaintance with pathological cases that very subtle forms of malfunctioning can vitiate or even negate altogether the agent's capacity to act with a normal degree of autonomy.

25. See, e.g., Carl Ginet, "Reasons Explanation of Action: An Incompatibilist Account," *Philosophical Perspectives* 3 (1989), pp. 17–46, reprinted as Chapter 5 in this volume.

26. "Indeterminism and Free Agency: Three Recent Views," *Philosophy and Phenomenological Research* 53 (no. 3, 1993), pp. 499–526.

27. See Honderich, *Determinism*, pp. 196–97.

28. See Stewart Goetz, "A Noncausal Theory of Agency," *Philosophy and Phenomenological Research* 49 (1988), pp. 303–16.

29. *Freedom and Belief* (Oxford: Oxford University Press, 1986), pp. 53–54. (This essay is reprinted as Chapter 1 in this volume.)

30. *Theodicy* (LaSalle, IL: Open Court, 1985), p. 421.

31. Helpful discussions of such choice scenarios are found in Robert Kane's *Free Will and Values* (Buffalo: SUNY Press, 1985) and Peter van Inwagen's "When Is the Will Free?" reprinted as Chapter 12 in this volume.

32. "Two Kinds of Incompatibilism," *Philosophy and Phenomenological Research* 50 (1989), pp. 219–54 (see, e.g., pp. 227–28). (This essay is reprinted as Chapter 8 in this volume.) Kane's remarks in this connection are endorsed by

Richard Double in *The Non-Reality of Free Will* (New York: Oxford University Press, 1991).

33. In a recent discussion, Randolph Clarke helpfully calls attention to the fact that a strong case has been made (quite apart from the special case of reasons explanation) by contemporary philosophers of science that explanation of an event needn't involve showing why it rather than *any* other possible outcome obtained. See his "A Principle of Rational Explanation?" *Southern Journal of Philosophy* 30 (no. 3, 1992), pp. 1–12, and the articles he cites there.

34. A similar claim is made by Irving Thalberg in "How Does Agent Causation Work?" in M. Brand and D. Walton, eds., *Action Theory* (Dordrecht: D. Reidel, 1976), pp. 213–38, esp. p. 234f.

35. I argue this claim at length in O'Connor, "Three Recent Views." See also ch. 4 of P. van Inwagen's *An Essay on Free Will* (New York: Oxford University Press, 1983).

36. As I suggested above, I am inclined to term the agent-causal event (*S's causation of e*) a "decision," the event component of which is the-coming-to-be-of-an-action-triggering-intention-to-V-here-and-now. It is plausible to take it that the intention one has concurrent with the full performance of the action (required in condition (iii) in the text) is a direct causal consequence of the action-triggering-intention that is directly brought about by the agent.

37. More precisely, *some* condition or other that is more or less like condition (iii) is needed to give a *sufficient* condition for acting in order to satisfy a prior desire.

38. Ginet, "Reasons Explanation."

39. Review of Ginet's *On Action* in *Mind* 100 (no. 3, 1991), p. 393.

40. Compare Ginet, *On Action*, p. 149.

41. An objection along these lines is presented by Alvin Goldman in *A Theory of Human Action* (Englewood Cliffs, N.J.: Prentice Hall, 1970).

42. For discussion of the possible use of the concept in the social sciences, see p. 84 of John Greenwood, "Agency, Causality, and Meaning," *Journal for the Theory of Social Behavior* 18 (no. 1, 1988), pp. 95–115.

43. "Free Will: Problem or Pseudo-Problem?" *Australasian Journal of Philosophy* 36 (1958), pp. 33–45.

44. *The View from Nowhere* (New York: Oxford University Press, 1986), ch. 7.

45. See note 5.

46. Ginet, *On Action*.

47. Donagan, surprisingly, is an agency theorist who professes to find the notion of directly *perceiving* one's causal activity unintelligible (*Choice: The Essential Element in Human Action* [London: RKP, 1987], pp. 181–82). Judging by his remarks there, however, I suspect that he would reach a similar verdict with respect to the notion of perceiving certain instances of event-causal activity.

# 11

# Toward a Credible Agent-Causal Account of Free Will

RANDOLPH CLARKE

Agent-causal accounts of free will, of the sort advanced in years past by Chisholm and Taylor,[1] are now widely regarded as discredited. Such accounts held that when an agent acts with free will, her action is not causally determined by any prior events. The agent herself was said to cause her action, and this causation by the agent was said not to consist in causation by an event or collection of events. An agent acting with this sort of freedom, it was claimed, acted with the ability to do otherwise. And what the agent did was not an accident or a matter of chance; the agent herself made it happen that she did what she did. She was an uncaused cause of her so acting.

Such accounts have been rejected chiefly for two reasons. First, they failed to provide an adequate account of the relations between an agent, her reasons for action, and her action, and hence they failed as accounts of rational free action.[2] Second, they did not provide an intelligible explication of what causation by an agent was supposed to be.[3]

It is, in my view, unfortunate that the notion of agent causation has been largely abandoned, and in this paper I hope to contribute to its rehabilitation. I will sketch an agent-causal account of free will that differs in important respects from those of Chisholm and Taylor; and I will argue that given this account, the first of the objections described above can be easily met, and that considerable progress can be made in meeting the second. If I am right, then the result is an important one, for a viable agent-causal account would provide an attractive alternative to compatibilist accounts of free will.

## I. Rational Free Action

On Chisholm's and Taylor's accounts, when an agent acts with free will, her action (or some event that is a part of her action) is not caused by any events.[4] Indeed, Chisholm seems to believe that *any* action must be caused by an agent and not by any event.[5] The rationality problem arises directly from these requirements, for if an agent's action is not caused by her having certain reasons for action, then it is unclear how she can be said to have acted on those reasons and how her action can be said to be rational (and rationally explicable).

There are, I believe, two errors in Chisholm's and Taylor's requirements regarding the causes of actions. First, agent causation should be seen as required for acting with free will, but not for acting. An agent-causal account of free will might then be made consistent with the familiar analyses of action. And second, an agent-causal account should not deny that free actions are caused by prior events. Both of these mistakes can be avoided without sacrificing what is of value in an agent-causal account. *Isn't that just compatibilism?*

According to one of our most familiar pictures of deliberation and action, it is frequently the case when an agent acts that there is a variety of things that she can do, and she brings it about that she does one of these things in particular. The chief virtue of an agent-causal view, I believe, is that it gives a non-Orwellian account of how these two conditions can obtain.

Like any libertarian view, an agent-causal account makes room for the first of these conditions by requiring that determinism be false. Given indeterminism, it may often be the case when an agent acts that there are several different actions each of which it is naturally possible that she perform, where "naturally possible" is explained as follows: at time t it is naturally possible that an event E occur (in our world) at time t' just in case there is at least one possible world with the same laws of nature as ours and with a history exactly like ours up through time t in which E occurs at t'.[6]

Unlike most other libertarian accounts, an agent-causal account secures the second condition by taking it seriously and quite literally. An agent's bringing it about that she performs one in particular of the naturally possible actions is taken as a condition of production, and producing is taken to be causally bringing about. An agent's causing her performing a certain action is taken to be really that, and not really something quite different, such as the causation of her action by an event involving the agent. Finally, since agents or persons are held not to

*causation by events*
*vs*
*causation by substances*

be themselves effects of prior causes, on agent-causal accounts agents constitute uncaused causes of their performing the particular actions they perform.

Agent-causal accounts thus secure an interesting condition of production, one that requires that, when an agent acts with free will, she is in a significant respect an originator of her action. This condition can be expressed as follows:

(CP) When an agent acts with free will, her action is causally brought about by something that (a) is not itself causally brought about by anything over which she has no control, and that (b) is related to her in such a way that, in virtue of its causing her action, she determines which action she performs.

When CP is fulfilled, an agent is a real point of origin of her action. She determines that she perform that action, and that determination by her is not determined by anything beyond her control.

Any account of free will that allows that all events (except perhaps the world's first event) are caused, that all causes are events, and that all causal chains go back in time, if not forever, then to the beginning of the universe will fail to secure CP, regardless of whether causal relations are deterministic or merely probabilistic. CP appears unsecured, too, if an uncaused event is the immediate cause of the agent's action. For then it is unclear how the agent could be related to that uncaused event in such a way that she controlled its occurrence, and by controlling its occurrence determined which action she would perform. CP *is* secured if the relation in question is taken to be identity. For then when an agent acts with free will, she herself causes her performing a certain action, and qua agent or person she is not the effect of any causes (although events involving her are).

Now, it is consistent with this much of the agent-causal account that earlier events, including the agent's having or coming to have certain reasons to act, cause her performing a certain action. For suppose that all events in our world (except perhaps a first event) are caused by earlier events, but that event causation is "chancy" or probabilistic rather than deterministic.[7] Then, given the events up until now, there might be a certain chance, or single-case, objective probability (say, for example, .6) that a certain event E occur now, as well as a certain chance (.4) that E not occur now. Whatever happens now, past events cause it; but since they do not causally necessitate it, something else might have happened instead, in which case past events would have caused that something else. Suppose, further, that frequently when a human agent acts, it is naturally possible that she perform any one of several different actions each of which precludes her performing any of the others. Whichever of these actions she performs, earlier events probabilistically cause that action. It is consistent wtih these suppositions that often when a human agent acts, *she* causes her performing one rather than any of the other naturally possible actions. She brings it about that she performs that particular action. Yet, until her performance of that action, the chance that she would perform it remained somewhere between zero and one.

A libertarian view that affirms this account of human agency allows that an agent's behavior, besides being caused by her, is caused also by earlier events, among which are her having or coming to have certain beliefs, desires, preferences, aims, values, and so forth. This difference from the agent-causal views of Chisholm and Taylor stems from the recognition, here, that event causation may be probabilistic, and that probabilistic causation is not the threat to free will that causal necessitation is.[8] CP can thus be secured even if it is allowed that all events are caused by prior events.

The agent-causal account that I have sketched, then, is itself a kind of reconciliationism. It reconciles a traditionally libertarian claim—that freedom consists in being an undetermined determinant of one's action—with the apparently undeniable fact that human beings are part of the causal order, that all events involving human beings are causally brought about by earlier events. Such a view reconciles free will not with determinism but with the highly plausible thesis of universal event causation. There is a clear advantage to be gained from this sort of reconciliation, for it allows for our ability to predict and explain human behavior.

The account suggested here thus provides a reply to the following version of the rational-explicability objection. The agent exists prior to, as well as during and after, the performance of any one of her actions. Yet the action occurs at a certain time. The fact that the action is caused by the agent, then, cannot explain why the action occurs when it does rather than earlier or later. Hence, it is objected, on an agent-causal account, the timing of human actions cannot be explained.[9]

The reply is that, on the view sketched here, the timing of an action is explained as well as it is on a wholly event-causal account of human agency, given the assumption that event causation is nondeterministic. On the view I suggest, the occurrence of certain prior events will be a necessary condition of an agent's causing a certain event. Absent those prior events, the later event will not be naturally possible, and an agent can cause only what is naturally possible. The agent-causal view thus has the same resources as does a wholly event-causal view of human agency to explain why an agent performs a certain action at a certain time, rather than earlier or later. If there is an event, such as her acquiring new reasons, that explains why she acted then and not at some other time, then both sorts of views have available an explanation. If there is no such event, then neither sort of view has available an explanation. As I explain in more detail in Section III, although agent causation adds nothing to our ability to explain human behavior, neither does it subtract anything.

On the agent-causal account sketched here, when an agent acts with free will, the agent's beliefs and desires are among the causes of her behavior. But if this is so, how are event and agent causation related, and can agent-caused actions still be rational?

The best reply here, I believe, is to maintain that what an agent directly causes, when she acts with free will, is her acting on (or for) certain of her reasons rather than on others, and her acting for reasons ordered in a particular way by weight, importance, or significance as the reasons for which she performs that action. Her acting for that ordering of reasons is itself a complex event, one that consists, in part, of her behavior's being caused by those reasons.[10] What is agent-caused, then, is her performing that action for that ordering of reasons rather than, say, that action for a different ordering of reasons or another action for different reasons.[11]

In the simplest case, an agent has her reasons and she acts on them. Pam attends a lecture on Mapplethorpe, say, primarily because she is interested in his work and secondarily because she knows the speaker. She might also have some desire to accompany a second friend to an interesting movie that is showing at the same time. But she causes her acting on the first set of reasons, and on a particular ordering of them, instead. What she directly causes is her attending the lecture primarily because of her interest in Mapplethorpe's work and secondarily because of her friendship with the lecturer.

Now, if an agent's action is rational, then her acting *for* a particular ordering of reasons will be rational in light of the reasons the agent *has* to act. It will be rational in light of her overall constellation of motivational states. And there are a couple of questions on this point that are waiting to be addressed.

One question concerning the rationality of agent-caused actions is whether, when an agent acts with this sort of freedom, there could be at least one ordering of the reasons *for* which she acts such that her acting for that ordering would be rational in light of the reasons she *has* to act. The answer to this question is an easy "yes." If Pam has better reasons to attend the Mapplethorpe lecture than to go to the movie, then it is rational for her to act for those better reasons. It will be rationally explicable why she went to the lecture, and rationally explicable as well why she went to the lecture instead of going to the movies. Such explanations need refer to no more than the reasons for which she acted in going to the lecture.

It is important for a libertarian view that on a significant number of the occasions when an agent acts with free will, there is more than one action that she might rationally perform. Although our freedom of the will might consist partly in an ability to behave irrationally, free will is more desirable if it is the freedom to determine which of several genuine alternatives one will rationally pursue. A second rationality question, then, is whether the view sketched here allows for such alternative rationality.

It is often rationally indeterminate what we shall do and for what reasons we shall act. We are, for example, sometimes faced with choices among alternatives about which we are utterly indifferent. If I am given a choice of any one of several fine-looking apples, I may have no reason to pick any one of them rather than any other. In this kind of situation, my choice of any one of the apples will be as rational as would have been the choice of any other one. We also often face decisions where we have equally good reasons for making either of two or more choices. If I have until now taken as great an interest in surfing as in downhill skiing, I might as rationally choose to vacation at the beach as I might choose to go to the mountains.

There are other sorts of cases in which it is rationally indeterminate not only *for* which reasons an agent will act, but also how the reasons an agent *has* to act will be ordered. In making a decision, an agent will sometimes change the order in which she ranks considerations as reasons for action, and sometimes it may be as rational for her to change an ordering as it is for her to maintain it. Someone who smokes, for example, might have long judged that the health risks are less important to her than the pleasure she derives from smoking and the irritability and disruption that would result from quitting. If such a decision could be rational in the first place, then this agent might rationally continue to smoke: but it would surely not offend rationality if she one day reversed her ordering of reasons and decided to quit. Finally, an agent may face a decision that requires her to order considerations that she has not previously compared with each other; in some such cases there may be two or more new orderings each of which would be equally rational given her previous constellation of motivational states.

The important point to be made about all cases of rational indeterminacy is that the presence or absence of agent causation makes no difference to the rationality of the action. Whether such an action is agent-caused or not, there will be no contrastive rational explanation of it, one that would answer the question, "Why did you choose this apple rather than that one?" or "Why did you go to the beach rather than to the mountains?" This absence is due entirely to the structure of the situation and the agent's reasons. Such actions are nevertheless rationally explicable. I chose this apple because I wanted to eat an apple and it was as good as any other; I went to the beach because I like to surf. There is nothing rationally defective about an action of this sort; given the circumstances, it is as rational as can be.

## II. *Causation by an Agent*

I turn now to the objection concerning the intelligibility of the notion of agent causation. Chisholm has offered a definition of agent causation in terms of 'undertaking' or 'endeavoring'.[12] However, both of these terms suggest that agent causation is a kind of intentional action; and if that is so, it is unclear that it deserves the name 'causation' at all, since event causation, about which there are at least intelligible accounts, is not any kind of intentional action. Van Inwagen has proposed a different kind of analysis, one on which the agent causation of an action is held to consist wholly in the performance of an action a component event of which is uncaused by any event.[13] However, this approach fails to tell us in positive terms in what the causation by the agent consists, and indeed why the component event could not be entirely uncaused.

Certain features drawn from the views of Chisholm and Taylor, as well as from the view I have sketched here, suggest the beginnings of an account of agent causation. Agent causation is a relation, the first relatum of which is an agent or person and the second relatum of which is an event. Agents enter into such relations only as first relata, never as second relata. And an agent that is a relatum of such a relation is not identical to any event, property, fact, or state of affairs, nor to any collection of such things.[14] What is directly caused by an agent is her acting for a particular ordering of reasons.

What remains is to say just what this relation is. The prevailing tendency among agent causalists and their critics alike on this point has been to stress how different agent causation is from event causation and indeed how "mysterious" the former is.[15] However, the proper line here, I believe, is to maintain that agent causation, if there is such a thing, is (or involves) *exactly* the same relation as event causation.[16] The only difference between the two kinds of causation concerns the types of entities related, not the relation. The question that needs to be addressed, then, is whether there is an intelligible account of the relation of causation that will serve in accounts of event causation as well as agent causation.

The most familiar accounts of event causation are reductionist, aiming to analyze causation in terms of such noncausal and nonnomological features as constant conjunction or counterfactual dependence, or in terms of the modalities of necessity and sufficiency. Certainly, if any of this type of account of event causation is correct, then agent causation cannot be the same relation as event causation. For agent causation plainly cannot be either the constant conjunction of an agent and an action type or the counterfactual dependence of an action on an agent, nor can it consist in an agent's being a necessary or sufficient condition for the performance of a particular action.[17] However, reductionist accounts are subject to grave difficulties,[18] and they are not the only sort of account around.

An attractive alternative is to take the causal relation to be among the basic constituents of the universe. Causation may be held to be a real relation between particulars, one that, although analyzable, is not reducible to noncausal and non-nomological properties and relations. There is a variety of such realist accounts of causation.[19] A common intuition underlying many is that reductionist accounts attempt to explain the more fundamental by the less fundamental. It is not, for example, because one event counterfactually depends on another that the second may be said to cause the first. Rather, according to a realist, such counterfactual dependence is to be explained in terms of causal relations and laws.[20]

One type of realist account of event causation can be sketched, in broad strokes, as follows. An event (particular) causes another just in case the relation of causation obtains between them. Two events can be so related only if they possess (or are constituted by) properties that are in turn related under a law of nature. Ultimately, then, causal relations are grounded in laws of nature, which consist of second-order relations among universals.

Such an account roughly resembles that favored by Tooley for event (or, as he would have it, state-of-affairs) causation.[21] Tooley maintains that the relations involved in this sort of account—causation, as well as the higher order relations among universals—can be adequately specified, without reduction, by a set of postulates indicating the roles of these relations within the domain of properties and states of affairs.[23] If he is correct about this, then we have an analysis of the causal relation that can be employed in an account of agent causation. An agent causalist can say that it is the relation thus analyzed that obtains between a person and her action when she acts with free will; it is the very relation that, within the domain of properties and events or states of affairs, occupies the specified role.[23]

Moreover, an account that runs parallel, at a certain level of description, to that suggested for event causation would seem to be available for agent causation. An agent may be held to cause a particular action (more precisely: an event of acting on a certain ordering of reasons) just in case the relation of causation obtains between these two particulars. And an agent can be said to be so related to one of her actions only if these two particulars exemplify certain properties. Perhaps the only agents who cause things are those who have the property of being capable of reflective practical reasoning,[24] and perhaps such an agent directly causes only those events that constitute her acting for reasons. There might, in that case, be a law of nature to the effect that any individual who acts with such a capacity acts with free will.

Here is one way in which such a law might be construed. Suppose that it is necessarily true that if an action is performed with free will, then the agent causes her acting on the reasons on which she acts. (That there is such a necessary truth seems to be what, at bottom, agent causalists have always argued.) Suppose, further, that a necessary, but not logically sufficient, condition of acting with free will is that an agent act with a capacity for reflective, rational self-governance. Now suppose that it is a law in our world that if an agent possessing that capacity acts on reasons, then she acts with free will.[25] Here we have a contingent statement of natural necessity. Together with the supposed necessary truth, it implies the obtaining of the causal relation between agent and action.

Natural law, then, may subsume all free action without undermining the freedom with which human beings act. On this sort of account, the agent causation on which free will is held to depend is seen as thoroughly natural.

On the suggested account, then, agent causation is the obtaining of a relation between two particulars; the relation involved is the very same one that is involved in event causation. An agent's exercise of her causal power is simply the obtaining of this relation between her and an event. An agent need not *do* anything—if by that is meant perform some action—in order to cause something. Thus, agent causation is not fundamentally the performance of some special kind of action that then causes one's bodily movements. Nevertheless, the causal power that such an account attributes to agents is no more "magical" than that which we attribute to events. For an event need not perform any action in order to cause another event, and event causation is not fundamentally the occurrence of some third event between cause and effect; it is fundamentally the obtaining of a relation between the two.

The upshot is that, on an agent-causal account, an agent's *control* over her behavior resides fundamentally in her *causing* what she does. Her control does not reside fundamentally in her performing some special sort of action. Since causing is bringing something about, producing it, or making it happen, causing seems to be the right sort of thing on which to base an agent's control over her behavior.

My suggestions concerning an account of agent causation are, of course, programmatic. It remains to be seen whether such an account can be fully worked out. Nevertheless, the alternative of a realist account of causation significantly weakens the charge that the notion of agent causation is mysterious or unintelligible. If a realist treatment of event causation is intelligible, then we fairly well understand, too, what is meant by the claim that agents cause their actions. And given a realist account of causation, what is expressed by the claim in question is, it seems to me, something that is true in some possible worlds. At this juncture, an objection that agent causation is metaphysically impossible would stand in need of some argument.[26]

## III. Why Believe It

Even if an agent-causal thesis is intelligible, however, and even if what it states is not something impossible, the question remains whether it is reasonable to believe that, in fact, human beings agent-cause at least some of their actions. I will first indicate what kind of argument is *not* available for such a view and then outline what seems to me the best argument that *can* be made.

First, if agent causation is as described here, then there is no observational evidence that could tell us whether our world is an indeterministic world with agent causation or an indeterministic world without it.[27] We do not introspectively observe agent causation, and even highly improbable behavior could occur in a world without agent causation.

A related point is that affirming agent causation would not improve our ability to predict and explain human behavior. Our beliefs about event causation play a crucial role in this kind of understanding of human agency. But those beliefs concern the conditions for the occurrence of some event, and beliefs about agent causation are about something quite different. Nevertheless, it should be evident that, since an agent-causal thesis does not require that there be any gaps in chains of event causes, agent causation does not undermine the predictive and explanatory significance of event causes. Indeed, agent causation is consistent with its being the case that probabilistic laws of nature apply as thoroughly to human beings and their behavior as such laws apply to anything else. Thus, contrary to what Chisholm claims, agent causation is not a reason why "there can be no complete science of man."[28]

If prediction and explanation are paradigmatic of scientific understanding, it appears that agent causation neither contributes to nor detracts from such understanding. Its contribution, rather, would be to our understanding of ourselves as moral agents. We believe, most of us, that we are morally responsible for much of what we do. Agent causation, it may be argued, is a condition of the possibility of morally responsible agency.[29] Affirming something like the view sketched here, then, would give us an explication of how we can be what we seem, from the moral point of view, to be. Importantly, the explication provided would be one that is consistent with how we view ourselves from the scientific point of view.

The broader case for this view, as these last remarks suggest, constitutes a kind of transcendental argument, one that, in outline, runs as follows: (1) we are morally responsible agents; (2) if we are morally responsible agents, then we act with free will; (3) if we act with free will, then determinism is false; (4) if determinism is false and still we act with free will, then we agent-cause our actions; and (5) if our acting with free will requires that we agent-cause our actions, then that freedom is as presented in the account sketched above.

I have not, of course, established these five propositions here. My aim has been only to argue for serious consideration of the account referred to in the last of them. The crucial steps of the argument are, of course, the rejection of compatibilism and of nonagent-causal libertarian views. What inclines many of us to follow those steps, I believe, is that we find unsatisfactory any view of free will that allows that everything that causally brings about an agent's action is itself causally brought about by something in the distant past. Certainly any freedom of the will that we enjoy on such a view, if not a complete fraud, is a pale imitation of the freedom that is characterized by an agent-causal account. If I am right that agent causation can be made intelligible and that agent-caused actions can be rational, then an agent-causal account certainly deserves close attention.

## *Notes*

I wish to thank audiences at Princeton University and North Carolina State University for comments on earlier versions of this paper. Many individuals provided helpful suggestions and criticisms; I am especially grateful to Gilbert Harman and David Lewis.

1. Roderick M. Chisholm, "Freedom and Action," in Keith Lehrer, ed., *Freedom and Determinism* (New York: Random House, 1966); "The Agent as Cause," in Myles Brand and Douglas Walton, eds., *Action Theory* (Dordrecht: D. Reidel, 1976); and *Person and Object* (La Salle, IL: Open Court, 1976), pp. 53–88. Richard Taylor, *Action and Purpose* (Englewood Cliffs, NJ: Prentice-Hall, 1966), pp. 99–152; "Determinism and the Theory of Agency," in Sydney Hook, ed., *Determinism and Freedom in the Age of Modern Science* (New York: Collier Books, 1979); and *Metaphysics* (Englewood Cliffs, NJ: Prentice-Hall, 1983), pp. 33–50.

2. The rationality objection is sometimes stated in terms of the intelligibility of the action or in terms of rational explicability. For versions of this objection, see C. D. Broad, *Ethics and the History of Philosophy* (London: Routledge & Kegan Paul, 1952), p. 215; Carl Ginet, *On Action* (Cambridge: Cambridge University Press, 1990), pp. 13–14; and Irving Thalberg, "Agent Causality and Reasons for Action," *Philosophia* 7 (1978), pp. 555–66, esp. p. 564.

3. For examples of the intelligibility objection, see R. Kane, *Free Will and Values* (Albany: State University of New York Press, 1985), p. 72; and Gary Watson, "Free Action and Free Will," *Mind* 96 (1987), pp. 145–72, esp. p. 167.

4. See, for example, Chisholm's "Freedom and Action," p. 17, and Taylor's *Action and Purpose*, p. 127.

5. Chisholm writes that "We must say that at least one of the events that is involved in any act is caused, not by any other event, but by the agent, by the man" ("Freedom and Action," p. 29).

6. In this paper I focus on cases in which an agent acts with an ability to do otherwise. Certain features of the account I will sketch are more visibly displayed in light of such cases. However, I emphasize here that I do not believe that a libertarian need require, for free will, that an agent be able to do anything significantly different from what she actually does. If an agent has very good reason to perform an action of a certain type (A'ing), and if she has no reason not to, then, although it may be causally indeterminate *when* she A's, or exactly *how* she A's, it may not be naturally possible that she not A. So long as she is an undetermined determinant of her A'ing, it seems to me that it ought to be allowed that she acts with free will.

7. For a sample of discussions of nondeterministic causation, see G. E. M. Anscombe, "Causality and Determination," in *The Collected Philosophical Papers of G. E. M. Anscombe*, vol. 2 (Oxford: Basil Blackwell, 1981); Ellery Eells, *Probabilistic Causality* (Cambridge: Cambridge University Press, 1991); David Lewis, "Causation," in *Philosophical Papers*, vol. 2 (Oxford: Oxford University Press, 1986), esp. pp. 175–84; and Michael Tooley, *Causation: A Realist Approach* (Oxford: Clarendon Press, 1987), pp. 289–96.

8. In fact, Chisholm, in one of his later discussions of free will, does draw a distinction that appears similar to this one. See Roderick M. Chisholm, "Comments and Replies," *Philosophia* 7 (1978), pp. 597–636, esp. p. 629. However, he and Taylor generally take causation to be causal necessitation, and they deny that free will is compatible with universal causation.

John Bishop, too, has argued that an agent causal view need not rule out universal event causation. See his "Agent-Causation," *Mind* 92 (1983), pp. 61–79, esp. pp. 76–79. However, there are two important differences between Bishop's approach and my own. First, his aim in "Agent-Causation" is to advance an agent-causal account of *action* and not just of acting with free will. (Hence, some of the problems with which he deals are not problems for me.) Second, Bishop suggests that agent causation is "conceptually primitive," and he does not attempt to explicate it. (In Section II, I take some steps toward such an explication.)

In his later work, Bishop defends an event-causal theory of action. See *Natural Agency: An Essay on the Causal Theory of Action* (Cambridge: Cambridge University Press, 1989).

9. This version of the rational-explicability objection is expressed by Broad, *Ethics*, p. 215, and by Ginet, *On Action*, pp. 13–14. Ginet notes that the objection can be stated as well in terms of explaining why one particular action rather than another is performed. The reply to this variation is analogous to that given to the variation concerning the timing of the action. Given the assumption that event causation is nondeterministic, the agent-causal view has the same resources as does a wholly event-causal account to provide the contrastive explanation. This point is covered in more detail in the remainder of Section I.

10. I say "in part" because acting on or for certain reasons consists in more than the fact that one's action is caused by those reasons. The action must be nondeviantly caused by the reasons, and the reasons must constitute at least part of an explanation of the action. For a fuller account, see Robert Audi, "Acting for Reasons," *Philosophical Review* 95 (1986), pp. 511–46.

11. Even if agents can cause events, is it credible that an agent can affect whether her having certain reasons will have a certain effect, viz., her performing a certain action? I think so. After all, events can affect whether other events will have certain effects. Suppose that human agency is a wholly event-causal process. If it is cloudy, I acquire the belief that it is cloudy and might rain. If I believe that it is cloudy and might rain, then I might take my umbrella, but it is very likely that I will not. However, if I believe that it is cloudy and might rain, and then if my companion remarks that it is cloudy, then I will very likely take my umbrella. My companion's remark, or the absence of it, may causally affect whether the clouds and my belief will cause a certain action. The agent-causal case is disanalogous in that the agent, unlike my companion's remark, is not an event. But if agents, like events, can cause events, then it appears that agents can affect which effects certain events will have.

12. Chisholm, "The Agent as Cause," and *Person and Object*, pp. 53–88.

13. Peter van Inwagen, "A Definition of Chisholm's Notion of Immanent Causation," *Philosophia* 7 (1978), pp. 567–81.

14. Only a very minimal commitment as to the nature of a person is implied here. All that is implied is a denial of the bundle view, the view that a person is simply a collection of qualities or events. It is certainly *not* implied here that a person is a Cartesian ego, or a monad, or any sort of nonphysical thing. Nor is it implied that a person is a bare particular; on the contrary, in the view sketched here, an agent's causal powers depend on her attributes.

15. Taylor expresses this sort of view, as do Kane and Watson. See Taylor, *Metaphysics*, p. 49; Kane, *Free Will and Values*, p. 72; and Watson, "Free Action and Free Will," p. 167.

16. Event causation may be probabilistic, and a single world might contain both kinds. The causal relation itself need not differ in the two cases; the difference between them might reside in the fact that the underlying laws involve different higher-order relations. For an account of this sort, see Tooley, *Causation*.

Perhaps it needs to be required that agent causation is deterministic. However, I am not sure that this is so. I see no problem in saying that, on the agent-causal account, the agent, together with her having certain reasons, jointly deterministically cause her acting on those reasons.

17. Certainly, if the agent had not existed, her action would not have occurred. However, it is not the agent's existing, nor her coming to exist, but rather the agent that is said to cause her action. Furthermore, no agent causalist wants to claim that an agent causes every event that would not have occurred had she not existed.

18. For criticism of reductionist accounts of causation, see Galen Strawson, "Realism and Causation," *The Philosophical Quarterly*, 37 (1987), pp. 252–77; Michael Tooley, "Causation: Reductionism Versus Realism," *Philosophy and Phenomenological Research* 50 (1990), pp. 215–36; and the works cited in note 19.

19. See, for example, John Bigelow and Robert Pargetter, "Metaphysics of Causation," *Erkenntnis* 33 (1990), pp. 89–119; Adrian Heathcote and D. M. Armstrong, "Causes and Laws," *Noûs* 25 (1991), pp. 63–73; and Tooley, *Causation*.

20. Bigelow and Pargetter write:

We take causation to be part of the basic furniture of nature, and as such it functions as an input into the explanation of modalities. It is widely agreed that the best account of modalities make appeal to the framework of possible worlds. There is less agreement on how possible worlds are to be construed. Most of the details on the nature of worlds are unimportant here. What is important is only the direction of explanation between causation and the nature of worlds. We support theories which use causation as part of an account of what there is in any given possible world. Thus causation enters into the explanation of modalities, and in particular, into the explanation of 'necessary and sufficient conditions', and also of probabilities. Hence modal or probabilistic theories, even if they could be adjusted until they became extensionally correct, would nevertheless proceed in the wrong direction from an explanatory point of view. ("Metaphysics of Causation," p. 98)

*not vice versa* (handwritten marginal note)

21. Tooley, *Causation*.

22. The terms defined in this manner themselves appear in the postulates, but they can be replaced by variables to give us a theory that employs only antecedently understood observational, quasi-logical, and logical vocabulary. The theory succeeds in defining causation and the (two) relations involved in laws just in case there is a unique ordered triple of relations that satisfies the open formula of the theory.

The approach is one that is generally available for a realist treatment of theoretical terms. The technique employed is the Ramsey/Lewis method. For discussion of this method see David Lewis, "How to Define Theoretical Terms," in *Philosophical Papers*, vol. 1 (Oxford: Oxford University Press, 1983).

23. I owe this suggestion to David Lewis.

24. Several compatibilist accounts identify free will with a capacity to direct one's behavior by reflective practical reasoning. See, for example, T. M. Scanlon, "The Significance of Choice," in Sterling M. McMurrin, ed., *The Tanner Lectures on Human Values*, vol. 8 (Salt Lake City: University of Utah Press, 1988), esp. p. 174; and Gary Watson, "Free Action and Free Will," esp. pp. 152–53. Acting with such a capacity is, I believe, a necessary condition of acting with free will, and an adequate libertarian account will need to affirm this. Whether having that capacity is lawfully associated with agent-causing one's actions is, of course, another matter.

25. This way of expressing the law seems to imply that intentionality enters into the law of nature that governs agent causation, and it might be objected that such an implication is incredible. I am not sure that it is. Many of us believe, anyway, that intentional states (or our having them) can enter into causal relations, and that it can be *because* a certain state has a certain intentional content that state causes what it does. If the intentionality of mental states really is relevant to their causal roles, then we have one good reason to believe that intentionality somehow enters into the laws of nature that govern the causal relations of those states.

On the other hand, what if the intentional is anomalous? In that case, anyone who claims that the intentionality of mental states is causally relevant owes us an account of how that relevance is captured in the laws of nature. When we have that account, an agent causalist can use it for her own purposes.

26. It may be objected that, even if it is not impossible that a person should be a cause, nevertheless, on the view I have suggested, entities of two ontologically different sorts are said to be causes, and that (so the objection goes) is absurd. I do not think that it is. When it comes to accounts of "ordinary" causation, some say the relata are events, some say aspects of events, some say states of affairs, and some say properties. Consider the hypothesis that, in fact, at least two of these sorts of entities are causes. I do not think that it asserts something that is impossible.

For an argument that entities of several ontologically different kinds are indeed relata of causation, see David H. Sanford, "Causal Relata," in Ernest LePore and Brian P. McLaughlin, eds., *Actions and Events: Perspectives on the Philosophy of Donald Davidson* (Oxford: Basil Blackwell, 1985). I note that Sanford does *not* admit persons as causal relata.

27. Perhaps we could have evidence that our world was a deterministic world; but I take it that we don't.

28. Chisholm, "Freedom and Action," p. 24.

29. There is a widespread conviction that it is just too much to believe that human beings have a causal power that is to be found nowhere else in nature. Here is one part of a reply to that conviction: If it is accepted that we are morally responsible for at least some of our actions, then it is already accepted that we are morally unique (at least among known natural agents). If it is, moreover, necessarily true that only an agent who agent-causes her actions is a morally responsible agent, then one cannot consistently believe that we are thus morally unique and at the same time reject the metaphysics of agent causation.

The second part of a reply is that, in fact, it is not necessary for an agent-causalist to maintain that only human agents are agent causes. It can be allowed that the laws governing agent causation are not as suggested above but also cover causation by agents who lack the reflective capacity that free agents have. In that case, agent causation is a necessary but not a sufficient condition for free will. A further necessary condition is that an agent act with a capacity rationally to reflect on the courses of action she might pursue and on the reasons for which she might pursue them, and to govern her behavior on the basis of such reflection.

# III

## Indeterminism
## and the Extent
## of Free Will

# III

Indeterminism
and the Extent
of Free Will

# 12

# When Is the Will Free?

PETER VAN INWAGEN

There is, it seems to me, something that might be called an "orthodox" or "classical" tradition in the history of thinking about the problem of free will and determinism. This tradition, as I see it, descends from Hobbes through Locke and Hume and Mill to the present day. I say "it seems to me" and "as I see it" because I am no historian and I freely grant that what appears to my untutored mind to be "the classical tradition" in the debate about free will and determinism may be an artifact of certain historians—or even of the editors of certain anthologies. (And, of course, in identifying this tradition as "classical," I exhibit the Anglo-Saxon bias that my education was designed to inculcate: Bergson, Heidegger, and Sartre are not going to appear in *my* list of the members of anything called "the classical tradition.")

However this may be, I speak as a member of this tradition, and I want to begin by describing its presuppositions—*my* presuppositions.

According to "the classical tradition," the history of the problem of free will and determinism is, primarily, the story of a debate between two schools of philosophers, the "compatibilists" and the "incompatibilists"; that is, between those who hold that free will is compatible with determinism and those who hold that free will is incompatible with determinism. Now I am going to have almost nothing to say about determinism in this paper. In fact, I am not going to talk about the problem of free will and determinism—or not directly about it. I begin with a brief characterization of the history of this problem because, while the paper is not about the problem of free will and determinism, it presupposes the correctness of a certain way of looking at that problem. I do not propose to defend that way of looking at the problem— the way adherence to which defines membership in what I am pleased to call "the classical tradition"—but I do want to make it clear what that way of looking at the problem is, and that it is my way. Since I shall have almost nothing to say about determinism, I shall not attempt to give any very careful explanation of this important idea. I will say only this. Determinism is the thesis that the past and the laws of nature together *determine* a unique future, that only one future is consistent with the past and the laws of nature. I am, however, going to have a great deal to say about free will and I will lay out in some detail the concept that the classical or orthodox tradition associates with the words "free will."

The term "free will" is a philosophical term of art. (It is true that this term occurs in ordinary English, but its occurrence is pretty much restricted to the phrase "of his own free will"—which means, more or less, "uncoerced." If someone uses the words "free will" and does not use them within this phrase, he is almost certainly a participant in a philosophical discussion.) The first thing to realize about the use of the words "free will" by philosophers belonging to the classical tradition is that, *now* at least, these words are a mere label for a certain feature, or alleged feature, of human beings and other rational agents, a label whose sense is not determined by the meanings of the individual words "free" and "will." In particular, the ascription of "free will" to an agent by a current representative of the classical tradition does not imply that the agent has a "faculty" called "the will." It was not always so. Once upon a time, to say that X "had free will" was to imply that X had something called a "will" and that this will was not only unimpeded by external circumstances (in which case the agent X *himself* was called "free"), but that X's internal constitution left him "free" to "will" in various alternative ways. (The title of this paper is a relic of those times.) A tradition, however, is a changing thing, and the classical tradition has abandoned these implications of the words "free will." When a *current* representative of the classical tradition says of, e.g., Mrs. Thatcher, that she "has free will," he means that she is at least sometimes in the following situation: She is contemplating incompatible courses of action A and B (lecturing the Queen and holding her tongue, say), and she *can* pursue the course of action A and *can also* pursue the course of action B.

Now the word "can" is one of the trickiest of all the little philosophically interesting Anglo-Saxon words. It is not only ambiguous; it is ambiguous in a rather complicated way. Accordingly, representatives of the classical tradition, when they are explaining the sense of their term of art "free will," generally prefer to use some other words, in addition to "can," to get their point across, rather as if they were trying to convey what someone looked like by displaying a photograph *and* a painted portrait *and* a pen-and-ink caricature. They say not only "can do A and can also do B," but "is able to do A and is also able to do B," and "has it within his power to do A and has it within his power to do B', and 'has a choice about whether to do A or to do B." They may also use language that is not ordinary English at all, but which seems somehow useful in conveying the sense they intend. They may, for example, talk of a sheaf of alternative possible futures that confront the agent, and say that he has free will just in the case that more than one of these futures is "open" to him or "accessible" to him.

Compatibilists, then, say that free will in this sense can exist in a deterministic world, and incompatibilists say that it cannot. The classical tradition sees the problem of free will and determinism as centered round the debate between the compatibilists and the incompatibilists. But what is at stake in this debate? Why should anyone care whether we have free will (in this special sense)? The answer is this: We care about morality, or many of us do, and, according to the classical tradition, there is an intimate connection between "free will" and morality. The connection is complicated, and various representatives of the classical tradition would describe it differently. But the following statement would, I think, be accepted by everyone within the classical tradition. Most within the traditional would want to say more; some *much* more. But this "highest common factor" by itself explains why many people care about whether we have free will.

> Some states of affairs are bad. They ought not to exist. And among these bad states of affairs are some that *are the fault of* certain human beings. These human beings are *to be blamed* for those states of affairs. The Nazis, for example, are to be blamed for the death camps: the existence of those camps is *their fault.* The Kennedy and Johnson and Nixon administrations are to be blamed for the U.S. involvement and actions in Vietnam. They (and perhaps others, but they at least) can be *held to account* for that involvement and many of its consequences. On a more homely and personal level, our profession is to blame for the fact that many young men and women are being graduated from universities who cannot compose an English sentence or tell you who Galileo was. And, doubtless, each reader of this paper knows of bad states of affairs that are his fault and his alone. But if there were no free will—if no one were able to act otherwise—then no state of affairs would be anyone's fault. No one would ever be morally accountable for anything. The actions of some people might indeed be among the causes of various bad states of affairs, but those things they caused would never be their fault. For example, suppose a father has raped his

nine-year-old daughter and, as a result, she has suffered immediate physical pain and terror and has experienced life-long psychological and emotional disorders. Unless the father had at least some measure of free will, the pain and terror and the rest are not his fault. He cannot be blamed for them. They are not something for which he can be held to account.

I have not argued for this position. I am only reminding you of what the classical tradition says about the relationship between being able to do otherwise than one does and moral accountability. It is because, rightly or wrongly, the members of the classical tradition believe in this relationship that they think it is an important question whether we have free will. Almost all of the members of the classical tradition have in fact believed in free will, although there are exceptions. Baron d'Holbach believed that determinism was true and that free will was incompatible with determinism and that there was thus no free will. C. D. Broad believed that free will was incompatible with both determinism and indeterminism, and was thus impossible. But d'Holbach and Broad were exceptions. Almost all of the members of the classical tradition believe in free will. What they differ about is what free will *is*—that is, about what it is to be able to do otherwise. Most incompatibilists, at least among trained philosophers, believe in free will. All compatibilists I am aware of believe in free will; there's not much point in being a compatibilist and not believing in free will.

Before going further, I want to point out what seems to me to be a blunder made by some writers on the problem of free will and determinism. Some writers speak of an "incompatibilist sense of 'can do otherwise' " and a "compatibilist sense of 'can do otherwise'." But when English-speaking compatibilists and incompatibilists argue about whether people could act otherwise in a deterministic world, they are using the words "could act otherwise" in exactly the same sense. Otherwise they wouldn't be disagreeing about anything, would they? Each of them, being a speaker of English, knows what "could have," "was able to," and so on, mean when they are used in everyday life, and each means to be, and is, using these words in that everyday sense. Their case may be compared with the case of the dualist and the materialist in the philosophy of mind. Each uses phrases like "feels pain" and "is thinking about Vienna" in the same *sense*—the sense provided by the English language—though the two of them have radically opposed opinions as to the nature of the events and processes to which these terms apply. Similarly with the compatibilist and the incompatibilist: the two of them use phrases like "could have acted otherwise" in just the same sense—the sense provided by the English language—and disagree about whether that one sense expresses something that could obtain in a deterministic world. Now it may be that a particular compatibilist or incompatibilist has a mistaken *theory* about what "could act otherwise" means. But, in such a case, that philosopher does not *himself* mean by "could act otherwise" what his mistaken theory says these words mean. For example, suppose that a certain compatibilist has published an essay the burden of which is that "*x* could act otherwise" means "*x* would act otherwise if he chose to." And suppose that this is wrong: suppose that this is not a correct account of the meaning of the English phrase "could act otherwise." Then that compatibilist is not only wrong about what others mean by "could act otherwise"; he is also wrong about what *he* means by these words. (Compare this case: if I mistakenly think that "knowledge" means "justified true belief," it does not follow that that is what I mean by "knowledge." If philosophers always used words to mean what their theories said those words meant, no philosopher would ever revise a definition because of a counterexample. But this occasionally happens. Now if all anyone means by talk of an "incompatibilist sense" or a "compatibilist sense" of the central terms in the free-will debate is that philosophers have sometimes proposed theories about the meanings of these terms, theories that support compatibilism (or, it may be, incompatibilism), I have no objection. But then we must remember that it remains an open question whether compatibilists use these terms in a "compatibilist sense" and whether incompatibilists use these terms in an "incompatibilist sense."

Finally, it is this single sense of "can do otherwise," the sense provided by ordinary English, that compatibilists and incompatibilists contend is so intimately connected with the possibility of moral accountability. This is the classical tradition.

Let me now turn to my title. My question is, just how often is it that we are able to do otherwise? A belief in one's free will is the belief that one can sometimes do otherwise. But then it is consistent to say of X that he has free will despite the fact that he can almost never do otherwise. The central thesis of this paper is that while it is open to the compatibilist to say that human beings are very often—hundreds of times every day—able to do otherwise, the incompatibilist must hold that being able to do otherwise is a comparatively rare condition, even a *very* rare condition.

It is almost self-evident that compatiblism entails that being able to do otherwise is as common as pins. Or, at any rate, it is evident that typical versions of compatibilism entail this. Typical versions of compatibilism entail that being able to do otherwise is some sort of conditional causal power. For example, one primitive version of compatibilism—a version pretty generally agreed to be unsatisfactory—holds that for one to have been able to act differently is for one to have been such that one would have acted differently if one had chosen to act differently. (More generally, for one to be able to do A is for one to be such that one would do A if one chose to.) And who could deny that at most moments each of us is such that he would then be acting differently if he had chosen to act differently?

The case is otherwise with incompatibilism. To see why this is so, let us remind ourselves of why people become incompatibilists. They become incompatibilists because they are convinced by a certain sort of argument. My favorite version of it—which I reproduce from my book *An Essay on Free Will*[1]—turns on the notion of "having a choice about." Let us use the operator 'N' in this way: 'N$p$' stands for "$p$ and no one[2] has, or ever had, any choice about whether $p$." The validity of the argument turns on the validity of two rules of deduction involving 'N':

> Rule Alpha: From $\Box p$ deduce N$p$. ('$\Box$' represents "standard necessity": truth in all possible circumstances.)
> Rule Beta: From N$p$ and N($p \supset q$) deduce N$q$.

Now let 'P' represent any true proposition whatever. Let 'L' represent the conjunction into a single proposition of all laws of nature. Let 'P$_0$' represent a proposition that gives a complete and correct description of the whole world at some instant in the remote past—before there were any human beings. If determinism is true, then $\Box(P_0 \text{ \& } L. \supset P)$. We argue from this consequence of determinism as follows.

| | |
|---|---|
| 1. $\Box(P_0 \text{ \& } L. \supset P)$ | |
| 2. $\Box(P_0 \supset (L \supset P))$ | 1; modal and sentential logic |
| 3. $N(P_0 \supset (L \supset P))$ | 2; Rule Alpha |
| 4. $NP_0$ | Premise |
| 5. $N(L \supset P)$ | 3, 4; Rule Beta |
| 6. $NL$ | Premise |
| 7. $NP$ | 5, 6; Rule Beta |

If this argument is sound, then determinism entails that no one has or ever had any choice about anything. Since one part of "anything" is what any given person does, this amounts to saying that determinism entails that no one could ever have done otherwise. No one, I think, could dispute the two premises or Rule Alpha. The question of the soundness of the argument thus comes down to the question whether Rule Beta is valid. It is not my purpose in this paper to defend Beta. I reproduce this argument only to point out the central role that Beta (or something equivalent to it) plays in the incompatibilist's reasons for accepting his theory. I will go so far as to say that, in my view, one could have no reason for being an incompatibilist if one did not accept Beta. If one accepts Beta, one should be an incompatibilist, and if one is an incompatibilist, one should accept Beta.

What I propose to show in the sequel is this: Anyone who accepts Beta should concede that one has precious little free will, that rarely, if ever, is anyone able to do otherwise than he in fact does. I shall argue for this position as follows. I shall first show that if Rule Beta is valid, then no one is able to perform an act he considers morally reprehensible. I shall then extend this argument; by a similar sort of reasoning, I shall show that, given Rule Beta, no one is able to do anything if he wants very much *not* to do that thing and has no countervailing desire to do it. Finally, by more or less the same reasoning, I shall show that the validity of Rule Beta entails that if we regard an act as the one obvious thing or the only sensible thing to do, we cannot do anything but that thing.

In *Elbow Room*,[3] Daniel Dennett has argued eloquently that he is simply *unable* to do anything he regards as morally reprehensible. Compatibilists may feel a bit uneasy about agreeing with Dennett about this. Really simple-minded and primitive compatibilists, those who hold that one can do something just in the case that one would do it if one chose to, *must* disagree with Dennett. Take Dennett's primary example, the torture of an innocent victim in return for a small sum. Dennett will concede, I am sure, that we can easily imagine situations in which he, being more or less as he is now, would succeed in carrying out such torture *if he chose to*. His point is that, being as he is, he would never choose to. *I* think that this is a perfectly good point, but, of course, it is a point that must be disallowed by the primitive compatibilist who identifies the ability to perform an act with the absence of environmental impediments to performing that act. Leaving aside the question of what more sophisticated compatibilists might say about such cases, let us turn to the incompatibilists. They, I maintain, must agree with Dennett. Dennett uses himself as an example. I will use myself. Let us consider some act I regard as reprehensible. I might, like Dennett, use torture as an example, but my acquaintance with torture is purely literary, and I should like to try to avoid that dreamlike sense of unreality that is so common in philosophical writing about morality. I will pick an example that touches my own experience. Recently, a member of my university, speaking on the floor of a College meeting, deliberately misrepresented the content of the scholarly work of a philosopher (who was not present), in an attempt to turn the audience against him. Suppose such a course of action were proposed to me. Suppose someone were to say to me, "Look, you don't want Smith to be appointed Chairman of the Tenure Committee, so tell everyone that he said in print that all sociologists are academic charlatans. (I've got a quotation you can use that seems to say that if you take it out of context.) Then the sociologists will block the appointment." Call the act that is proposed A. I regard lying about someone's scholarly work as reprehensible. And, while I should prefer not to see Smith appointed, I certainly wouldn't *think* of blocking his appointment by any such means. In short, I regard the proposed act A as being indefensible. (I mean in the actual circumstances: I might lie about the content of someone's scholarly work to prevent World War III, but the start of World War III is not *in fact* what hangs on my performing or not performing A.) I may even say that I regard doing A as being "indefensible, given the totality of information available to me." And, of course, I do not so regard *not* doing A: there's nothing much to be said against that. We may also suppose that I am unable (as things stand) to search out any further relevant information—the vote will come in a moment, and I must speak at once if my speaking is to affect it. Now consider the following conditional:

> C If X regards A as an indefensible act, given the totality of rele-
> vant information available to him, and if he has no way of
> getting further relevant information, and if he lacks any positive
> desire to do A, and if he sees no objection to *not* doing A (again,
> given the totality of relevant information available to him), *then*
> X is not going to do A.

What is the modal status of C? It seems to me to be something very like a necessary truth. What would be a conceivable circumstance in which its antecedent is true and its consequent false (i.e., X proceeds to do A)? If X changes his mind about the indefensibility of A (perhaps because of the intervention of some "outside" agent or force, or because of an access of new information, or because he suddenly sees some unanticipated implication of the information available to him)? If X just goes berserk? If so, build the nonoccurrence of these things into the antecedent of C: he is not going to change his mind about the indefensibility of A and he is not going to go berserk.

It seems to me that there is no possible world in which C is false. What would it be *like* for C to be false? Imagine that X does do A. We ask him, "Why did you do A? I thought you said a moment ago that doing A would be reprehensible." He replies:

> Yes. I did think that. I still think it. I thought that at every moment up
> to the time at which I performed A; I thought that while I was perform-
> ing A; I thought it immediately afterward. I never wavered in my
> conviction that A was an irremediably reprehensible act. I never
> thought there was the least excuse for doing A. And don't misunder-
> stand me: I am not reporting a conflict between duty and inclination. I
> didn't *want* to do A. I never had the least desire to do A. And don't
> understand me as saying that my limbs and vocal cords suddenly began
> to obey some will other than my own. It was *my* will that they obeyed.
> It is true without qualification that *I* did A, and it is true without
> qualification that I *did* A.

This strikes me as absolutely impossible. It's not, of course, impossible for someone to say these words—just as it's not impossible for someone to say, "I've just drawn a round square." But it is impossible for someone to say these words and thereby say something true.

Now consider the proposition that I consider the act A to be indefensible. I think it's pretty clear that I have—right now—no choice about how I feel about A. Like most of my beliefs and attitudes, it's something I just find myself with. (Which is not to say that I don't think that this attitude is well grounded, appropriate to its object, and so on.) If you offered me a large sum of money, or if you promised—and I believed you could deliver—the abolition of war, if only I were to change my attitude toward A, I should not be able to take you up on this offer, however much I might want to. It is barely conceivable that I have the ability to change my attitude toward A over some considerable stretch of time, but we're not talking about some considerable stretch of time; we're talking about right now.

Let us now examine a certain Beta-like rule of inference, which I shall call Beta-prime:

From N $x$, $p$ and N $x$,($p \supset q$) deduce N $x$,$q$.

Here 'N' is a two-place operator, and 'N $x$,$p$' abbreviates '$p$ and $x$ now has no choice about whether $p$'. The one-place operator 'N' served my purposes in *An Essay on Free Will*, because there the premises of my argument concerned only propositions that were related in just the same way to all human beings, past, present, and future: laws of nature and propositions about the state of the world before there were any human beings. It is clear, I think, that whatever relation any given human being bears to such a proposition, any other given human being bears that relation, too. Since I was interested only in such propositions, I employed the impersonal and timeless one-place 'N'; it was simpler to do so. The arguments I wish to consider in the present paper, however, involve propositions about particular human beings and what they do at particular times, and their attitudes toward what they do at those times. For that reason, I need to use the person- and time-relative rule Beta-prime, and I must forgo the convenience of Beta. And Beta-prime seems hardly less evident than Beta. The same intuitive considerations that support Beta seem to support Beta-prime, and it is hard to imagine a philosopher who accepts Beta but rejects Beta-prime.

Consider the following instance of Beta-prime:

N I, I regard A as indefensible
N I, (I regard A as indefensible $\supset$ I am not going to do A)
*hence,*
N I, I am not going to do A.

In this argument, "I regard A as indefensible" is short for "I regard A as an indefensible act, given the totality of relevant information available to me, and I have no way of getting further relevant information, and I lack any positive desire to do A, and I see no objection to *not* doing A, given the totality of relevant information available to me." (Compare the antecedent of the conditional *C*, above.) The conclusion of this argument, written out in full, is "I am not going to do A and I now have no choice about whether I am not going to do A." Now the second conjunct of this sentence is a bit puzzling. But we may note that the sentences "I have a [or *no*] choice about whether *p*" and "I have a [or *no*] choice about whether not-*p*" would seem to be equivalent. Therefore, we may read the conclusion of the argument as "I am not going to do A and I now have no choice about whether I am going to do A." (The reason the original version of the conclusion seems puzzling is this: the mind looks for a function for that final "not" to perform and finds none.)

The first premise of this argument is true, because, as we have seen, I (right now, at any rate) have no choice about whether I regard A as indefensible. The second premise is true because as we have seen, the conditional "I regard A as indefensible ⊃ I am not going to do A" is a necessary truth, and no one has any choice about the truth-value of a necessary truth.

The general lesson is: if I regard a certain act as indefensible, then it follows not only that I *shall not* perform that act but that I *can't* perform it. (Presumably, "I am not going to do A and I have no choice about whether I am going to do A" is equivalent to "I can't do A."

This conclusion is not intuitively implausible. To say that you can do A (are able to do A, have it within your power to do A) is to say something like this: there is a sheaf of alternative futures spread out before you; in some of those futures you do A; and some at least of those futures in which you do A are "open" to you or "accessible" to you. Now if this picture makes sense (as a picture; it's only a picture), it would seem to make sense to ask what these futures are like. You say you can do A; well, what would it be like if you did? You say that a future in which you do A is "open" to you or "accessible" to you? Well, in what circumstances would you find yourself if you "got into" or "gained access to" such a future? If you can't give a coherent answer to this question, that, surely, would cast considerable doubt on your claim to be able to do A.

And suppose I do regard doing A as indefensible (for me, here, now). Then, I think, I cannot give a coherent description of a future (one coherently connected with the present) in which I proceed to do A. I have already considered what such an attempt would sound like ("Yes. I did think that . . .") and have rejected it—rightly—as incoherent.

We must conclude, therefore, that (given the validity of Beta-prime) I *cannot* perform an act I regard as indefensible, and that this is a perfectly intuitive thesis. Its connection with incompatibilism is displayed in the following argument.

(1) If the rule Beta-prime is valid, I cannot perform an act I regard as indefensible.

(2) If the rule Beta is valid, the rule Beta-prime is valid.

(3) Free will is incompatible with determinism only if Beta is valid. *hence,*

(4) If free will is incompatible with determinism, then I cannot perform an act I regard as indefensible.

Throughout this little argument, "I cannot perform an act I regard as indefensible" is to be understood in a *de re,* not a *de dicto* sense. It does not mean, "Not possible: I perform an act I regard as indefensible"; it means, "For any act *x,* if I regard *x* as indefensible, then I do not have it within my power to perform *x.*" (I don't mean to deny the *de dicto* statement; it is in fact true, but it doesn't figure in the argument.)

The defense of premise (1) of this argument has been the main task of the paragraphs preceding the argument.

Premise (2) seems undeniable because, as I have said, the intuitions that support Beta also support Beta-prime.

Premise (3) can be defended on this ground: the only reason known for accepting incompatibilism is that it follows from Beta. This, of course, does not *prove* that (3) is true. But it is unlikely that anyone would accept incompatibilism and reject Beta.

Let us now leave the topic of indefensibility and turn to desire—to cases of simple, personal desire having no moral dimension whatever.

Suppose that someone has an (occurrent) desire to perform some act. Suppose that this desire is very, very strong, and that he has no countervailing desire of any sort. (We have considered the case in which duty is unopposed by inclination. We now turn to the case in which inclination is unopposed by inclination.) Consider the case of poor Nightingale in C. P. Snow's novel *The Masters.* Nightingale wants to be a Fellow of the Royal Society—in the current idiom, he wants this distinction so badly he can taste it. Every year, on the Royal Society's election day, Nightingale strides out to the porter's lodge of his Cambridge college and leaves *strictest* instructions that, if a telegram arrives for him, he is to be notified *immediately.* (He threatens the porter with summary dismissal if there is the slightest delay.) Now suppose that poor Nightingale, on the day of the election, is sitting in his rooms biting his nails and daydreaming about being able to call himself 'F.R.S.'. The telephone rings. He snatches it from its cradle and bawls, "Nightingale here," doubtless deafening his caller.

What I want to know is: *Could* he have refrained from answering the telephone? Was he able not to touch it? Did he have it within his power to let it ring till it fell silent? If what we have said above (in connection with indefensibility) is correct, he could have refrained from answering the telephone only if we can tell a coherent story (identical with the story we *have* told up to the point at which the telephone rings) in which he *does* refrain from answering the telephone. Can we? Well, we might tell a story in which, just as the telephone rings, Nightingale undergoes a sudden religious conversion, like Saul on the road to Damascus: all in a moment, his most fundamental values are transformed and he suddenly sees the Fellows of the Royal Society as cocks crowing on a dunghill. Or we might imagine that Nightingale's mind snaps at the moment the telephone rings and he begins to scream and break up furniture and eventually has to be put away. But, remember, neither of these things *did* happen. Let's suppose that they did not even come close to happening. Let's suppose that there was at the moment we are considering no disposition in the mind of God or in Nightingale's psyche (or wherever the impetus to religious conversion is lodged) toward a sudden change in Nightingale's most fundamental values. Let's suppose also that the moment at which the telephone rang was the only moment at which there was *no* possibility of Nightingale's mind snapping—it was a moment of sudden, intense hope, after all. Build these suppositions into our story of how it was with Nightingale up till the moment at which the telephone rang. Build into it also the proposition that no bullet or lightning bolt or heart attack is about to strike Nightingale. Call this story the Telephone Story. I am inclined to think that there is no possible world in which the Telephone Story is true and in which Nightingale does not proceed to answer the telephone. We have the following instance of the rule Beta-prime (imagine that the present moment is the moment at which the telephone rings):

> N Nightingale, the Telephone Story is true.
> N Nightingale, (the Telephone Story is true ⊃ Nightingale is going to answer the telephone)
> *hence,*
> N Nightingale, Nightingale is going to answer the telephone.

The conclusion may be paraphrased, "Nightingale is going to answer the telephone, and he has no choice about whether to answer the telephone." And the premises seem undeniably true.

The lesson would seem to be: If the rule Beta-prime is valid, then if a person has done A, and if he wanted very much to do A, and if he had no desires whatever that inclined him towards not doing A, then he was unable not to do A; not doing A was simply not within his power. An argument similar to the one given above shows that the incompatibilist ought to accept this consequence of Beta-prime.

Let us, finally, turn to a third kind of case. On many occasions in life, with little or no deliberation or reflection, we simply do things. We are not, on those occasions, in the grip of some powerful desire, like poor Nightingale. The things just seem—or would seem if we reflected on them at all—to be the obvious things to do in the circumstances. I suppose that on almost all occasions when I have answered the telephone, I have been in more or less this position. On most occasions on which I have answered the telephone, I have not been biting my nails in a passion of anxiety and impatience like Nightingale. On most such occasions, I have not been expecting the telephone to ring (not that its ringing *violates* any expectation of mine, either); with my mind still half on something else, I pick up the receiver and absently say, "Hello?" Obviously, mere habit has a lot to do with this action, but I do not propose to inquire into the nature of habit or into the extent of its involvement in such acts.

Now consider any such occasion on which I answered the telephone. I was sitting at my desk marking papers (say); the telephone rang. (I had not been expecting it to ring. I had no reason to suppose it would *not* ring.) I answered it. Without reflection or deliberation. I simply put down my pen and picked up the receiver.

Can we tell a coherent story in which (in just those circumstances) I simply ignore the telephone and go on marking papers till it stops ringing? Well, we might. Since the matter is a minor one, we need not postulate anything on the order of a religious conversion. We might simply assume that some good reason for not answering the telephone suddenly popped into my mind. (Didn't I have a letter recently from a man who claimed to be able to prove mind-body dualism from the fact that he had made several trips to Mercury by astral projection? Didn't he say that he would be calling me today to make an appointment to discuss the implications of his astral journey for the mind-body problem?) Or, again, we might imagine that I suddenly go berserk and begin to smash furniture. Or we might postulate a sudden Divine or meteorological or ballistic alteration of my circumstances. But we might also imagine that there exists no basis either in my psyche or my environment (at the moment the telephone rings) for any of these things. We may even, if you like, suppose that at the moment the telephone rings it is causally determined that no reason for not answering the phone will pop into my mind in the next few seconds, and that it is causally determined that I shall not go berserk or be struck dead.

This set of statements about me and my situation at the moment the telephone rang (and during the two or three minutes preceding its ringing) we may call the Second Telephone Story. It seems to me to be incoherent to suppose that the Second Telephone Story is true and that I, nevertheless, do not proceed to answer the telephone. And, of course, we have the following instance of Beta-prime:

N I, The Second Telephone Story is true.
N I, (The Second Telephone Story is true ⊃ I am going to answer the telephone).
*hence,*
N I, I am going to answer the telephone.

The conclusion may be read: "I am going to answer the telephone and I have no choice about whether to answer the telephone." Its connection with incompatibilism can be established by an argument not essentially different from the one already given.

It seems clear that if the premises of this third instance of Rule Beta-prime are true, then we have precious little free will—at least assuming that Beta-prime is valid. For our normal, everyday situation is represented in the Second Telephone Story. It is perhaps not clear how many of the occasions of everyday life count as "making a choice." The light turns green, and the driver, his higher faculties wholly given over to thoughts of revenge or lunch or the Chinese Remainder Theorem puts his car into gear and proceeds with his journey. Did he do something called "making a choice between proceeding and not proceeding"? Presumably not: the whole thing was too automatic. The young public official, unexpectedly and for the first time, is offered a bribe, more money than he has ever thought of having, in return for an unambiguous betrayal of the public trust. After sweating for thirty seconds, he takes the money. Did he make a choice? Of course. Between these two extremes lie all sorts of cases, and it is probably not possible to draw a sharp line between making a choice and acting automatically. But I think it is evident that, wherever we draw the line, we are rarely in a situation in which the need to make a choice confronts us and in which it isn't absolutely clear what choice to make. And this is particularly evident if we count as cases of its being "absolutely clear what choice to make" cases on which it is absolutely clear *on reflection* what choice to make. A man may be seriously considering accepting a bribe until he realizes (after a moment's reflection on the purely factual aspects of his situation) that he couldn't possibly get away with it. Then his course is clear, because it has become clear to him that there is nothing whatever to be said for taking the bribe and a great deal to be said against it. He has not *decided* which of two incompatible objects of desire (riches and self-respect, say) to accept; rather he has *seen* that one of the two—riches—wasn't really there.

There are, therefore, few occasions in life on which—at least after a little reflection and perhaps some investigation into the fact—it isn't absolutely clear what to do. And if the above arguments are correct, then an incompatibilist should believe that on such occasions the agent cannot do anything other than the thing that seems to him to be clearly the only sensible thing.

Now there are *some* occasions on which an agent is confronted with alternatives and it is not clear to him what to do—not even when all the facts are in, as we might put it. What are these cases like? I think we may distinguish three cases.

First, there are what might be called "Buridan's Ass" cases. Someone wants each of two or more incompatible things and it isn't clear which one he should (try to) get, and the things are interchangeable; indeed their very interchangeability is the reason why it isn't clear to him which to try to get. (I include under this heading cases in which the alternatives are importantly different but look indistinguishable to the agent because he unavoidably lacks some relevant datum. Lady-and-tiger cases, we might call them.) Closely allied with Buridan's Ass cases, so closely that I shall not count them constituting a different kind of case, are cases in which the alternatives are not really interchangeable (as are two identical and equally accessible piles of hay) but in which the properties of the alternatives that constitute the whole of the difference between them are precisely the objects of the conflicting desires. We might call such cases "vanilla/chocolate cases." They are often signaled by the use of the rather odd phrase "I'm trying to decide which one I want"—as opposed to ". . . which one to have." I want chocolate and I want vanilla and I can't (or won't or don't want to) have both, and there is no material for deliberation, because my choice will have no consequences beyond my getting vanilla, or, as the case may be, chocolate. (Note, by the way, that someone who is trying to decide whether to have chocolate, to which he sometimes has an allergic reaction, or vanilla, which he likes rather less than chocolate, does not constitute what I am calling a "vanilla/ chocolate case.") Both vanilla/chocolate cases and "Buridan's Ass proper" cases are characterized by simple vacillation. Hobbes's theory of deliberation, whether or not it is satisfactory as a general theory, is pretty uncontroversially correct in these cases. One wavers between the alternatives until one inclination somehow gets the upper hand, and one ends up with a chocolate cone or the bale of hay on the left.

The second class of cases in which it is not obvious what to do (even when all the facts are in) are cases of duty versus inclination. Or, better, cases of general policy versus momentary desire. (For what is in conflict with the agent's momentary desire in such cases need have nothing to do with the agent's perception of his moral duty; it might have no higher object than his long-term self-interest.) I have made for myself a maxim of conduct, and no sooner have I done this than, in St. Paul's words, ". . . I see another law in my members, warring against the law of my mind." Our story of the young official and the proffered bribe is an example; further examples could be provided by any dieter. This class of cases is characterized by what is sometimes called moral struggle, although, as I have said, not all cases of it involve morality.

The third class of cases involves incommensurable values. (I owe this point to the work of Robert Kane.[4]) A life of rational self-interest (where self-interest is understood to comprise only such ends as food, health, safety, sex, power, money, military glory, and scientific knowledge, and not ends like honor, charity, and decency) versus a life of gift and sacrifice; caring for one's aged mother versus joining the Resistance; popularity with the public versus popularity with the critics. All these are cases of incommensurable values. Other cases would have to be described with more care to make sure that they fit into this class. The case of a young person wondering whether to become a lawyer or a concert pianist might belong to this class. But not if the question were, "In which profession should I make more money?", or "In which profession should I make the greater contribution to human happiness?" In those cases, values are not at issue, but only how maximize certain "given" values; the matter is one of (at best) calculation and (at worst) guesswork. The general form of the question that confronts the agent in true cases of the third type is, What sort of human being shall I be?, or What sort of life shall I live? And, of course, this does not mean, What sort of life is dictated for me by such-and-such values (which I already accept)? *That* question is one to be decided by calculation or guesswork. In cases of the third type, the agent's *present* system of values does not have anything to tell him. His values may tell him to become a professional rather than a laborer and an honest rather than a dishonest professional, but they do not tell him whether to become a lawyer or a pianist. (It may be that the values he could expect to have as a result of the choice would confirm that choice—see Kierkegaard on the moral versus the "aesthetic" life—but that's of no help to him *now.*) The choices in the third category are those that many philosophers call "existential," but I will not use this term, which derives from a truly hopeless metaphysic. As the cases in the first category are characterized by vacillation, and the cases in the second by "moral" struggle, so the cases in the third are characterized by *indecision*—often agonized indecision. The period of indecision, moreover, may be a long one: weeks, months, or even a really significant part of the agent's life.

I believe that these three cases exhaust the types of case in which it is not obvious to the agent, even on reflection, and when all the facts are in, how he ought to choose. Therefore, if our previous arguments are correct, the incompatibilist should believe that we are faced with a genuinely free choice only in such cases. (That is: in these cases, if in any. The incompatibilist may well believe that in some of *these* cases we have no choice about how to act, or, like d'Holbach and C. D. Broad, that even in these cases we have no choice about how to act.) It is not clear to *me* that in cases of the first type—"Buridan's Ass" cases—there is any conceivable basis for saying that we have a choice about what to do. Doubtless when we choose between identical objects symmetrically related to us, or when we choose between objects that differ only in those properties that are the objects of our competing desires, there occurs something like an internal coin-toss. (My guess, for what it's worth, is that we contain a "default" decision maker, a mechanism that is always "trying" to make decisions—they would be wholly arbitrary decisions if it were allowed to make them—but which is normally overridden by the person; I speculate that when "vacillation" occurs, the person's control over the "default" decision maker is eventually suspended and it is allowed to have its arbitrary way.) I think that it's pretty clear that in such cases one has no choice about how one acts. If one tosses a coin, then one has no choice about whether it will land heads or tails. And, indeed, why should one want such a power—if the alternatives really are indifferent?

If this is correct, then there are at most *two* sorts of occasion on which the incompatibilist can admit that we exercise free will: cases of an actual struggle between perceived moral duty or long-term self-interest, on the one hand, and immediate desire, on the other; and cases of a conflict of incommensurable values.

Both of these sorts of occasion together must account for a fairly small percentage of the things we do. And, I must repeat, my conclusion is that this is the *largest* class of actions with respect to which the incompatibilist can say we are free. The argument I have given shows that the incompatibilist ought to deny that we have free will on any occasions other than these. It has no tendency to show that the incompatibilist should say that we do act freely on these occasions. The argument purports to show that, given the principles from which the incompatibilist derives his position, it is impossible for us to act freely on occasions other than these. It has no tendency to show that—given the incompatibilist's principles—it is possible for us to act freely on any occasion whatever. It's like this: A biologist, using as premises certain essential features of mammals and some facts about Mars, proves that there could not be mammalian life on Mars; such a proof, even if it is beyond criticism, has no tendency to show that there *could* be any sort of life on Mars. That's as may be. His proof just tells us nothing about nonmammalian life.

I will not discuss (further) the question of how much free will we might have *within* these two categories. In the sequel, I wish to discuss the implications of what I have argued for so far for questions of moral blame.

I have argued that, if incompatibilism is true, free action is a less common phenomenon than one might have thought. It does not, however, follow that moral accountability is a less common phenomenon than one might have thought. And this is the case even on the traditional or "classical" understanding of the relationship between free will—that is, the power or ability to do otherwise than one in fact

does—and accountability. Nothing that has been said so far need force
the incompatibilist (the incompatibilist whose view of the relation between free will and blame is that of the classical tradition) to think that
moral accountability is uncommon.

Let us see why. Would anyone want to say that the classical tradition
is committed to the following thesis? "An agent can be held accountable
for a certain state of affairs only if either (a) that agent intentionally
brought that state of affairs about and could have refrained from bringing it about, or (b) that agent foresaw that that state of affairs would
obtain unless he prevented it, and he was able to prevent it." I don't
know whether anyone would want to say this. My uncertainty is due
mainly to the fact that philosophers discussing problems in this general
area usually talk not about accountability for states of affairs—the *results*
of our action and inaction—but accountability (or "responsibility") for
*acts*. This way of talking about these matters is confusing and tends to
obscure what I regard as crucial points. However this may be, the classical tradition is not committed to this thesis, though it may be that some
representatives of the tradition have endorsed it. This is fortunate for the
tradition, because the thesis is obviously false. This is illustrated by
"drunk driver" cases: I could not have swerved fast enough to avoid
hitting the taxi, and yet no one doubts that I am to blame for the
collision. How can that be? Simple: I was drunk and my reflexes were
impaired. Although I was unable to swerve to avoid hitting the taxi, that
inability (unlike, say, my inability to read minds) was one I could have
avoided having. Or again: Suppose that when I am drunk it is not within
my power to refrain from violently assaulting those who disagree with
me about politics. I get drunk and overhear a remark about Cuban
troops in Angola and, soon, therefore, Fred's nose is broken. I was,
under the circumstances, unable to refrain from breaking Fred's nose.
And yet no one doubts that I am to blame for his broken nose. How can
that be? Simple: Although I was unable to avoid breaking his nose, that
inability is one I could have avoided having. What these examples show
is that the inability to prevent or to refrain from causing a state of affairs
does not logically preclude being to blame for that state of affairs. Even
the most orthodox partisan of a close connection between free will and
blame will want to express this connection in a principle that is qualified
in something like the following way:

> An agent cannot be blamed for a state of affairs unless there was
> a time at which he could so have arranged matters that that
> state of affairs not obtain.

And this principle is at least consistent with its being the case that, while
we are hardly ever able to act otherwise than we do, we are nevertheless
accountable for (some of) the consequences of *all* of our acts. (No one, I

suppose, would seriously maintain that we can be blamed for *all* of the consequences of *any* of our acts. If I am dilatory about returning a book to the library and this has the consequence—apparent, I suppose, only to God—that a certain important medical discovery is never made, the thousands of deaths that would not have occurred if I had been a bit more conscientious are not my fault. And who can say what the unknown consequences of our most casual acts may be? Obviously, I can be blamed only for those consequences of my acts that are in some sense "foreseeable.") Consider this case. A Mafia hit-man is dispatched to kill a peculating minor functionary of that organization. The victim pleads for his life in a most pathetic way, which so amuses the hit-man (who would no more think of failing to fulfill the terms of a contract than you or I would think of extorting money from our students by threats of failing them) that he shoots the victim in the stomach, rather than through the heart, in order to prolong the entertainment. Could he have refrained from killing the victim? Was it, just before he shot the victim, within his power to pocket his gun unfired and leave? If what has been said so far is true, probably not. Would it follow that he was not morally responsible for the victim's death? By no means. Given the kind of man he was, he was unable, in that situation, to have acted otherwise. But perhaps he could have avoided having that inability by avoiding being the kind of man he was. It is an old, and very plausible, philosophical idea that, by our acts, we make ourselves into the sorts of people we eventually become. Or, at least, it is plausible to suppose that our acts are *among* the factors that determine what we eventually become. If one is now unable to behave in certain ways—I am not talking about gross physical inabilities, like a double amputee's inability to play the piano—this may be because of a long history of choices one has made. Take the case of cold-blooded murder. The folk wisdom has it (I don't know if there is empirical evidence for this) that most of us have been born with a rather deep reluctance to kill helpless and submissive fellow human beings. But, if there is such a reluctance, it can obviously be overcome. And (so the folk wisdom has it) each time this reluctance is overcome it grows weaker, until it finally disappears. Suppose our Mafia hit-man *did* have a free choice the first time he killed a defenseless victim. He might have experienced on that occasion—though doubtless these terms were not in his vocabulary—something like a conflict between momentary inclination and long-term self-interest. Suppose he did kill his man, however, and that he continued to do this when it was required of him until he had finally completely extirpated his reluctance to kill the helpless and submissive. If he is now unable to pocket his gun unfired and walk away, this is, surely, partly because he has extirpated this reluctance. The absence of this normal reluctance to kill is an essential component of his present inability not to kill. If the folk wisdom is right, and let us suppose for the sake of the example that it is, then it is conceivable he could have avoided having his present inability. And, therefore, it may be, for all we have said, that he can properly be held to account for the victim's death. Given the causal and psychological theses contained in the folk wisdom, he may be accountable for the victim's death for the same reason that a drunk driver is accountable for an accident traceable to his impaired reflexes. (But, of course, I don't mean to suggest that the case of a man who has turned himself into a sociopath by a long series of free choices over many years is morally *very* much like the case of a man who has turned himself into a temporarily dangerous driver by one or two acts of free choice in the course of an evening.)

I have nothing more to say on the subject of moral blame. This is a difficult topic, and one that involves many other factors than the ability to act otherwise. (Coercion and ignorance, for example, are deeply involved in questions of accountability. And there is the dismally difficult question of what it is for a consequence of an act to be "foreseeable" in the relevant sense.) My only purpose in these last few paragraphs has been to give some support to the idea that the radically limited domain of the freedom of the will that the incompatibilist must accept does not obviously commit him to a similarly radically limited domain for moral blame. It may be that we are usually right when we judge that a given state of affairs is a given person's fault, even if people are almost never able to refrain from bringing about the states of affairs they intentionally bring about, and even if people are almost never able to act to prevent the states of affairs that they know perfectly well will obtain if they do not act to prevent them. For it may be that they could have avoided having these inabilities.

## Notes

This paper was read at a conference on "Freedom and Mind" at McGill University in September, 1986, and as an invited paper at the 1987 meeting of the Central Division of the American Philosophical Association. On the latter occasion, the commentator was R. Kane. The paper was also read to the Philosophy Department at Virginia Polytechnic Institute and State University. The audiences on these occasions are thanked for their useful comments, as are those who have been kind enough to correspond with me about the topics discussed herein. Special thanks are due to Daniel Dennett, Robert Kane, and Lawrence H. Davis.

1. Oxford: The Clarendon Press, 1983. See pp. 93–105.

2. That is, no human being. We shall not take into account the powers of God or angels or Martians.

3. Cambridge, MA: Bradford Books, 1984. See pp. 133ff.

4. See Part II of *Free Will and Values* (Albany: State University of New York Press, 1985).

# 13

# When the Will Is Free

## JOHN MARTIN FISCHER and MARK RAVIZZA

Incompatibilists usually direct their attention to the following worry: if the thesis of causal determinism is true, then none of us is free to do other than what he actually does. But although causal determinism poses the most frequently discussed threat to freedom for incompatibilists, it may not be their only source of worry, at least not for those incompatibilists who also accept the common intuition that most of us, most of the time, are free to do otherwise.

In his article "When Is the Will Free?"[1] Peter van Inwagen offers a creative and systematic development of this less often discussed side of incompatibilism. He maintains (1) that anyone who is an incompatibilist should accept a rule of inference which he calls 'Beta,' and (2) that "anyone who accepts Beta should concede that [even if causal determinism is false] one has precious little free will, that rarely, if ever, is anyone able to do otherwise than he in fact does" (p. 405).[2] We will call the position suggested by van Inwagen's arguments 'restrictive incompatibilism' or 'restrictivism' for short. This name seems appropriate because restrictive incompatibilists hold both that incompatibilism is true, and that anyone who accepts the truth of incompatibilism must also (in virtue of accepting Beta) accept radical restrictions on one's ability to do otherwise.[3] According to this position, if causal determinism is true, we never are free to do otherwise, and if causal determinism is false, we "rarely, if ever" are free to do otherwise.

The conclusion that all incompatibilists allegedly must accept—that we, at best, are only rarely free to do otherwise—will come as a shock to many. However, this conclusion becomes even more disquieting when it is combined with another assumption of the "classical tradition" which van Inwagen and many other incompatibilists embrace. This is the assumption that freedom to do otherwise is a necessary condition of moral responsibility. Accept this premise and the following worry quickly arises: If the restrictivist is right—if incompatibilists are committed to a severe restriction on one's ability to do otherwise—then must they not also accept a similar limitation on the range of states of affairs for which one can be held morally responsible? And if this is the case, then would not incompatibilism itself seem to be incompatible with many of our most deeply held beliefs about the type of respect, praise and blame merited by persons?

In what follows we will address these issues by outlining the arguments for restrictive incompatibilism and then by discussing some responses to this position. In particular, we will argue that one can accept incompatibilism without *a fortiori* being committed to the restrictivist position. That is, we will maintain that one can accept the thesis that freedom to do otherwise is incompatible with causal determinism without implicitly being committed to the further conclusion that "rarely, if ever, is anyone able to do otherwise than he in fact does" (p. 405). In taking this position, we do not intend to argue *for* the truth of causal determinism or incompatibilism, but rather to argue *against* the restrictivists' claim that the logic behind the incompatibilist position requires that any incompatibilist also accept severe restrictions on freedom to do otherwise. Finally we will argue that, irrespective of our earlier criticisms, restrictive incompatibilists cannot (as van Inwagen suggests they can) provide a satisfying theory of moral accountability while still remaining within the classical tradition (which accepts that such accountability requires freedom to do otherwise).

## I. From Incompatibilism to Restrictive Incompatibilism

Let us begin by considering why incompatibilists purportedly must find themselves with little, if any, freedom to do otherwise. The restrictivist argues that the incompatibilist position rests upon a rule of inference termed 'Rule Beta'. Beta says that "from Np and N(p $\supset$ q) deduce Nq" (where " 'Np' stands for 'p and no one has or ever had any choice about whether p' ") (pp. 404–5). To appreciate the reason for this stress on Rule Beta we need only digress for a moment to consider one form of the Consequence Argument which persuades the restrictive incompatibilist that free will is not compatible with causal determinism:[4]

Rule Alpha: From $\Box$p deduce Np.

('$\Box$' represents "standard necessity": truth in all possible circumstances.)

Rule Beta: From Np and N(p $\supset$ q) deduce Nq.

Now let 'P' represent any true proposition whatever. Let 'L' represent the conjunction into a single proposition of all laws of nature. Let 'Po' represent a proposition that gives a complete and correct description of the whole world at some instant in the remote past—before there were any human beings. If determinism is true, then $\Box$(Po & L. $\supset$ P). We argue from the consequence of this as follows.

| | |
|---|---|
| 1. $\Box$(Po & L. $\supset$ P) | |
| 2. $\Box$(Po $\supset$ (L $\supset$ P)) | 1; modal and sentential logic |
| 3. N(Po $\supset$ (L $\supset$ P)) | 2; Rule Alpha |
| 4. NPo | Premise |
| 5. N(L $\supset$ P) | 3,4; Rule Beta |
| 6. NL | Premise |
| 7. NP | 5,6; Rule Beta |

If the above argument is sound, then determinism entails that no one has a choice about what she does; hence, determinism is incompatible with freedom to do otherwise. Since the restrictive incompatibilist insists that no one reasonably could take issue with either of the premises or Rule Alpha, he concludes that the soundness of the incompatibilist argument depends upon the validity of Beta. Indeed van Inwagen goes so far as to say that "if one accepts Beta, one should be an incompatibilist, and if one is an incompatibilist, one should accept Beta" (p. 405).

The next step in the restrictivist argument is to claim that any person who accepts Beta should also accept a similar rule of inference termed 'Beta-prime'. Beta-prime tells us that "from Nx,p and Nx,(p $\supset$ q) deduce Nx,q" (where the two-place operator 'N' is used as follows: 'Nx,p' abbreviates 'p and x now has no choice about whether p') (p. 408). When an agent has no choice about whether a proposition (or statement) obtains we will say that that proposition is "power necessary" for him.

Finally the restrictivist presents three arguments to show that if Beta-prime is valid then (even if causal determinism is false) we are not able to do otherwise in three types of cases which represent the majority of all actions. We will discuss the details of these arguments in Section III; here we need only note the three cases. The first is one of duty unopposed by inclination; that is, "no one is able to perform an act he considers morally reprehensible" (p. 405). The second case is one of unopposed inclination; thus, "no one is able to do anything that he wants very much *not* to do and has no countervailing desire to do it" (p.

406). The third case is one in which we act without reflection or deliberation; thus "if we regard an act as the one obvious thing or the only
sensible thing to do, we cannot do anything but that thing" (p. 406).
Given these points, the restrictivist concludes that the only times an
agent *is* free to do otherwise are times in which the agent is confronted
with conflicting alternatives such that, even after reflection, it is not
obvious to him what to do. Such conflict situations, van Inwagen tells
us, occur *rarely* and can be divided into three general categories: (1)
"Buridan's Ass" cases,[5] (2) cases in which duty or general policy conflicts with inclination or momentary desire, and (3) cases in which one
must choose between incommensurable values.[6]

Since the restrictivist holds that all incompatibilists must accept Beta
and hence Beta-prime, and that anyone who accepts Beta-prime must
concede that we cannot do otherwise in the cases which make up the
majority of all our actions, he therefore concludes that "the incompatibilist must hold that being able to do otherwise is a comparatively rare
condition, even a *very* rare condition" (p. 404).

## II. Who Needs Beta?

Before getting involved in the details of the restrictivist's individual arguments, we should note that an immediate way to circumvent his conclusion is simply to deny the initial contention that ". . . if one is an
incompatibilist, one should accept Beta."[7] To support this denial a nonre-
strictive incompatibilist could simply refer to any of a number of formulations of the Consequence Argument for incompatibilism which do not
explicitly make use of modal principles akin to Beta.[8] If valid, these
arguments apparently would give one reason to accept incompatibilism
without also requiring one to accept Beta or Beta-prime. Then, even if
all of the restrictivist's remaining arguments should prove to be valid,
one could accept incompatibilism without having any corresponding
commitment to accept the restrictivist's conclusion that we rarely, if ever,
have free will.

In response to this type of objection the restrictive incompatibilist
might insist that all formulations of the Consequence Argument, even
those which aren't explicitly formulated using Beta, must implicitly depend upon *some* rule of inference similar to Beta. Such a response is
suggested by van Inwagen's own claim that all three of his formulations
of the Consequence Argument in *An Essay On Free Will* should "stand or
fall together."[9] This claim is particularly germane to our discussion,
because only van Inwagen's third argument explicitly depends upon
Beta. Nevertheless, he writes: "I am quite sure that any specific and
detailed objection to one of the arguments can be fairly easily translated

into specific and detailed objections to the others; and I think that any objection to one of the arguments will be a good objection to *that* argument if and only if the corresponding objections to the others are good objections to *them.*"[10]

Van Inwagen is not alone in holding this view. Even some compatibilists, who in other respects want to take issue with van Inwagen's reasoning, agree with his intuition that any respectable form of the argument for incompatibilism must depend upon some type of inference akin to Beta. Pursuing this intuition, such compatibilists have sought to attack the incompatibilist's position by blocking the modal inference on which it purportedly rests. One such "beta-blocker," Michael Slote, writes: "I want to argue, in particular, that the arguments of GLVW [Carl Ginet, James Lamb, Peter van Inwagen, and David Wiggins] all rest on the questionable form of inference, the very inference from the double modality of 'Np' and 'N(p ⊃ q)' to 'Nq' which marks the superiority of the new kind of argument to earlier defenses of incompatibilism."[11] Further support for this position is found in Terence Horgan's comment that "Slote has described well the deep family resemblances among the various formulations [of the Consequence Argument for incompatibilism], and he too has suggested that the different versions probably stand or fall together."[12] This shared opinion on the part of compatibilists and incompatibilists alike, along with the debate over the validity of Beta to which it has given rise, support the restrictivist's contention that anyone who accepts any formulation of the Consequence Argument implicitly is committed to accepting Beta. Thus, the restrictivist might seem to be on firm ground when he insists that "if one is an incompatibilist, one should accept Beta" and with it (assuming the soundness of his subsequent arguments) restrictive incompatibilism.

Nevertheless, we want to argue that this claim is false. Admittedly, many formulations of the Consequence Argument do depend upon intuitions similar to those which underlie Beta. However, the argument for incompatibilism can be formulated in such a way that it does not explicitly make use of Beta, and hence the onus remains on the restrictivist to show how such arguments do, in fact, commit their proponents to accepting Beta.[13]

To illustrate this point consider the following sketch of an argument which is adapted from a parallel argument concerning the incompatibility of God's foreknowledge and free will.[14] The argument rests upon two principles which are controversial though not implausible. The first principle expresses the fixity of the past; it says not only that one cannot causally affect the past, but also that one cannot so act that the past would have been different from what it actually was. The fixity of the past principle can be formulated as follows:

(FP)  For any action Y, agent S, and time T, if it is true that if S were to do Y at T, some fact about the past relative to T would not have been a fact, then S cannot at T do Y at T.

The second principle expresses the fixity of the laws; in a manner similar to FP it says not only that one cannot causally change the laws, but also that one cannot so act that the laws of nature would have been different from as follows:

(FL)  For any action Y, and agent S, if it is true that if S were to do Y, some natural law which actually obtains would not obtain, then S cannot do Y.

Now consider some act X which agent A actually refrains from doing at $T_2$. Taking determinism to be the thesis that a complete description of the world at T in conjunction with a complete formulation of the laws entails every subsequent truth, then if determinism is true, and $S_1$ is the total state of the world at $T_1$, one of the following conditionals must be true:

(1)  If $A$ were to do X at $T_2$, $S_1$ would not have been the total state of the world at $T_1$.
(2)  If A were to do X at $T_2$, then some natural law which actually obtains would not obtain.
(3)  If A were to do X at $T_2$, then either $S_1$ would not have been the total state of the world at $T_1$, or some natural law which actually obtains would not obtain.

But if (1) is true, then (via FP) A cannot do X at $T_2$; similarly, if (2) is true, then (via FL) A cannot do X at $T_2$. Finally, if (1)'s truth implies that A cannot do X at $T_2$ and (2)'s truth implies that A cannot do X at $T_2$, then it follows that if (3) is true, then A cannot do X at $T_2$. The conclusion of this argument is that if determinism is true, then A cannot do anything other than what he actually does at $T_2$. Generalizing this result, the incompatibilist claims that if determinism is true none of us is free to do other than what he does.

The importance of the argument for our purposes, however, it not to raise yet one more banner for incompatibilism.[16] Rather, the argument serves to illustrate that the debate over incompatibilism should not be reduced to a discussion about the validity of Beta. Incompatibilists share basic beliefs about the relationships between free will, determinism, the fixity of the past and the fixity of the laws. But these beliefs can find expression in different forms of argument, not all of which necessarily involve the same commitments. Such arguments show that an incompatibilist can consistently adhere to her position without automatically being committed to Beta or restrictive incompatibilism.[17]

As we pointed out above, van Inwagen claims that incompatibilism depends upon Beta, but we have presented an argument for incompatibilism which does not appear to depend in any way upon Beta. We thus conclude that van Inwagen's claim is false. Further, if we are correct, then Slote's strategy (in what has been described by Dennett as a "pioneering article") is not nearly so promising as it might have been supposed to be.[18] Slote alleges that there are counterexamples to modal principles structurally analogous to Beta, and he suggests that Beta is similarly flawed. He concludes that incompatibilism should be rejected. We take issue with Slote's claim that Beta is flawed.[19] But what is relevant to our discussion here is that *even if Slote were correct and Beta were invalid,* one could generate versions of the troubling argument for incompatibilism. Thus, a Beta-blocking strategy cannot easily assuage the panic that might issue from the incompatibilist's argument.

There is another approach which claims that Beta is not necessary in order to generate the incompatibilist's argument. Bernard Berofsky has recently argued that one can develop the argument without the use of Beta.[20] Berofsky presents what he calls a 'system of contingent necessity'. This sort of system validates the following kind of principle, with certain restrictions:

$$P$$
$$N(P \supset Q)$$
hence, $N(Q)$

Whereas it is often alleged that this sort of move involves a modal fallacy, Berofsky attempts to justify this inference (with suitable restrictions on the substitution-instances of the propositional variables), and he claims that it provides a way of formulating the incompatibilist's argument in a valid fashion. We share with Berofsky the claim that the incompatibilist's argument does not require Beta. But if we are correct, then the incompatibilist's argument does not even require the validity of Berofsky's principle and his system of contingent necessity.[21] It is useful to see that the incompatibilist's argument does not require *any* modal principle similar to Beta.

Clearly, the above considerations—that the incompatibilist's argument can be formulated in various ways without the use of Beta—do not in any way bear on the validity of Beta.[22] We, in fact, are of the opinion that Beta might well be one of those intractable principles which seems valid but which can neither be easily proved nor disproved. Recognizing this, the restrictive incompatibilist might contend that, independently of its decisive role in many arguments for incompatibilism, Beta should be accepted by all incompatibilists simply because Beta is valid. And these grounds alone would be sufficient to confirm the restrictivist's position.

For the sake of argument, let us entertain this claim. Let us consider that Beta may well be valid, or at the very least that incompatibilists of the van Inwagen sort are committed to its validity. Does it now follow that such incompatibilists must also be restrictive incompatibilists? To evaluate this question, we turn to van Inwagen's three arguments that purportedly establish that if Beta is valid, then rarely, if ever, is one free to do otherwise.

### III. *Free to Ignore the Obvious*

In order to show that most of the time one is not able to do otherwise, the restrictivist presents a series of three arguments. In the first, he argues that no one is able to act in a manner that he considers morally indefensible. The argument runs as follows:

(1)  N I, (I regard A as indefensible).
(2)  N I, (I regard A as indefensible ⊃ I am not going to do A).

Hence (via Beta),

(3)  N I, (I am not going to do A) (p. 409).

The intuitive idea behind the argument is that at this moment I don't have any choice about the fact that I now consider some action A indefensible, and I also don't have any choice about its being the case that if I regard an action as being morally indefensible then I am not going to do it; these two premises being true, it follows that at this moment I'm not going to do A and I don't have any choice about this. In short, it is power necessary for me that I am not going to do A. Generalizing the results of this argument the restrictivist concludes that "no one is able to perform an act he considers morally reprehensible" (p. 405).

Van Inwagen (our model restrictive incompatibilist) then extends the type of reasoning used in this argument about morally indefensible actions to two other cases which, he claims, constitute the majority of all actions: (1) cases of unopposed inclination in which we want very much to do one thing and have no opposing desires; and (2) cases of unreflective action in which we know what the obvious thing to do is after little if any deliberation. In the case of unopposed inclination, we are asked to consider an example in which a person, Nightingale, is anxiously awaiting a phone call which he very much desires to receive. Nightingale has a very strong desire to answer the phone, and no countervailing desires not to do so. The question is: Can Nightingale refrain from answering the phone? The restrictivist reasons that he cannot, and in support of this conclusion he offers the same argument-form used above. Skipping the formalization, the rough idea behind the argument is as follows: (1) At this moment Nightingale does not have any choice about the fact that he very much desires to answer the phone, and (2) he also has no choice about its being the case that if he very much desires to answer the phone (and he has no countervailing desire to refrain from doing so), then he is going to answer the phone; these two premises being true, it follows that at this moment Nightingale is going to answer the phone and he doesn't have any choice about this. Van Inwagen concludes that "no one is able to do anything that he wants very much *not* to do and has no countervailing desire to do it" (p. 406).

In the last argument, which is supposed to cover the broadest range of actions, the restrictivist turns to actions which "with little or no deliberation . . . just seem—or would seem if we reflected on them at all—to be the obvious thing to do in the circumstances" (p. 412). Again we are asked to consider a situation in which a phone rings and a person immediately answers it without giving the matter a second thought. Following the same style of reasoning as in the Nightingale example, the argument claims that the agent is not free to refrain from answering the phone. Roughly the argument runs as before: (1) At the moment the phone rings, the person has no choice about the fact that he has no reason not to answer the phone immediately or to deliberate about answering it; (2) furthermore, he has no choice about its being the case that if he hasn't any reason not to answer the phone then he is going to answer it. From these two premises it follows that at the moment the phone rings, the agent is going to answer it and he has no choice about this. Generalizing this conclusion and that of the preceding argument van Inwagen concludes:

> There are therefore, few occasions in life on which—at least after a little reflection and perhaps some investigation into the facts—it isn't absolutely clear what to do. And if the above arguments are correct, then an incompatibilist should believe that on such occasions the agent cannot do anything other than the thing that seems to him to be clearly the only sensible thing to do. (P. 415)

Does an incompatibilist have to accept this conclusion? We think not. To challenge these arguments, we want to take issue with the second premise in each. The most detailed defense of premise (2) is offered in the first argument; here van Inwagen maintains that the second premise is true because the following conditional is a necessary truth and no one has a choice about a necessary truth.

(C1) If X regards A as an indefensible act, given the totality of relevant information available to him, and if he has no way of getting further relevant information, and if he lacks any positive desire to do A, and if he sees no objection to *not* doing A (again, given the totality of relevant information available to him), then X is not going to do A (p. 407).[23]

Van Inwagen claims that the restrictivist's three arguments are similar, and thus we assume that van Inwagen imagines that there are conditionals parallel to (C1) which are supposed to support the parallel premises of the latter two arguments. Here, we will begin by discussing the latter two arguments—pertaining to unopposed inclination and unreflective action. We will deny the claim that the relevant conditionals successfully support the second premises of these arguments. We shall focus our remarks on the argument concerning unopposed inclination; this argument appears to us to be the stronger of the latter two restrictivist arguments, and the considerations adduced against it can readily be applied to the third argument. Then we will turn to van Inwagen's first argument—concerning indefensible actions. Although we are departing from van Inwagen's order of presentation, our criticism can be developed more naturally in this fashion.

In his second argument, the restrictivist argues that in cases of unopposed inclination the agent cannot do other than what he actually does (despite the intuitive impression that he can so act). The argument has the same form as the argument concerning indefensible actions sketched above, but now the second premise (upon which we shall concentrate) is:

> (2)  N X, (X has an unopposed inclination to do A $\supset$ X is going to do A).

And parallel to the conditional which allegedly supports the second premise of the argument about indefensibility, we have:

> (C2)  If X very much desires to do some act A given the totality of relevant information available to him, and if he has no way of getting further relevant information, and if he lacks any positive desire to perform any act other than A, and if he sees no objection to doing A and refraining from doing anything else (again, given the totality of relevant information available to him), then the person is not going to do anything other than A.

Now, the only way in which (C2) can support premise two of the argument is if (C2) is *power necessary* for the relevant agent. That is, (C2) must be true and X must have no choice about whether C2 is true. (This is parallel to the point made above that it is in virtue of the fact that no one has any choice about the truth of (C1) that premise (2) of the first argument is supported.)

The problem with the argument can be made clear by employing the following rather familiar sort of strategy. (C2) admits of two interpretations. On one interpretation, (C2) is plausibly thought to be true and power necessary, but it does not support the second premise of the argument. And on the other interpretation the second premise is supported but (C2) is not plausible. Thus, there is *no* interpretation according to which it is the case that both (C2) is plausibly thought to be power necessary and the relevant premise of the argument is true.

Let us first consider the interpretation according to which (C2) is plausibly taken to be true and power necessary. This interpretation is motivated by the basic idea that action requires some sort of "pro-attitude"—say, a desire. That is, it might be argued that actions are distinguished from mere events in virtue of being preceded (in a suitable way) by special sorts of events: "volitions." Further, it might be claimed that a volition must be based (in a suitable way) on at least *some* desire. If these claims were true, it would follow that it would be impossible for an agent to perform an *action* without having some desire to do so. We suppose that the necessity of desire for action could be posited even by a theorist who does not believe in volitions. In any case, it is a plausible conceptual claim that it is impossible for an agent to perform an action without having some desire to perform the action in question.[24]

The key point is that the alleged conceptual truth cannot support premise two of the argument. Note that the alleged conceptual truth can be regimented as follows:

(C2*) It is not possible that the following state of affairs obtain: that X performs an act other than *A* without having any desire to perform such an act.

And note further that (C2*) does *not* imply

(2) N, X (X has an unopposed desire to do A ⊃ X is going to do A).

As long as there is no *obstacle* to the agent's having the desire to do other than A during the relevant temporal interval, we believe that (2) can be false compatibly with the truth of (C2*). (2) would be false if, despite the fact that X has an unopposed desire to do A, he *could* refrain from doing A; and, given that (during the relevant temporal period) X can acquire this sort of desire, we believe that it is reasonable to suppose that X can do other than A. (We will argue for this below.)

That (C2*) fails to imply (2) can be seen by considering this simple analogy. It is uncontroversially true that it is not possible that the following state of affairs obtain at all points in some temporal interval: Jones is sitting and Jones is standing up. But this conceptual truth does *not* imply that, if Jones is sitting at some point in some temporal interval, then Jones cannot stand at some point in that interval. Thus, even if (C2*) were true—and it does seem plausible to us—it would not successfully secure the truth of the second premise of van Inwagen's argument.

Now let us interpret (C2) such that it does entail (2):

(C2**) If X does not desire to do other than A, X cannot do other than A.

We concede that (C2**) supports (2), but at the price of plausibility. This is because, even if an agent does not actually desire to do other than A, he might well have the ability (during the relevant temporal interval) to generate such a desire, and to act on this desire. And it is extremely implausible to suppose that agents quite generally lack the *power* to generate the relevant sorts of desires.

We elaborate. Just about anybody can summon up the worry that he is not free to do otherwise. That is, one can worry that, despite the pervasive intuitive feeling that frequently we have genuine freedom to do various things, we do not in fact have such freedom. (Indeed, anyone who thinks about the restrictivist's argument certainly has reason to worry that he might not be free to do otherwise in many contexts.) This worry can then generate *some* reason (perhaps, a desire) to do otherwise simply to prove that one can do so.[25] Thus, barring special circumstances—to which the restrictivist does not allude in his arguments—even an agent who actually does not have any desire to do other than A can have the power to generate such a desire (during the relevant temporal interval). And insofar as: (i) the agent *can* generate the desire to do other than A, (ii) the agent can try to act on this desire, and (iii) if he were to try to act on this desire, he would succeed, then we believe that the agent *can* (during the relevant temporal interval) do other than A.[26] The leading idea here is that there is no reason to suppose that agents *generally* lack the power to generate (in some way or another) reasons to do otherwise, the power to try to act on those reasons, or the power to succeed in so acting.

Consider van Inwagen's own example in which Nightingale wants very much to answer the phone as soon as it rings. If Nightingale can call to mind the doubt that he is able to do otherwise in such situations, this very doubt can give him a reason to pause before picking up the receiver. (Perhaps he simply does not answer the phone on the first ring, but waits until it rings five times; this suffices, he might feel, to prove he was free to do otherwise.) In this scenario, Nightingale's worry has transformed a normally routine phone call into a situation in which Nightingale must decide between two conflicting desires: (1) a desire to answer the phone as soon as it rings, and (2) a desire to prove to himself that he doesn't have to answer it as soon as it rings. We claim that insofar as: (i) the agent can generate a desire of the second sort, (ii) he can try to act on this desire, and (iii) if the agent were to try to act on this sort of desire, he would succeed in doing other than A, then the agent *can* (during the relevant temporal period) do other than A, even though he actually lacks any desire to do other than A.[27]

We believe that the above considerations show that, even if an agent actually lacks any desire to perform a given act, he *can* perform that action, insofar as certain conditions are met. These conditions involve the ability to generate certain reasons and to translate these reasons into action. Further, we suggested that it is extremely plausible to suppose that (absent special assumptions about causal determinism or particular psychological or physical impairments) these conditions are frequently met.[28] Thus, we believe that (C2**) is not in general true. We have argued, then, that whereas (C2*) is plausible, it does not imply (2); and whereas (C2**) implies (2), it is not plausible.

In order more clearly to highlight our position, it is useful to consider the complaint that we have simply missed van Inwagen's point.[29] Van Inwagen's claim is that *if* in some possible world, W1, Nightingale has a strong, unopposed inclination to answer the phone as soon as it rings then, Nightingale is going to answer the phone as soon as it rings and he is not able in W1 to do otherwise. But—the objector continues— all your reconstruction of the example shows is that if in some other possible world, W2, Nightingale's motivational set is changed so that he has two conflicting inclinations, then Nightingale in W2 is able to refrain from answering the phone as soon as it rings. Nightingale's ability in W2, however, is a function of his having opposing inclinations, and in itself this doesn't show that Nightingale in W1, without the opposing inclinations, is able to do otherwise. The issue, then, is not what Nightingale can do in W2 with a different motivational set, but rather what Nightingale can do in W1 given that his motivational set is just as van Inwagen stipulates.

We reply that, as long as Nightingale is genuinely *able* (during the relevant temporal interval) in W1 to generate a desire to answer the phone, then he is *able* in W1 to answer the phone. Insofar as W2 is *genuinely accessible* to Nightingale, then W2 is relevant to what Nightingale *can* do in W1. It is only if W2 is not so accessible that it is irrelevant to Nightingale's abilities in W1. Of course, we rely here on the fact, if some world W2 is in the appropriate sense accessible to W1, then W2 may be relevant to the modal properties of individuals in W1.

## IV. *Free To Act Indefensibly, Free To Act Crazily*

Thus far we have argued against the restrictivist's argument that in cases of unopposed inclination the agent is not free to do otherwise. We believe that the same considerations apply, *mutatis mutandis*, to the argument concerning unreflective actions. Thus, we believe that we have pointed to a way of salvaging the intuition that, even if Beta were true, individuals are often free to do otherwise in contexts of unopposed desire and unreflective action. Now let us turn to van Inwagen's parallel argument concerning indefensible actions.

Having developed the criticism of the argument pertaining to unopposed desire, it is now extremely simple to explain what is wrong with the argument concerning indefensible actions. In fact, our objection to the argument concerning indefensible actions is precisely the same as the objection to the argument concerning unopposed desires.

Recall that van Inwagen adduces (C1) in support of premise (2) of the argument:

> (C1)  If X regards A as an indefensible act, given the totality of relevant information available to him, and if he has no way of getting further relevant information, and if he lacks any positive desire to do A, and if he sees no objection to *not* doing A (again, given the totality of relevant information available to him), then X is not going to do A (p. 407).

Given that van Inwagen adduces (C1) in support of (2), it is clear that he is interpreting the second premise of the argument in the following way:

> (2)  N, X (X regards A as an indefensible act and X lacks any desire to do A ⊃ X does not do A).

To proceed as above. (C1) can be interpreted so as to claim that the following state of affairs is not possible: that X regards A as indefensible, has no desire to perform A, and performs A. But (C1), so interpreted, does not imply (2). Alternatively, (C1) could be interpreted so as to claim that if X regards A as indefensible and X lacks any desire to do A, then X cannot do A. But, so interpreted, (C1) is false, insofar as X can (in the relevant temporal interval) generate the desire in question.

But in the context of unopposed desire discussed above, it is not supposed that the agent believes that the act in question is *indefensible*. Might this belief constitute an obstacle to generating a reason (or desire of the sort discussed above) to perform the act? That is, is the context of indefensible acts relevantly different from the contexts of unopposed desire and unreflective action?

The examples adduced by van Inwagen in support of (C1) suggest that morally indefensible actions *do* have some special status such that one literally is unable to bring oneself to desire to do (and to do) them.[30] To make this point, van Inwagen begins with an example presented by Daniel Dennett in which Dennett makes the claim that he is unable to torture innocent victims for small sums of money.[31] Van Inwagen observes that the point of the example is not so much that Dennett would not be able to torture these innocents if he so chose, but rather that, given Dennett's character, he simply is *unable to make such a choice* (and, presumably, unable to generate the relevant desire). Van Inwagen wishes to extend this line of reasoning to show that he also could not slander a colleague to prevent that colleague's appointment to Chairman of the Tenure Committee, and similarly that none of us could do anything that he considers indefensible.

Now, we certainly grant that there may be *some* actions—call them "unwillable" actions—which a particular agent literally cannot bring himself to choose to do (and to do); and some (although not necessarily all) of these unwillable actions may be ones that are morally indefensible.[32] Indeed, Dennett's example of torturing innocents seems to be just such a case. We wish to emphasize, however, that it does not follow from an action's being morally indefensible that is is *unwillable*. That is, we suggest that the Dennett/van Inwagen point here gains plausibility from their focusing on a proper subset of the relevant cases: those morally indefensible actions which are *also* unwillable. But an indefensible action is not *eo ipso* unwillable. Thus, we wish to block the move from the specific case of one's not being able to torture innocents to the general claim that "no one is able to perform an act he considers morally reprehensible" (p. 405).

We believe that there *can* be cases in which an agent believes that an act is morally indefensible and nevertheless has a desire to perform it (of the sort mentioned above) and indeed successfully acts on this desire. And it is in general plausible to suppose that agents have the *power* to generate this sort of desire. In order to support our claim that the context of indefensible action is not relevantly different from the other two contexts, we present the following examples in which an individual believes that the act in question is indefensible but nevertheless has a desire to perform it and does indeed perform it.

Consider first Augustine's famous account of the theft of pears in his boyhood. Shortly before this passage, Augustine is wondering about the reason for his stealing pears for which he had no desire, and after acknowledging the view that all action must be for the sake of some apparent good, he dismisses this explanation in his own case:

> now that I ask what pleasure I had in that theft, I find that it had no beauty to attract me. . . . It did not even have the shadowy, deceptive beauty which makes vice attractive [*Confessions* II, vi, Pine-Coffin translation] . . . Let my heart now tell you what it sought when I was thus evil for no object, having no cause for wrongdoing save my wrongness. The malice of the act was base and I loved it—that is to say I loved my own undoing, I loved the evil in me—not the thing for which I did the evil, simply the evil. [*Confessions* II, iv, Sheed translation]

Augustine's reflections are disturbing precisely because they exemplify one man's ability not only to do something he takes to be morally indefensible, but to be drawn to the action precisely because it is so indefensible. This is not to say that Augustine did not see the robbery as having some desirable consequences. He himself admits that he would not have committed the crime had it not been for his companions and the "thrill of having partners in sin" (*Confessions* II, viii).

However, simply because Augustine wanted something from his thieving, this does not show that he saw the thieving as good, or that he
believed it conformed to an overall system of values he was willing to
defend. A person might see the pilfering of pears as wholly indefensible
and still desire to do it, if for no other reason than to assert one's ability
to act against moral value. Indeed Augustine's comments suggest that
he saw his attraction to evil as being intimately connected to this desire
for a perverse sort of freedom and power—a freedom to ignore the
Good:

> What was it, then, that pleased me in that act of theft? Which of my
> Lord's powers did I imitate in a perverse and wicked way? Since I had
> no real power to break his law, was it that I enjoyed at least the
> pretence of doing so, like a prisoner who creates for himself the illusion
> of liberty by doing something wrong, when he has no fear of punish-
> ment, under a feeble hallucination of power? Here was a slave who ran
> away from his master and chased a shadow instead! What an abomina-
> tion! What a parody of life! What abysmal death! Could I enjoy doing
> wrong for no other reason that that it was wrong? . . . I loved nothing
> in it except the thieving, though I cannot truly speak of that as a
> "thing" that I could love, and I was only the more miserable because of
> it. [*Confessions* II, vi–viii, Pine-Coffin Translation]

A different type of rebellion, but one which expresses a related
yearning to flout moral prohibitions, is found in the story of a character
quite distinct from St. Augustine: Dostoevsky's Raskalnikov. Recall that
at the outset of the story, Raskalnikov is contemplating killing and robbing the old pawnbroker, Alena Ivanovna, and as he does so, he is
keenly aware of the evil at hand; he knows such acts are morally reprehensible and he is repulsed by his own musings:

> "Oh God, how repulsive! Can I possibly, can I possibly . . . no, that's
> nonsense, it's ridiculous!" he broke off decisively. "How could such a
> horrible idea [i.e., to rob and murder Ivanovna] enter my mind? What
> vileness my heart seems capable of! The point is, that it is vile, filthy,
> horrible, horrible!" [*Crime and Punishment*, I.1]

In spite of this moral aversion, Raskalnikov nonetheless finds that
he is able to do the indefensible: he takes a borrowed axe to the head of
not only Alena Ivanovna but her sister as well. Later, as he thinks back
on the murder and robbery, Raskalnikov dismisses the only reasonable
motive for the crime: "If it all has been done deliberately and not idioti-
cally," he ponders, "if I really had a certain and definite object, how is it I
did not even glance into the purse and don't know what I had there, for
which I have undergone these agonies and have deliberately undertaken
this base, filthy, degrading business?" (*Crime and Punishment*, II.2).
Raskalnikov knows that he did not kill the old woman, as a more typical

criminal might have, for her money. And later, as he confesses to Sonya, the deeper motivation behind the crime comes out:

> "I realized then, Sonya," he went on enthusiastically, "that power is given only to the man who dares stoop and take it. There is only one thing needed, only one—to dare . . . I wanted to *have the courage*, and I killed . . . I only wanted to dare, Sonya, that was the only reason!" . . . "what I needed to find out then, and find out as soon as possible, was whether I was a louse like everybody else or a man, whether I was capable of stepping over the barriers or not. Dared I stoop and take the power or not?" . . . "Listen: when I went to the old woman's that time, it was only to *test myself* . . . Understand that!" [*Crime and Punishment*, V.5]

Raskalnikov's remarks are of interest to us because they give an example of a man who (1) knows that robbery and murder are morally indefensible, (2) is not driven to perform these acts in the pursuit of some good which can be separated from the crime itself, and (3) nonetheless does rob and murder two people. Indeed, what is most important about Raskalnikov for our purposes, is that, given a straightforward reading, he seems drawn to murder the aging pawnbroker, precisely to see if he *can* do it: He wants to discover if he has the power to ignore moral prohibitions; he wants to know if he is free to do the morally indefensible.[33]

What is striking about the crimes of both Augustine and Raskalnikov is that, unlike a more mundane robbery in which the wrongdoing is merely a means to material gain, the motive behind their crimes is inextricably bound up with a desire to do wrong and to flout moral constraints. This is not to say that the motivations of Augustine and Raskalnikov can be assimilated in every respect. Whereas Augustine seeks the freedom to do evil in order to rebel against the good, Raskalnikov seeks this freedom to show that he is beyond good and evil. But the crucial point for our discussion is that both men claim to do what the restrictive incompatibilist says they cannot—freely perform an act that is perceived by the agent to be morally indefensible.

We have argued, then, that the context of indefensibility is not relevantly different from the context of (say) unopposed desire: an agent can generate a certain sort of desire to perform an action even though he believes that the action is morally indefensible. Thus, our critique of van Inwagen's argument about contexts of unopposed desire (and unreflective action) can be extended to apply to his argument about contexts of indefensible actions. Someone might object that our examples only pertain to contexts in which agents believe that the relevant actions are *morally* indefensible, rather than indefensible from some broader (perhaps "all-things-considered") perspective.[34] But it is clear that van

Inwagen has in mind the notion of moral indefensibility. Further, if the broader notion of indefensibility were employed, this would substantially reduce the incidence of contexts of indefensibility (thus vitiating the restrictivist's claim that we are rarely free to do otherwise). Finally, we do not see why individuals cannot generate desires (perhaps they would be "weak-willed desires") to do things which they consider to be indefensible, all things considered.

Before leaving the question of whether or not we are free to act indefensibly, we want to consider a final worry about such freedom which is suggested by two interesting examples recently formulated by Susan Wolf. Wolf asks us to consider what it would mean for an agent to have the ability to act against everything he believes in and cares about:

> It would mean, for example, that if the agent's son were inside a burning building, the agent could just stand there and watch the house go up in flames. Or that the agent, though he thinks his neighbor a fine and agreeable fellow, could just get up one day, ring the doorbell, and punch him in the nose. One might think that such pieces of behavior should not be classified as actions at all—that they are rather more like spasms that the agent cannot control. If they are actions they are very bizarre, and an agent who performed them would have to be insane. *Indeed, one might think he would have to be insane if he had even the ability to perform them.* For the rationality of an agent who could perform such irrational actions as these must hang by a dangerously thin thread.[35]

Before directly discussing these examples, a word of qualification is in order. Wolf originally presents these examples to illustrate what it would mean for an agent's actions not to be determined by any interests whatsoever. One of the points she is making, if we have understood her properly, is that a person whose actions weren't determined by *any* interests could hardly be said to be acting at all. Rather his behavior, since it did not reflect any interests or intention, would seem more like spasms or the bizarre movements of an insane person. Understood in this fashion Wolf's claim is certainly unobjectionable; indeed, this insight seems merely to reflect the (alleged) conceptual truth discussed above that all behavior, if it is to be considered action at all, must reflect some pro-attitude.

Our interest in Wolf's examples comes from another more substantive claim which is also suggested by her examples and subsequent comments; this is the suggestion that anyone who even had the *ability* to perform indefensible acts (like allowing her children to burn, or punching her neighbor in the nose for no good reason) would have to be insane. This claim is not the trivial one that anyone whose bodily movements did not reflect her interests would be insane; rather it is the more interesting and substantive claim that anyone who even had the ability to act against all seemingly good interests would be insane. A similar sentiment is found in the following passage by Daniel Dennett: "But in other cases, like Luther's, when I say I cannot do otherwise I mean I cannot because I see so clearly what the situation is and because my rational control faculty is *not* impaired. It is too obvious what to do; reason dictates it; I would have to be mad to do otherwise, and since I happen not to be mad, I cannot do otherwise."[36] Both Wolf and Dennett seem inclined to slide from the claim that "doing X would be crazy" to stronger claim that "anyone who had the ability to do X would be crazy." If this "Wolf/Dennett slide" were correct, then, since most of us are not crazy, it would seem to follow that most of us are not able to act in a crazy, indefensible manner—a conclusion which the restrictive incompatibilist would of course welcome.

We think the conclusion reached via the Wolf/Dennett slide is false. In fact, a strategy similar to the one used earlier to expose the fallacy in van Inwagen's arguments also can be deployed here to make clear the problem with this slide. The conclusion that sane people are not free to do insane things is supposed to follow from the claim that it is not possible for someone to do something that is crazy without actually being crazy. But there are two ways to interpret this claim. On one interpretation, the claim is true, but it fails to support the desired conclusion; on the other interpretation, the conclusion does follow, but the claim is false.

On the first interpretation, the initial claim is construed to mean that the following state of affairs is not possible: that an agent be sane and perform a crazy action. So interpreted the claim may be true, but it certainly does not imply the conclusion that no sane person has the *ability* to act crazily. In order to reach this conclusion, the initial claim needs to be strengthened so as to claim that if an agent is sane then it is not possible for her to do crazy things. But so interpreted the claim seems false. After all, what reason is there to think that the mere *ability* to act crazily should call one's rationality into question?

With respect to other vices, it is customary to accept a distinction between having an ability and exercising it. For example, having the ability to eat and drink to excess does not imply that one is intemperate; nor does having the ability to flee from the battlefield, a coward make. Indeed this distinction seems applicable to a wide range of character traits—having the ability to act generously does not make one generous, having the ability to act dishonestly does not make one a liar, and so forth. The point here is simply that having the power to act in a certain way does not entail that someone is the type of person who will act that way. And given this general fact, why should we expect the case to be otherwise with indefensible actions like punching one's neighbor for no good reason?[37] Why should simply having the ability to act crazily render one crazy? Why should there be this asymmetry between the "ability to act crazily" and other dispositional notions?

An example might be helpful here. A traditional view has it that if we have a free will at all, we must have a perfect, God-like free will. Roughly the idea behind the view is that whereas there can be impediments to action—i.e., one can be unable to act in accordance with one's will—there cannot be any impediments to willing.[38] We raise this view not to defend it, but rather to assume, for the purposes of this example, that it is true. (If one prefers science fiction and fantasy to tradition, then simply imagine that you happen upon a magical ring, and after placing it on your finger, you discover that it has bestowed upon you the infinitely free will described by the traditional view above: a will that enables you to choose or not choose any option you desire irrespective of your morals or best interests.) Now one thing should be clear: simply because the range of your choices has been increased (thanks to the ring), your ability to listen to reason has not been decreased. Having this freedom does not somehow mute the voice of conscience, or leave you with no way to know which course of action is the most rational; it merely gives you the ability to pick a less optimal path if you so will. Like the motorist who reaches a junction from which she can take either a scenic parkway heading directly toward her destination, or a one-lane dirt road that crawls through acres of sanitary landfill in the wrong direction, you more than likely will pick the most reasonable alternative. But surely we won't judge the motorist to be crazy simply because she is at a junction were she can choose a route which is not in her interests, and neither should we judge you crazy simply because you have the power to choose against your interests.

"Still"—one might complain—"being at a crossroads scarcely shows that one is free to turn as she pleases. After all, no sane motorist ever *will* take the dirt path, and similarly no sane person ever *will* knowingly act against her interests. Indeed having the freedom to act this way would appear to be less a blessing than a curse; for why would anyone ever want the ability to behave in such a contrary fashion? It short it would seem that the power to act both irrationally and immorally, if we have it at all, is hardly as much of an ability, as it is a *dis*ability—a character flaw which needs to be overcome."[39]

Two points are raised by this worry. One is easily dealt with; the other broaches a broader issue which we can only touch upon in the context of this discussion. As to the first point—that a sane motorist will never actually choose the dirt road, and a sane person will never actually act against her best interests—we can agree that in most cases this is true.[40] Nevertheless, as we saw above, the fact that someone never *will* act against her interests does not entail that she *cannot* do so. For surely there is nothing incoherent about a person having a power which she never exercises. Having given this response, however, we are lead straightaway to the second, more complicated worry: why would a sane person ever want to have a power that she will never exercise, especially a power to act against all of her morals and best interests?[41]

But, lamentably, to ask whether we would *want* to have something is, of course, not the same as asking whether we *have* it, for it might turn out that we have the freedom to act indefensibly even though this is hardly a freedom we *would like* to have. Hence, this worry cannot aid the restrictive incompatibilist in securing his position.[42]

The Wolf/Dennett slide *is* a slide, and it is not well motivated; the fact that doing X would be crazy does not (in itself and without further argumentation) imply that anyone who had the *ability* to do X would be crazy. Just as agents with the *power* to be gluttonous need not *be* gluttons, agents with the *power* to act crazily need not be considered crazy.

## V. Restrictive Incompatibilism and Moral Responsibility: Tracing

Thus far we have argued that incompatibilists need not accept the restrictive incompatibilist's claim that "rarely, if ever, is anyone able to do otherwise than he in fact does." But what if our criticisms have not persuaded? What if incompatibilists still believe that they are conceptually committed to the thesis of restrictive incompatibilism? In closing we want to entertain this possibility and in particular to direct our attention to the following question: how would an incompatibilist account of moral responsibility be affected if one were convinced that most of the time we are not able to do otherwise? Answering this question will show that, even if incompatibilists did not find our previous objections compelling, they should wish they had.

As we mentioned at the outset of this paper, the restrictive incompatibilist identifies himself with what van Inwagen terms the 'classical tradition.' This tradition holds that there is an intimate connection between free will and moral responsibility, such that if there were no free will—if nobody were ever able to do otherwise—then there would be no moral responsibility. This requirement does not, of course, mean that there aren't particular instances in which a person might still be held accountable even though at the time of the action he was unable to do otherwise. (Van Inwagen's example of the drunk driver is such a case.) However, it does suggest that any state of affairs for which we are responsible must be able to be traced back to some prior free action. To capture this "tracing" principle, van Inwagen offers the following rule:

> An agent cannot be blamed for a state of affairs unless there was a time
> at which he could so have arranged matters that that state of affairs not
> obtain. (P. 419)

This type of principle does not bode well for any incompatibilist who feels compelled to accept the restrictivist's conclusions, but still hopes to remain within the classical tradition. Remember the restrictive incompatibilist must hold that there are only three situations in which we are able to do otherwise: Buridan cases, cases in which duty conflicts with inclination, and situations of conflict between incommensurable values. Conjoin this premise with the above tracing principle, and now the restrictive incompatibilist is committed to showing that all states of affairs for which we are responsible can be traced back to one of these three kinds of situations. But why should we think that everything for which we are responsible can be traced back to some free choice between equally attractive alternatives, duty and inclinations, or incommensurable values?

The most promising strategy for the incompatibilist to adopt at this point is to argue that these kinds of conflict situations are precisely the ones through which our characters are formed; hence, we can accept his theory and still be responsible for all states of affairs which come about as a result of actions that are produced by our characters. In the end, however, even this strategy must fail. Much of our character results from the habituation we receive in early life, and these portions of our character don't seem to be necessarily connected with situations of conflict between duty, inclinations, or incommensurable values.

Consider a young woman, call her Betty, who has spent all of her life in a small, rural community. Like most of the citizens of her town, Betty's family is still proud to be American, and over the years Betty has gradually, almost imperceptibly, internalized a certain degree of patriotism. Being raised mostly during the apathy of the Reagan years, Betty has never been in any situation where her mild patriotism has come into conflict with any of her short-term inclinations or other values. Indeed she has never given the matter much thought—for Betty, being a loyal American has come as naturally as flying the flag on Independence Day. Even though this mild patriotism is a fixed feature of Betty's character, the restrictivist must hold that she is not yet responsible for it; he is committed to this view because Betty has not yet been in a conflict situation in which she was able to make a free choice that would have prevented her from having her patriotic disposition. Imagine now that Betty travels abroad for the first time, and through a series of strange coincidences, a singularly incompetent foreign agent mistakes her for a young American soldier who has expressed an interest in selling government secrets. He approaches Betty and asks her, in so many words, to betray her country. Of course, Betty thinks that treason is morally indefensible; she has a strong desire not to do it, and with scarcely a moment's deliberation she turns down the agent's offer without waiting for any further explanation. For the restrictive incompatibilist, Betty clearly was not able to do anything but what she did. Moreover given that her action resulted from features of her character which in turn could not be traced back to some earlier free decision, it seems that he should say that Betty is not responsible for the ensuing state of affairs that Betty declined to betray her country. But such a conclusion runs directly counter to our actual practices of holding people responsible. Indeed if Betty is not responsible in this case, then it would appear that the restrictivist's position requires that he severely limit the domain of moral responsibility, for a great many of our everyday actions result from other character traits and dispositions which, like Betty's patriotism, are not able to be traced back to one of these situations of conflict between duty and inclination or between incommensurable values.

Of course, the restrictive incompatibilist might object that Betty really is responsible for her disposition to patriotism. "Undoubtedly"—the argument goes—"there must have been many more small conflict situations in her life than you have allowed for (or she is even aware of), and these situations taken together account for her present disposition." However, to make such a concession would prove fatal to the restrictivist's position, for it would undermine his central thesis that rarely, if ever, are we in one of these situations in which we are free to do otherwise. Thus, we leave the restrictive incompatibilist with a dilemma: either accept a severe restriction on the range of states of affairs for which we can be held morally accountable, or else reject the claim that most of the time we are unable to do otherwise. Van Inwagen claims that restrictive incompatibilism can be embedded within a traditional approach to moral responsibility via a tracing theory; we have argued this claim is false.

## VI. Conclusion

We have not in this paper intended to argue for incompatibilism, nor have we attempted to explain how the will can be free in an indeterministic world. Rather, we have tried to make several more minimal points. First we sought to undermine the restrictive incompatibilist's position by challenging van Inwagen's initial claim that "if one accepts Beta, one should be an incompatibilist, and if one is an incompatibilist, one should accept Beta" (p. 405). In particular we presented an argument to show that accepting Beta is not a necessary condition of incompatibilism. (In passing we also cited several compatibilist strategies which allege that accepting Beta is not a sufficient condition of incompatibilism.) The argument that one can be an incompatibilist without having to accept Beta has ramifications beyond the scope of our discussion of restrictive incompatibilism. If incompatibilism can be secured without explicitly using Beta, then a recent trend—exemplified by

Slote—which sees a deep family resemblance among various formulations of the argument for incompatibilism and which hopes to undermine them all by questioning the validity of Beta must be seen to have a
more limited scope than its proponents might previously have hoped.

Second, we argued that even if an incompatibilist does accept Beta,
he need not accept the restrictivist's thesis that one rarely, if ever, is free
to do otherwise. Specifically we challenged the restrictivist's claim that
persons are unable to (1) perform actions they consider morally indefensible, (2) refrain from performing actions which they strongly desire to
perform, and (3) refrain from performing actions which they take to be
the only sensible thing to do. In connection with these arguments we
questioned a slide (suggested in the writings of Wolf and Dennett) which
sought to move from the claim that "doing X would be crazy" to the
stronger conclusion that "anyone who can do X must be crazy."

Finally we examined the consequences that restrictive incompatibilism would have for a traditional theory of moral responsibility. We
concluded that if incompatibilists were indeed committed to the thesis
that we rarely are able to do otherwise, such a commitment would bode
ill for any incompatibilistic theory of responsibility which still hoped to
remain within the classical tradition.[43]

## Notes

We are grateful to Sarah Buss, David Copp, Carl Ginet, Jonathan Lear, Nancy
Schauber, and Eleonore Stump for their helpful comments on a previous draft of
this paper. Previous versions of this paper were read at the UCLA Law and
Philosophy Discussion Group, and at the University of California, San Diego.

1. Peter van Inwagen, "When Is the Will Free?" in James Tomberlin, ed.,
*Philosophical Perspectives, vol. 3, Philosophy of Mind and Action Theory* (Atascadero,
California: Ridgeview Publishing, 1989), pp. 399–422 (also reprinted as Chapter 12 in this volume). All subsequent page references will be to this article
unless otherwise noted.

2. We will follow van Inwagen's usage and treat 'free will' as "a philosophical term of art." According to van Inwagen to say of someone that she "has
free will" means roughly that she sometimes is free to do other than what she, in
fact, does.

3. In "When Is the Will Free?" van Inwagen primarily argues for the
second half of this thesis; he doesn't purport to offer a detailed defense of the
argument that free will is incompatible with causal determinism. He does, however, provide such a defense in his excellent book *An Essay on Free Will* (Oxford:
Clarendon Press, 1983). Hence we believe that when taken together "When Is
the Will Free?" and *An Essay on Free Will* can reasonably be construed as a
defense of the position we are calling 'restrictivism'.

4. The following formulation of the Consequence Argument is quoted

from "When Is the Will Free?" p. 405. See also *An Essay on Free Will*, pp. 55–105, and Carl Ginet, "In Defense of Incompatibilism," *Philosophical Studies* 44 (Nov. 1983), pp. 391–400.

5. Van Inwagen uses this term broadly to include both standard Buridan cases in which "one wants each of two or more incompatible things and it isn't clear which one he should (try to) get, and the things are interchangeable" (p. 415), and cases that he calls "vanilla/chocolate cases." These are situations in which "the alternatives are not really interchangeable (as two identical and equally accessible piles of hay) but in which the properties of the alternatives that constitute the whole difference between them are precisely the objects of the conflicting desires" (p. 415).

6. Because the central thrust of our criticisms lies elsewhere, we will not directly take issue with this claim. However, it is worth noting that van Inwagen's contention that these sorts of cases (i.e., cases in which we are free) occur only *rarely* is highly debatable. Indeed it seems more plausible to suppose that these cases occur as often, if not more often, than the three types of cases in which van Inwagen claims we are *not* free. We are grateful to Carl Ginet and Nancy Schauber for calling this point to our attention.

7. Van Inwagen claims that "if one accepts Beta one should be an incompatibilist, and if one is an incompatibilist, one should accept Beta" (p. 405). In what follows we discuss how certain incompatibilists would take issue with the latter half of this claim—i.e., "if one is an incompatibilist, one should accept Beta." However, it is worth noting that the former half of the claim—"if one accepts Beta, one should be an incompatibilist"—would also be contested by certain compatibilists. Such compatibilists argue that one can accept Beta and still take issue with the basic argument for incompatibilism; they do so either by challenging the fixity of the past (van Inwagen's premise 4) or by challenging the fixity of laws (van Inwagen's premise 6). (For a discussion of the former type of compatibilism, which might be called "multiple-pasts" compatibilism, see Jan Narveson, "Compatibilism Defended," *Philosophical Studies* 32 [July 1977], pp. 83–87; André Gallois, "van Inwagen on Free Will and Determinism," *Philosophical Studies* 32 [July 1977], pp. 99–105; Richard Foley, "Compatibilism and Control Over the Past," *Analysis* 39 (March 1979), pp. 70–74; Keith Lehrer, "Preferences, Conditionals, and Freedom," in Peter van Inwagen, ed., *Time and Cause* (Dordrecht: Reidel, 1980); and John Martin Fischer, "Incompatibilism," *Philosophical Studies* 43 (Jan. 1983), pp. 127–37. For a discussion of the latter type of compatibilism, which might be called "local-miracle" compatibilism, see David Lewis, "Are We Free to Break the Laws?" *Theoria* 47 (1981, pt. 3), pp. 113–21; Ginet, "In Defense of Incompatibilism"; Fischer, "Incompatibilism"; Fischer, "Freedom and Miracles," *Noûs* 22 (June 1988), pp. 235–52; and Kadri Vihvelin, "How We Are (and Are Not) Free to Break the Laws of Nature" (manuscript).

8. Indeed, van Inwagen himself offers two formulations of the argument for incompatibilism that do not depend on any rule of inference like Beta. See van Inwagen's presentation of his First Formal Argument and his Second "Possible Worlds" Argument in *An Essay on Free Will* pp. 55–93. For another example see Carl Ginet, *On Action* (Cambridge: Cambridge University Press, 1990), pp. 90–123.

9. *An Essay on Free Will*, p. 57.

10. Ibid.

11. Michael Slote, "Selective Necessity and the Free-Will Problem," *Journal of Philosophy* 79 (Jan. 1982), p. 9.

12. See Terence Horgan, "Compatibilism and the Consequence Argument," *Philosophical Studies* 47 (1985), p. 339.

13. Pace van Inwagen, Slote, and Horgan, we want to argue that a "finer-grained" approach to the various arguments for incompatibilism is needed that recognizes that not all formulations make use of the same inference rules or involve the incompatibilist in the same commitments. For example, whereas van Inwagen's modal argument makes use of principle Beta (*Essay on Free Will*, p. 94), his First Formal Argument uses a different "entailment" principle: "If s can render r false, and if q entails r, then s can render q false" (*Essay on Free Will*, p. 72). Other arguments for incompatibilism rely on still a different type of "transfer" principle: "S cannot do X; In the circumstances doing X is doing Y; Therefore, S cannot do Y." (See Fischer's discussion in "Scotism," *Mind* 94 [April 1985], pp. 231–43). Other philosophers also employ similar principles. For discussions of such principles and their roles in incompatibilistic arguments see: Philip L. Quinn, "Plantinga on Foreknowledge and Freedom," in James E. Tomberlin and Peter van Inwagen, eds., *Alvin Plantinga* (Dordrecht: Reidel, 1985); Thomas B. Talbott, "Of Divine Foreknowledge and Bringing About the Past," *Philosophy And Phenomenological Research* 46 (March 1986), pp. 455–69; David Widerker, "On an Argument for Incompatibilism," *Analysis* 47 (Jan. 1987), pp. 37–41; and Widerker, "Two Forms of Fatalism," in John Martin Fischer, ed., *God, Foreknowledge, and Freedom* (Stanford: Stanford University Press, 1989); and Ginet *On Action*. Although all of these Beta-like principles bear some resemblance to one another, it is clear that (on the surface at least) they are not identical. Moreover, as we argue below, the incompatibilist's argument can be formulated in such a way that it makes use of neither Beta, van Inwagen's entailment principle, nor any transfer principle. In addition to the argument we shall present, van Inwagen's second argument—the "Possible Worlds" argument—is an example of an incompatibilist argument that does not depend on any principles of this sort.

14. For a detailed presentation and discussion of this argument see Fischer, "Scotism."

15. The issues here are complex and delicate: see Lewis, "Are We Free to Break the Laws?"; Ginet, "In Defense of Incompatibilism"; Fischer, "Incompatibilism" and "Freedom and Miracles"; and Vihvelin, "How We Are (and Are Not) Free to Break The Laws."

16. In fact, we do not take this argument to be a definitive proof of incompatibilism. For one type of compatibilist response to this argument, see John Martin Fischer, "Power Over the Past," *Pacific Philosophical Quarterly* 65 (1984), pp. 335–50. The criticisms in this article suggest that a stronger version of the argument for incompatibilism might well be something like the "Possible Worlds" argument van Inwagen develops in *An Essay on Free Will*. This argument has the advantage that it relies on neither Beta nor on an overly strong fixity of the past claim that denies one even noncausal power over the past.

17. One might object that although the above argument does not explicitly

employ Beta, it would not be sound unless Beta were valid because some principle like Beta is what leads one to accept FL and FP. We, however, do not see how this objection could be developed to show that FP or FL is indeed formally dependent on Beta, nor do we see how the alleged counterexamples to Beta could be successfully translated into criticisms of the above argument. Rather it seems to us that such principles about the fixity of the past and the laws have an independent appeal, and hence one could accept FP and FL without having to accept anything like Beta as a general rule of inference.

18. See Daniel C. Dennett, *Elbow Room: The Varieties of Free Will Worth Wanting* (Cambridge, MA: The MIT Press, 1984), p. 148; and Slote, "Selective Necessity."

19. John Martin Fischer, "Power Necessity," *Philosophical Topics* 14 (Fall 1986), pp. 77–91.

20. Bernard Berofsky, *Freedom from Necessity: The Metaphysical Basis of Responsibility* (New York: Routledge & Kegan Paul, 1987).

21. Indeed, recognizing that the incompatibilist's argument can be formulated without either Beta or Berofsky's principle calls into question much of the motivation for developing such a system of contingent necessity. The machinery of the system of contingent necessity developed by Berofsky is useful insofar as one wishes to have a modal version of the incompatibilist's argument; but it is important to see that this machinery is not necessary in order to generate the incompatibilist's argument.

22. For further discussion concerning the validity of Beta see John Martin Fischer, "Introduction: Responsibility And Freedom," in John Martin Fischer, ed., *Moral Responsibility* (Ithaca, NY: Cornell University Press, 1986), pp. 9–61; and Fischer "Power Necessity."

23. Although van Inwagen calls this conditional, '(C)', it will be useful for our purposes to call it, '(C1)'.

24. It is, of course, not clear that this conceptual claim is true. A Kantian theorist of action might argue that actions can be motivated by reason alone and that desire is not a necessary precursor of genuine action. Thus, we do not wish to suggest that the (Humean) conceptual claim is obviously true; rather, we only suggest that it has a certain plausibility. Further, it is clear that if the Humean conceptual point is indeed false, then van Inwagen's argument is even in worse shape: in this case even the weaker interpretation would issue in a falsehood and thus no support for (2).

25. In *De Fato* Alexander suggests that when one's freedom is called into question it can be reasonable to do something (that might on other occasions be seen as irrational) simply in order to demonstrate one's ability to do otherwise:

> Next it is not by compulsion that the wise man does any one of the things which he chooses, but as himself having control also over not doing any one of them. For it might also sometimes seem reasonable to the wise man *not* to do on some occasion what would reasonably have been brought about by him—in order to show the freedom of his actions, if some prophet predicted to him that he would of necessity do this very thing. (*De Fato* 200.2–7)

26. The notion of successfully acting on a desire is ambiguous between being moved by the desire and actually succeeding in getting the object of one's desire. We mean to adopt the latter interpretation.

27. Of course, a critic might object that this scenario presupposes that we always do have the ability to call such a worry to mind. However, nothing the restrictivist has said suggests that an incompatibilist must deny that we have *this* ability, and until such an argument is given it seems reasonable to adhere to the common wisdom that we are free to think as we will. And one cannot here point out that *if* causal determinism were true—together with incompatibilism—it would follow that we would not have the power in question. This is because the restrictivist's argument is supposed to show that Beta implies that we are rarely free to do otherwise, even if determinism were false.

28. Admittedly van Inwagen does want to construe his example in such a way that the incompatibilist must agree that the person is unable to call to mind any reason for not answering the phone. To ensure this condition, he writes:

> But we might also imagine that there exists no basis either in my psyche or my environment (at the moment the telephone rings) for any of these things [i.e., things that would give me a reason not to answer the phone or that would keep me from answering it]. We may even, if you like, suppose that at the moment the telephone rings it is causally determined that no reason for not answering the phone will pop into my mind in the next few seconds. . . . (p. 413)

We will agree that if a person's motivational set is such that he has no reason to or pro-attitude toward answering the phone, then he will not answer the phone. This is simply an instance of the sort of consideration that supports the alleged Humean conceptual point. However, what is at issue is whether a person with such a motivational set *can* answer the phone. As far as we can tell, the restrictivist has not presented any argument to show that a person with this motivational set lacks the power to call to mind the worry that he might be unable to refrain from answering the phone. If a person has this power, then (even if he actually has no reason or desire to refrain from answering the phone) he does have the power to call to mind a reason not to answer the phone. Given that certain other conditions are satisfied, it is plausible to suppose that he has the power to refrain from answering the phone.

Of course, if it is supposed that causal determinism obtains, then the incompatibilist must say that the agent does not have the power to generate the relevant reasons and thus lacks the power to refrain from answering the phone. But in the context of an assessment of restrictivism, it is not fair to assume causal determinism; after all, the restrictivist's claim is that, even if causal determinism were false, we would rarely be free to do otherwise.

29. We are grateful to Sarah Buss, Nancy Schauber, and Eleonore Stump for each calling this objection to our attention.

30. Van Inwagen, "When Is the Will Free?" pp. 406–7.

31. Dennett, *Elbow Room*, pp. 133ff.

32. Harry Frankfurt uses the term "unthinkable" to describe actions that an agent cannot bring himself to will to perform. According to Frankfurt, some acts

will be unthinkable for an agent because of his moral inhibitions, but "on the other hand, the considerations on account of which something is unthinkable may be entirely self-regarding and without any moral significance." See Harry G. Frankfurt, "Rationality and the Unthinkable," in *The Importance of What We Care About* (Cambridge: Cambridge University Press, 1988), p. 182. Another reason why an agent may be unable to will something is given by Lehrer's examples of agents who cannot bring themselves to choose to do something because they suffer from a pathological aversion. See Keith Lehrer, "Cans Without Ifs," *Analysis* 29 (Oct. 1968), pp. 29–32, and Lehrer, " 'Can' In Theory And Practice: A Possible Worlds Analysis," in Myles Brand and Douglas Walton, eds., *Action Theory* (Dordrecht: Reidel, 1976), pp. 241–70.

33. We do not mean to suggest that this is a complete analysis of Raskalnikov's complex character; rather for the sake of brevity we want to limit our comments about his motivations to those that emerge from the passages cited. A more complete analysis would undoubtedly have to consider among other things: (1) the fact that Raskalnikov claims to have felt *beforehand* that he would know *after* the crime that he was only a louse and not an extraordinary man (III.6) and his later demise that seems to confirm this suspicion; (2) his later insistence that challenges the previous claim and suggests that he now, like the extraordinary man, feels no guilt for his crime (Epilogue.2); (3) his claim to have suffered his downfall through "some decree of blind fate" (Epilogue.2); and (4) the promised repentance at the end of the book. All these facts point to the need further to define and revise our abbreviated sketch of Raskalnikov; however, we leave this task to more capable literary critics. For an interesting discussion of these issues, see the collection of critical essays on Raskalnikov in George Gibian, ed., *Norton Critical Edition of Crime and Punishment* (New York: W. W. Norton & Company, 1975).

34. For example, one might object that Raskalnikov commits his crime to show that he is the "extraordinary man" for whom all things are permitted, and therefore he must view his act as being defensible from the broader perspective available to such a person. Even in this reading, however, Raskalnikov still must be seen as doing something he takes to be indefensible given the constraints of conventional morality, for to want to be the "extraordinary man" is to want nothing less than to be free to ignore such moral imperatives.

35. Susan Wolf, "Asymmetrical Freedom," in Fischer, ed., *Moral Responsibility*, p. 206, emphasis added. Watson outlines this worry in his excellent article "Free Action and Free Will," *Mind* 96 (April 1987), pp. 145–72.

36. Dennett, *Elbow Room*, p. 133.

37. It is interesting to note that Wolf, like van Inwagen, begins with an example—that of allowing one's children to be incinerated—that is an action most people would find both indefensible and unthinkable, and then moves to an example—that of punching one's neighbor—that most people would just find indefensible. Since we want to focus on the question of whether the mere ability to do indefensible things does indeed make one crazy, we will concentrate on her second example.

38. For example, Descartes in his Fourth Meditation claims: "It is free will alone or liberty of choice which I find to be so great in me that I can conceive no

other idea to be more great; it is indeed the case that it is for the most part this will that causes me to know that in some manner I bear the image and similitude of God." For a modern defense of the view that idea of an unfree will is inconceivable see Brian O'Shaughnessy, *The Will: A Dual Aspect Theory* (Cambridge: Cambridge University Press, 1980); and Rogers Albritton, "Freedom of Will and Freedom of Action," Presidential Address, *Proceedings of the American Philosophical Association* 59 (Nov. 1985), pp. 239–51. As Watson points out, the truth behind such claims seems to be that "our concept of the will is such that there is no such thing as failing to will; willing is necessarily successful"; from this point, however, "it does not follow that one cannot be prevented from willing, not by having obstacles placed in the path, but by having one's will pushed as it were toward one path or another." See Gary Watson, "Free Action and Free Will," *Mind* 96 (April 1987), p. 163.

39. Watson raises this worry in "Free Action and Free Will," p. 164.

40. Although we have suggested that examples like those of Augustine challenge even this intuition: for if we take Augustine at his word, he seems to be a case of someone who did act against his best interests, in a manner he believed to be indefensible, and still was not crazy. And if this is true, if one can exercise this freedom and not be insane, then surely one can simply possess this freedom without being crazy.

41. Wolf puts this latter point well when she asks: "Why would one want the ability to pass up the apple when to do so would merely be unpleasant or arbitrary? Why would one want the ability to stay planted on the sand when to do so would be cowardly and callous? . . . To want autonomy in other words, is to want not only the ability to act rationally but also the ability to act *ir*rationally—but this latter is a very strange ability to want, if it is an ability at all" (*Freedom Within Reason* [Oxford: Oxford University Press, 1990], pp. 55–56.)

42. Although authors like Dennett and Wolf have argued that the freedom to act indefensibly is not only not wanted by rational agents, but further that it may even be a liability to them, other writers have viewed this freedom in quite an opposite fashion; they have pointed to it as a primary source of human dignity. Jeffrie Murphy asks: "Does not each person want to believe of himself, as a part of his pride in his human dignity, that he is *capable* of performing, freely and responsibly performing, evil acts that would quite properly earn for him the retributive hatred of others? And shouldn't he at least sometimes extend this compliment to others?" (See Jeffrie G. Murphy and Jean Hampton, *Forgiveness and Mercy* [Cambridge: Cambridge University Press, 1988], p. 102.) Presumably, part of the intuition here is that our respect for others stems from seeing them as responsible agents who, even though they are able to do the bad, refrain from doing so and choose instead to act in accord with morality. Indeed Watson suggests (in his article "Free Action and Free Will") that a Kantian conception of moral agency that emphasizes an ability to set ends requires this type of freedom. On this view, we want the freedom to act indefensibly, not because we want to be irrational, but rather because this freedom underlies our unique status as moral agents; it gives us the ability to reorder our values and to change radically the ends that govern our actions.

43. With respect to this last point, it is worth noting that there are good

reasons for abandoning this tradition. For a representative sample of articles discussing this position, see Fischer, *Moral Responsibility,* pp. 143–249. Also see John Martin Fischer, "Responsiveness and Moral Responsibility," in Ferdinand Schoeman, ed., *Responsibility, Character, and the Emotions* (Cambridge: Cambridge University Press, 1987), pp. 81–106; Mark Ravizza, "Is Responsiveness Sufficient for Responsibility?" (manuscript); and Fischer and Ravizza, "Responsibility and Inevitability" *Ethics* 101 (Jan. 1991), pp. 258–78.

# Name Index

Adler, M., 112 n.2
Albritton, R., 268 n.38
Alexander, 265 n.25
Allison, H., 149 n.21
Anscombe, G.E.M., 37, 143,
  212 n.7
Aquinas, St. T., 99
Aristotle, 24, 30 n.20, 119, 170 n.19
Armstrong, D., 197 n.1, 213 n.19
Audi, R., 65 n.7, 130–31, 134,
  147 n.1, 149 nn.15–16, 212 n.10
Augustine, St., 112 n.3, 253–55,
  168 n.40
Aurobindo, 114 n.17
Austin, J. L., 168 n.5
Ayer, A. J., 49, 55 n.4, 74, 75, 80,
  91 n.5

Baier, K., 168 n.5
Barker, S., 171 n.20
Bayle, P., 155
Beauchamp, T., 171 n.20
Beckermann, A., 198 n.8
Bennett, J., 42 n.3

Bergmann, F., 70–71, 75, 91 n.3,
  92 n.21
Bergson, H., 219
Berlin, I., 30 n.20
Bernstein, M., 147 n.1, 149 n.24
Berofsky, B., 245, 265 nn.20–21
Bigelow, J., 213 nn.19–20
Bishop, J., 181, 198 n.17, 212 n.8
Blumenfeld, D., 147 n.1, 149 n.24
Boutroux, E., 139
Bradley, R. D., 196
Bramhall, Bishop, 152
Brand, M., 100 n.1, 148 nn.8, 10,
  149 n.16, 200 n.34, 211 n.1,
  267 n.32
Broad, C. D., 116–17, 148 n.10, 183–
  84, 199 n.19, 211 n.2, 212 n.9, 222,
  234
Brody, B., 199 n.19
Burkhardt, H., 100 n.2
Buss, S., 262, 266 n.29

Campbell, C.A., 113 n.9, 148 n.8, 196
Carr, E. H., 24, 30 n.20

*271*